Functional Skills
ICT

Levels 1 & 2

Microsoft® Office 2007 & Windows® XP

Created and published by:

CiA Training Ltd
Business & Innovation Centre
Sunderland Enterprise Park
Sunderland
SR5 2TA
United Kingdom

Tel: +44 (0) 191 549 5002
Fax: +44 (0) 191 549 9005
E-mail: info@ciatraining.co.uk
Web: www.ciatraining.co.uk

ISBN: 978-1-86005-948-3
Release: FS01v2

LONDON BOROUGH OF WANDSWORTH	
9030 00003 0290 3	
Askews & Holts	10-Jan-2013
	£13.50
	WWX0010352/0001

Acknowledgements

Microsoft® is a registered trademark and *Windows*® is a trademark of the Microsoft Corporation. Screen images reproduced by permission of the Microsoft Corporation. All other trademarks in this book are acknowledged as the property of their respective owners.

Websites

Websites are constantly changing. At the time of writing, all addresses and links are correct, but this may change. If a named website is unavailable, you will need to search for an alternative. A list of *Useful Links* to other websites is provided online at www.bigplanetsupport.co.uk.

Contents

About this book

Hello and welcome to *Big Planet Theme Park* – the world's first *Functional Skills* amusement park. From high-speed rollercoasters to haunted castle rides, there really is something for everyone.

This book is split up into 8 separate sections. In each section you will visit a different area of the theme park and meet one of the people who work there. Each person will tell you a little bit about themselves and the job that they do, and then ask you to help them complete a number of simple, everyday ICT tasks.

The practical, functional skills that you learn in each section can then be used to solve ICT problems in your own life – at home, in education and at work.

Enjoy your visit to *Big Planet Theme Park* and have fun!

Monty Spangles

Park Director

Introduction

Functional Skills ICT

You live in a world where Information and Communication Technology (ICT) is used in almost every aspect of modern life, from business, education, media and banking to social networking and shopping. Computers in particular can be found everywhere you look – at home, at work, at school, at college and at university.

To get the most out of your own education and employment opportunities, you therefore need to be able to use computers confidently, effectively and independently. The *Functional Skills* syllabus seeks to give you that ability, providing the professional ICT skills needed to successfully use computers in every aspect of your daily life. In general this includes using ICT systems to accurately find, work with and communicate information of various types.

Aim of this book

The aim of this book is to provide the knowledge and skills necessary to achieve the *Functional Skills ICT* qualification. Step-by-step exercises are provided to guide you through the most useful features of popular *Microsoft Office 2007* applications and to help build confidence in their use. Additional problem solving activities specific to your level are also included to reinforce learning.

Remember that achieving a *Functional Skills ICT* qualification is not just about knowing how to use a computer, but realising how to apply that practical knowledge to solve unfamiliar problems in all aspects of your life. The eight sections in this book are therefore based on a number of authentic work-related scenarios drawn from real life, each of which teaches a relevant set of skills that are highly valued in further education and employment.

After completing this book you will be able to:

*   select and use the best ICT tools and techniques to complete a given task

*   find and select the most appropriate information to complete a task

*   apply your knowledge and skills to plan, develop and evaluate suitable solutions

*   solve unfamiliar problems using a range of complex software features

*   manage information correctly and respond to problems

*   present and communicate information and engage with others

*   stay safe and respect laws and regulations.

Software and data files

This guide was written using *Microsoft Office 2007* running on *Windows XP*. If you are using a different version of *Office* or *Windows* you will still be able to complete the activities in this book, but some features may look or function slightly differently to that described.

 Data files accompanying this book enable you to practice new skills without the need for data entry. These files must be downloaded from our website. To do this, go to **www.ciatraining.co.uk/data** and follow the simple on-screen instructions.

Your *FastCode* for this guide's data is: FS02

The data files will be installed to the following location on your computer:

My Documents \ DATA FILES \ Functional Skills ICT

If you prefer, the data files can also be supplied on CD at an additional cost. Contact our sales team at **info@ciatraining.co.uk**.

Notation used

Key presses are included within angled brackets. For example, <**Enter**> means press the **Enter** key on your computer's keyboard. Also, unless otherwise specified, clicking the mouse means click the *left* mouse button *once*.

Recommendations

Each section in this book is split up into individual exercises. Most exercises consist of a written explanation of a specific software feature or technique followed by a stepped activity. Work through all of the exercises in sequence so that one feature is understood before moving on to the next.

Also try to read the whole of each exercise before starting to work through it. This aids the learning process and helps to prevent unnecessary mistakes.

Planning and evaluating

Tasks specific to your level are available at the end of each section. To help you plan and organise your solutions for these activities, a planning checklist is provided at the end of this book. A review checklist is also provided to help you evaluate how well your solutions work in practice, how they can be improved, and how you might approach the problems differently next time.

Skills and Assessment

At the end of each section you will be given two activities to complete on your own which require you to demonstrate the functional skills you have learned. Level 1 students should only attempt the first task, but level 2 students are encouraged to complete both. Each task is similar to the type of question you can expect to find in the assessment for this qualification. Sample solutions are also provided in the data files folder to allow you to compare your answers against the expected pass standard.

> **Note:**   Don't forget to use the planning and review checklists at the back of the book to organise and evaluate your work.

Level 1

To achieve *Functional Skills ICT* at level 1 you must be able to demonstrate your ability to:

* identify the ICT requirements needed to plan and solve a simple, straightforward task

* use your own judgement to interact with ICT systems to meet the requirements of the task (and also know when to ask others for help and guidance)

* find and select information relevant to the task and apply a range of techniques to manage, develop, present and communicate that information

* act safely and securely and be able to evaluate your selection and use of ICT tools.

Level 2

To achieve *Functional Skills ICT* at level 2 you must be able to demonstrate your ability to:

* plan solutions to complex, non-routine problems and select the correct ICT systems to meet the needs of the task

* break the ICT requirements down into smaller parts and tackle each using the most suitable tools available

* solve problems without requiring help and show that you can find, select, edit and manage information on your own

* apply a variety of advanced ICT techniques across several different applications in order to develop, present and communicate a solution

* act safely and securely and overcome challenges to produce successful solutions.

Basics of ICT

1 | Basics of ICT

I'm a member of the customer services team at *Big Planet Theme Park*. Located at the park entrance, it is our responsibility to welcome visitors and organise ticket sales. We even have a gift shop selling a wide variety of books and souvenirs.

To do my job, I need to be able to work well in a team and deal with customers in a helpful and professional manner. I also need to regularly use a computer to register sales, print tickets and manage stocks. It's exciting work and I get to use a computer to do some really interesting things. In fact, as I'd only ever used a computer to browse the Internet and play games at home, I never knew you could do so much with them!

However, I must admit that I was surprised to learn about all of the rules and regulations that affect me as a computer user. Before I started working at the park I'd never heard about copyright law or the Data Protection Act, and I had no idea how important health and safety was. Fortunately, it turns out these simple rules are easy to understand and – as you will find out in this section – really do make a whole lot of sense.

What you will learn:

In this short section you will explore the basics of ICT and learn how to safely and legally use the computing technology available to you. You will also briefly examine a range of professional software applications and learn to choose the most appropriate one for a task.

Knowledge, skills and understanding:

* Appreciate the practical uses of ICT in business, education and at home

* Identify important health and safety issues which apply when using ICT

* Understand the laws and regulations that affect you

* Evaluate and use information correctly and legally

* Recognise the problems that viruses can cause and learn how to avoid them

* Find out how to keep personal details and sensitive information safe

* Select the right software application(s) to complete a task

* Work accurately, safely and securely

1.1 What is ICT?

The term **ICT** stands for **Information and Communication Technology**. Pretty much any device or computer program that creates, stores, interacts with or exchanges digital information can be considered an ICT system, including:

* Hardware such as desktop PCs, laptops, servers, games consoles and digital TV

* Software applications such as web browsers, word processors, spreadsheets, databases, e-mail systems, graphics programs and even games

* Internet technologies such as *Google*, *Twitter*, *Facebook* and *Flickr*

* Mobile devices such as smart phones, digital cameras, iPads and iPods

* Peripheral items such as printers, scanners and network equipment

As computer and communications equipment continues to get smaller and cheaper to make, it is becoming more and more common for manufacturers to combine multiple technologies in one device. For example, many modern mobile phones now include a digital camera, voice recorder, multimedia player and Internet browser. This is a trend that is likely to continue and expand into other areas of everyday life.

> Note: ICT systems are used in more places than you may realise: car engines, vending machines, home heating systems. Even some "smart" refrigerators have built-in Internet connections to automatically reorder groceries, and as you are reading this scientists are working hard to make "wearable computers" a reality!

1.2 Why is ICT important?

Computers and mobile technology have completely transformed how people live their lives – at home, in education and at work. It has changed how people communicate with each other, how they store and access information, how they work and how they spend their spare time. ICT systems allow people to better explore ideas, find answers, solve problems, and ultimately become more productive in both their personal and professional lives.

If you want to be an active member of your own society and succeed in a future career, your ability to fully understand and use ICT technology safely and effectively will be an essential functional skill.

1.3 Health and Safety

Before you start working with equipment of any kind, you first need to know how to use it safely and responsibly. ICT devices are no different, and whether you use them at home, in education, or as part of your job, you are required <u>by law</u> to take reasonable care of your own safety and the safety of others.

> **Note:** When you are at work, employers are legally required to make sure all of their employees are well-protected and well-trained. For ICT users, this means providing you with equipment that is safe, secure and comfortable to use.

Modern ICT systems present a number of health and safety hazards that you <u>must</u> be aware of. Whenever you use a computer, no matter where it is, you should watch out for the following hazards:

* Electrical injuries and fires from damaged wires or incorrect connections

* Electrical injuries and fires from overloaded power sockets (i.e. too many plugs connected to one outlet)

* Injuries and fires caused by improperly stored materials (i.e. paper and other items piled up and around equipment)

* Breakdowns and breathing problems due to poor ventilation (many ICT devices need to be kept cool and some laser printers can emit hazardous fumes)

* Trips and slips due to trailing cables or problems accessing your work area

> **Note:** Never eat or drink at a computer. Food and liquids can easily be dropped or spilled which can damage equipment or cause severe electrical injuries.

When on the move you also need to watch out for other potential hazards. For example, do not ignore obvious trip or fall dangers in your environment when using an ICT device, and never use your mobile phone when driving or operating dangerous machinery.

> **Note:** Never misuse ICT equipment or attempt to repair a broken device yourself. If you experience any problems always contact a qualified technician.

Of course, depending on how and where you work, there will also be a number of other health and safety dangers to watch out for. As you will see in this book, ICT equipment can be used in many different locations and situations, and so the concerns listed above need to be considered in addition your other health and safety responsibilities.

> **Note:** Always tell someone in charge about any health and safety concerns you have. If you do hurt yourself or damage a piece of equipment you <u>must</u> report it.

Activity:

1. Look around you. Check that there are no cables lying across the floor that you or someone else could trip over.

2. Check that there are no cables hanging down behind your desk that could entangle your feet as you work. This includes power cables and Internet connection wires.

> **Note:** Take care when adjusting cables. Always make sure your computer equipment is turned off and unplugged before you start.

3. Look out for and immediately replace worn or frayed cables. <u>Never</u> touch a suspect wire until the device it is connected to has been turned off and unplugged.

4. Check for sockets or power extensions that have too many plugs in them. Overloaded electrical sockets can easily cause fires or injury.

5. Remove any unnecessary clutter from around your computer and avoid storing items where they could fall and cause injury or damage.

6. Finally, check your surroundings for any other potential dangers: obstructions and trip hazards (e.g. wires, boxes, bins and bags), fire hazards, nearby laser printers, and so on.

> **Note:** In every building that you work, you should always know where the fire exits and extinguishers are located.

1.4 Your Work Space

If you sit at a computer or use ICT equipment for long periods of time, it can start to get uncomfortable and – in severe cases – cause injury. To stay safe and well you need to learn how to avoid these problems *before* they start. Remember: prevention is *always* better than cure!

> **Note:** The most common complaints reported by computer users are eye strain, aches and pains in the arms, neck and back, and headaches. If you start to experience these problems regularly you need to act fast to prevent them getting worse.

When using general ICT equipment, always remember the following simple precautions:

*   Take regular breaks away from all of your ICT devices (one or two minutes every hour)

*   Look away from screens regularly (and remember to blink often)

*   Vary your work activities so that you do not perform the same task for too long

*   Don't sit with a poor posture or hold heavy ICT devices for long periods of time

*   Use simple stretching exercises to relax your muscles and stay active

If you use a desktop or laptop computer for any length of time it is also important that you set up your work space correctly. The following advice will help:

*   Position your computer screen directly in front of you with the top of the screen at roughly the same height as your eyes

*   Adjust your screen to reduce glare and reflections from lights or windows

*   Adjust the position of your chair so that you can sit upright at your desk about one arm's length away from your screen (50 to 80 centimetres is recommended)

*   Set up your chair so that it fully supports your back and make sure your feet rest firmly on the floor. Foot and wrist rests can be used to help if necessary

*   Place your keyboard and mouse directly in front of you and do not stretch to reach them. Your forearms and hands should always remain parallel with the floor

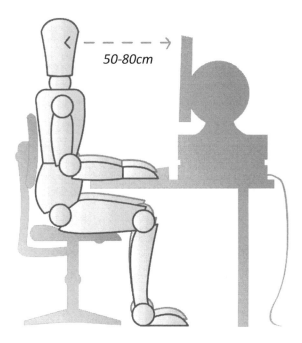

50-80cm

Activity:

1.   Adjust your chair so that your back is straight and your hands are placed comfortably over the mouse and keyboard. Your feet should be flat on the ground.

2. Check that the computer screen you are using is positioned at a comfortable height and angle so that you can see it without straining. Make sure there is no glare or reflections.

3. Adjust the position of the screen, keyboard and mouse so that you are comfortable operating the computer.

> **Note:**   Employers are required by law to do all they can to look after their employees. This includes helping them to sit at and use ICT equipment correctly and safely.

1.5 Hardware and Software

ICT devices come in a variety of forms: digital cameras, smart phones, MP3 players, and of course desktop and laptop computers. All of these devices are known as **hardware**, which is a term that refers to any piece of physical technology that you can touch.

The term **software** is used to describe a set of commands that can be used to tell an ICT device what to do, how to do it, and when. Software does not exist in the real world and can't be touched, but it can be used to perform a specific task when "run" on a device. Without software, most modern computing hardware wouldn't be much use at all.

> **Note:**   Specific pieces of software are also known as **programs** or **applications**.

All of the information that you enter or copy onto an ICT device is known as **data**. Together, software and data are held in a permanent storage area on your device (for example, a hard disk or external USB memory stick) and are moved into memory when required.

> **Note:**   Data held in memory will be lost when a computing device is switched off. To keep this data you must save it as a **file** on an available storage device.

1.6 Basic ICT Security

Computers and mobile ICT devices have totally changed the way we work and communicate with each other. Unfortunately, this widespread use and reliance on technology has also created a number of important privacy and security issues which you – as an ICT user – need to be aware of and fully understand.

Firstly, your personal photos, videos, music and documents are all very important and it can be a disaster if you lose them. At work, however, business documents, customer data, credit card details and passwords are even more valuable. Consider what would happen if this data was lost due to hardware failure, equipment loss or accidental deletion.

Secondly, personal and business information is also very valuable to criminals. If "hackers" are able to gain access to an ICT device and get hold of sensitive and confidential data, they can and will use it for their own purposes. This will cause a lot of trouble and embarrassment and may even end up costing a great deal of money!

> **Note:** **Hacking** is the term used to describe unauthorised access into an ICT system.

To protect yourself and others you must take steps to safeguard all ICT devices <u>and</u> the data they contain from being lost or stolen. There are a number of ways to do this, including:

* Using strong passwords and PIN numbers to prevent unauthorised access

* Storing and using data safely and sensibly (and backing it up regularly)

* Using antivirus programs to prevent software damage or theft of data

* Taking care to make sure hardware devices are not stolen

You will find out more about these important issues in the following exercises.

1.7 Passwords

To prevent other people from gaining access to your ICT devices you need to protect them with a **password** or **PIN** (Personal Identification Number). If a device is stolen or left unattended for a time, passwords and PINs will act as your own personal entry codes and stop unauthorised use.

> **Note:** As well as a password, most computer systems require the use of a user ID (a **username** or log-in name) which uniquely identifies you on a computer or network. It is a name that represents you and only you, and together with your password proves your identity and right to access information.

A good password should be made up from a combination of numbers and both lowercase <u>and</u> uppercase letters. It should also be *at least* 8 **characters** long.

> **Note:** The term "character" is used to describe a single letter, number or symbol.

It is a good idea to use a password that you can easily remember, but not one that is easy for others to guess. For example, don't use your dog's name or the word **password**. The same rule applies to PINs: don't use **1234** or any other combination that is easy to guess.

> **Note:** PIN numbers are usually 4 digits long and only contain the numbers 0 to 9. PINs are most often used to secure mobile devices or bank cards.

Always keep your password and PIN information safe and try to avoid writing them down. It is also good practice to change your passwords and PINs often and avoid using the same details for different purposes. Remember: never give your security information to other people.

> **Note:** If you use a computing device that is connected to the Internet, there is a very small chance that a hacker could access it from another computer elsewhere. However, if you use a good password or PIN, they will not be able to do this.

1.8 Information Security

As most people and businesses now rely on ICT systems, it is important that the information they contain is kept safe. The following simple guidelines will help you do this:

* Always respect and value information – whether it is yours or someone elses – and treat it with care.

* Don't disclose private or sensitive information to anyone, especially if that information belongs to someone else or the business you work for.

* Protect your ICT devices from unauthorised access by using a strong password or PIN.

* Protect your computing devices from viruses using antivirus software (which you will learn more about in later exercises).

* Further protect your computing devices from hackers by using a **firewall**.

> **Note:** **Firewalls** are used to stop unauthorised users from accessing computer systems remotely across the Internet (and attempting to guess your passwords). Don't worry: *Windows* has a built-in firewall that automatically protects you.

* Password protect sensitive documents that you send by e-mail or place on a mobile device (you will see an example of how to do this in section 3).

* Back up your own data regularly in case it is lost or accidentally deleted (in a business this should be done for you by the person in charge of your network).

> **Note:** An easy way to backup your own personal data is to use a portable device such as a USB memory stick or external hard drive. Simply plug it into your computer's USB port and copy files straight from your computer to the backup device. That's all there is to it – you can then keep your backup in a safe and secure place.

1.9 Hardware Security

Mobile ICT devices are very expensive, but the information they contain is sometimes even more valuable. You need to protect and take care of your equipment and make sure it doesn't fall into the wrong hands. The following simple guidelines will help you do this:

* Handle ICT hardware with care – it's easy to damage computer equipment

* Don't expose devices to heat, cold or water

* Store ICT devices in a secure place

* Never leave your ICT devices unattended where other people can see them

* Special cables can be used if required to tether computing devices to desks

Mobile storage devices and removable media such as CD or DVDs are an excellent way to transport files. However, these are also very easy to lose. Take extra care with these and try to avoid using them to store sensitive, confidential or valuable information.

1.10 Viruses and Malware

The most well known and feared threat in modern computing is the **virus** – a small piece of "malicious software" (or **malware**) designed to "infect" and cause harm to a computer. All viruses are man-made and get their name from the way they automatically copy themselves onto other ICT devices.

The effects of a virus can vary enormously. Some simply change a web browser's home page, others decrease the performance of a computer, and a small few cause real damage to file

1

systems by destroying data and preventing *Windows* from working correctly. Even more seriously, some malware can identify sensitive personal information within files and then transmit that data to another person via the Internet!

Some other common forms of computer malware you may hear about are:

* ✱ **Spyware**. This type of software hides on your computer and interferes with your use of the system. Spyware can also record secure and personal information and send it to another person via the Internet.

* ✱ **Adware**. This type of software displays advertisements from the Internet automatically.

* ✱ **Worms**. This type of software can damage programs on your computer, and like viruses are able to copy themselves to other devices (often via e-mail).

* ✱ **Trojans**. These are files that look harmless (e.g. pictures, documents, spreadsheets) but contain any number of the threats shown above.

> **Note:**   A virus is not the same thing as a **bug**. A bug is simply an error or fault in a piece of software code.

Always remember that computer viruses can only be introduced to a system from outside (they do not suddenly appear from nowhere). Common sources of viruses are e-mail attachments, Internet downloads, pirate CDs or DVDs, and even external USB devices.

1.11 Antivirus Software

One way to defend against viruses is to install **antivirus software**. This is a small program that runs in the background on your computer and scans all files and incoming data – including e-mail attachments and Internet downloads – for <u>known</u> malware.

Unfortunately, new viruses appear every day. To make sure your antivirus program learns about these new threats it needs to be kept up-to-date. This involves downloading the latest **updates**, which your antivirus program will probably already be set up to do automatically.

> **Note:**   Antivirus software can also be used to scan files "on-demand", including your entire computer, which is useful for checking downloaded files and e-mail attachments <u>before</u> you open them.

At the time of writing some common antivirus programs include *Norton Internet Security*, *McAfee VirusScan*, *NOD32*, *Trend Micro Internet Security*, and *AVG*. Once installed, these programs will watch for and *immediately* delete any malware that enters your system.

> **Note:**   You will learn more about protecting yourself from malware in section 8.

1.12 Laws and Regulations

IT and electronic communications now form an important part of many people's lives, so it is not surprising that a large number of laws exist to control it. The most relevant to you as an ICT user are shown in the table below.

Law/Regulation	Description
User Licences	When you buy a piece of software you get a **licence** to use it, so giving away copies of programs for others to use (or downloading them yourself) is illegal. Organisations will often purchase multiple user licences allowing them to run a certain number of copies.
Copyright	This law protects any original work (text, images, music, videos, etc.) from being copied or used by other people. To obtain a "licence" to use them you must first get the permission of the owner (and often pay a small fee). In practice, this law prevents you from copying text and images from the Internet for use in your own work.
Data Protection Act	This law protects all personal data that a business or organisation stores about people. In particular, it requires that only information that is required for a "specific purpose" can be stored (and only when the owner has given permission). The law also requires that information is kept safe and secure and isn't given away to other people.
Computer Misuse Act	This act makes it illegal to try to gain unauthorised access to – or in any way damage – an ICT system.
Health and Safety	The *Health and Safety at Work* laws protect you and your employer from physical harm. Most of these regulations have been described in earlier exercises.

You must always respect the confidentiality of information that you have access to. All organisations, both business and educational, should have a **privacy policy** to show you how to do this. They should also have an **e-mail and Internet use policy** and **health and safety** guidelines for you to follow.

1.13 Choosing Software

In the course of your personal and working life you will often come across problems that can be solved using IT (*Information Technology*). Although not every problem that you encounter will require a computer-based solution, many could benefit from the significant speed and accuracy advantages that IT systems offer.

However, you need to be able to choose the best software application(s) for the task you have been given. The notes on the following page will help you to understand the differences between the most popular types of common software applications available.

1

> **Note:** Each of the software applications described in this exercise will be looked at in more detail in the following sections of this book.

Software Type	Description
Windows	*Windows* allows you to organise all of your files into folders, start other applications, and manage your computer's settings.
Word Processing	Word processing software lets you create professional documents such as letters, essays, reports and books.
Spreadsheets	Spreadsheet software allows you to work with numbers and calculate a variety of different types of sums. It is useful for doing simple accounts and budgets.
Presentations	Presentation software can be used to create slideshows to accompany a spoken lecture or talk. It can also be used to create handouts for students, or automatic presentations that run in a loop.
Publications	Publication software can be used to create high quality printed materials with lots of graphics. This includes flyers, posters, banners, brochures, magazines, greeting cards and advertisements.
Databases	Databases can be used to store and work with large quantities of information (e.g. customer or product details). You can also query a database to find out information quickly and create reports.
Web Browsing	Web browsing software allows you to access the vast amounts of information and file downloads available on the Internet.
E-mail	E-mail software allows you to send messages and file attachments to other computer users anywhere in the world. You can also use this software to organise the messages you receive into folders.

There are also many other software applications available that can be used to help with a wide variety of specific tasks, including image, music and video editing. However, these applications are very specialised and are generally only used by professionals.

> **Note:** It is often helpful to plan your work before you start and then review it again afterwards. To help you do this, checklists are provided at the back of the book.

1.14 Next Steps

Well done! You have now completed all of the exercises in this section. If you feel you are ready to test your knowledge and understanding of the topics covered, move on to the following **Develop Your Skills** activities. If there are any subjects covered in this section that you are unsure about, you should revisit the appropriate exercises and try them again before moving on.

Develop Your Skills...

At the end of every section you will get the chance to complete two full tasks without my assistance. This will help to reinforce learning and develop your skills. Don't forget to use the planning and review checklists at the back of the book to organise and evaluate your work.

> **Note:** Sample solutions for both tasks are provided in this section's data files folder.

Level 1: Security and Safety

In this task you will be asked to consider a few simple security and safety issues for *Hassan*. You will need to use the ICT skills you have learned in this section to plan, develop and present an appropriate solution. You can ask for help from friends, colleagues or a teacher if you get stuck.

Level 1 Task

To inform customers of new promotions and offers in the future, my manager has asked me to record the contact information of visitors to the park. To do this, I've been given a brand new computer. However, before I can use it to store information, I first need to protect it with a password – which of the following do you think I should use and why?

    A. **bigplanet**
    B. **password**
    C. **HassanKhan**
    D. **HKhan3487**
    E. **3487**

Are there any issues that I need to consider when recording customer information?

I'm also thinking of plugging my new computer into a socket on the other side of the room. If the wires don't stretch I'll use an extension. Do you have any concerns about this?

Notes:

Level 2: Software Decisions

In this task you will be asked to help *Hassan* choose the best software applications for a number of different activities. You will need to use the ICT skills that you have learned in this section to recommend and present a suitable solution. Only level 2 students should attempt this task and it should be completed without help from others.

Level 2 Task

Next Wednesday the park is running a special "Buy 1 Get 1 Free" offer on all tickets. To advertise and promote the event, I've been asked to use my new computer to do a number of different tasks.

Unfortunately, I just can't decide which software application to use for each job. Can you help? Each task that I must complete is shown below on the left, and all of the applications I can use are shown on the right. Can you suggest *the best* application to use for each task?

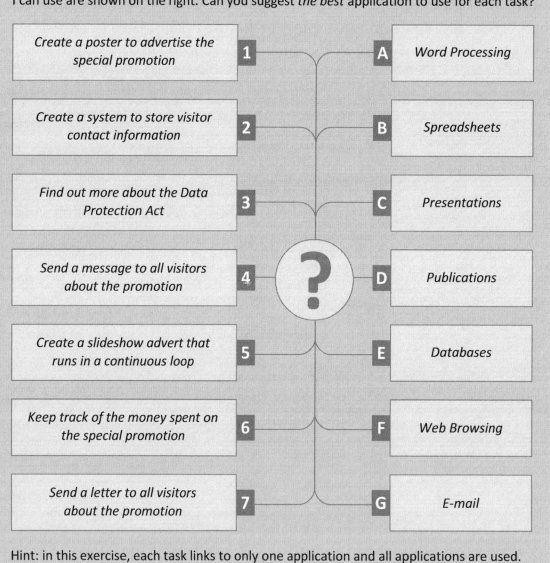

Create a poster to advertise the special promotion	**1**	**A** Word Processing
Create a system to store visitor contact information	**2**	**B** Spreadsheets
Find out more about the Data Protection Act	**3**	**C** Presentations
Send a message to all visitors about the promotion	**4**	**D** Publications
Create a slideshow advert that runs in a continuous loop	**5**	**E** Databases
Keep track of the money spent on the special promotion	**6**	**F** Web Browsing
Send a letter to all visitors about the promotion	**7**	**G** E-mail

Hint: in this exercise, each task links to only one application and all applications are used.

Microsoft Windows

2 | Microsoft Windows

I'm a member of the *Big Planet Theme Park's* reception desk team. We deal with all incoming and outgoing park communications and receive a variety of customer enquiries by telephone, e-mail and post. It's a rewarding job and working with the general public is really good fun.

My specific role in the office is to interact with park visitors and answer any questions that they may have. Of course, to be able to do this accurately, I need to be able to find and access information on my computer *fast*. I therefore use *Microsoft Windows* to organise files into different folders so that everything is easy to find.

I also use *Windows* to start programs so that I can create and edit files. With a little practice you'll quickly discover how to do this yourself and how to customise *Windows* to work best for you. Although *Windows* isn't the only operating system available, it's definitely the most widely used at home, in education and at work.

What you will learn:

In this section you will use the operating system *Microsoft Windows XP* to help *Fiona* complete a number of everyday tasks at *Big Planet Theme Park*. You will see how to log on and off, change computer settings, respond to common problems, start programs, and perform a variety of simple file management tasks.

Knowledge, skills and understanding:

* Perform simple file management tasks and create efficient file storage systems

* Use *Windows* effectively, start programs, and change computer settings

* Work accurately, safely and securely

Data files

Data files needed to complete the activities in this section are provided in the **Section 2** data files folder. Files and folders that you create or edit can be saved to the same folder.

2.1 About Microsoft Windows

Microsoft Windows is an **operating system** that enables you to interact with and use a computer. It is a very powerful piece of software that controls all of the hardware connected to the computer such as the monitor, the keyboard, the mouse, the hard disk, and so on. More importantly, you can also run **programs** that can be used to perform a number of specific tasks.

> **Note:** Known collectively as **software**, computer programs can be used to perform a variety of useful jobs within *Windows*. Simple desktop calculators, Internet browsers, e-mail managers, word processors and antivirus software systems are all examples of computer programs.

2.2 Logging On

Windows allows more than one person to sign on to a computer. Each person has their own settings and private storage spaces in which to keep files.

My Documents   My Pictures   My Music

To access your own files and start using the computer, you first need to **log on** to *Windows*. This involves entering a **username** and a **password** that is known only by you.

> **Note:** If you are using *Windows* at home, have not yet set up a password and do not share your computer with others, you may not need to log on.

At home you may only need to select a user name and, if required, enter a password. If your computer is connected to a network (at work, school or university for example) you will first be prompted to press the key combination **<Ctrl Alt Del>**.

> **Note:** You will need to press and hold the **<Ctrl>**, **<Alt>** and **<Delete>** keys down together.

> **Note:** If there is a light on your computer but nothing on the screen, the computer is probably "sleeping". Move the mouse or press a key on the keyboard to wake it up.

2.3 The Windows Desktop

When you have successfully logged on, the *Windows* **Desktop** will be displayed. This is the starting point for all tasks performed in *Windows*. From here it is possible to start all the programs installed on the computer and access all of the features of *Windows*.

Icons

Desktop

Taskbar

Start Button

Notification Area

> Note: The *Windows* **Desktop** is an example of a **Graphical User Interface**, or **GUI**. A GUI allows you to interact with your computer using pictures, symbols and icons rather than complicated and hard-to-remember text commands.

> Note: As you will see later, *Windows* can be customised according to your own preferences and that of the organisation which owns and runs the computer. Nearly every aspect of its appearance can be changed. For this reason, the screens shown in this book may not quite match that of your computer. The basic layout and functionality, however, should be exactly the same.

The **Icons** that appear on the **Desktop** represent the programs, folders and files stored on the computer. They are small pictures that you usually **double click** to start or open.

My Computer   Recycle Bin   My Documents   Internet

> Note: Don't worry if you see a different set of icons. The items that appear on a **Desktop** depend on how the computer was set up and the programs that are installed on it. As you will see later, you can also add your own icons to the **Desktop**.

> **Note:** To change the position of an icon on the **Desktop** you can simply drag and drop it to another location. Alternatively, to quickly arrange your icons, right-click on an empty area of your **Desktop** and select a layout option within **Arrange Icons By**.

Along the bottom of the **Desktop** is a bar known as the **Taskbar**. This is used to access and manage running programs and usually remains on screen at all times.

Start button   *Show hidden icons*

Active program   *Grouped program*

The **Start** button on the left of the **Taskbar** is used to start nearly all programs and *Windows* features. More than one program can be run at the same time (this is known as **multi-tasking**), and as each program is started, an icon for it appears on the **Taskbar**. If the same program (or folder) is opened many times, *Windows* may group icons together to save space.

> **Note:** If *Windows* groups similar items, a full list of those items can be viewed by clicking the group's button on the **Taskbar** once.

The **Notification Area** on the right of the **Taskbar** displays the time. On occasion, short status messages and alerts from *Windows* may also appear here. These are usually important and you should pay attention to them.

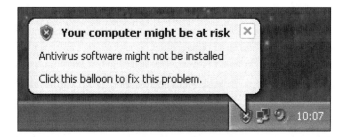

Some programs also install small icons in the **Notification Area** to provide status updates and allow you to quickly access settings. These may be hidden by default, but you can see them by clicking the **Show hidden icons** button.

> **Note:** You can right-click an empty area of the **Taskbar** and select **Show the Desktop** to display the **Desktop** at any time.

2.4 The Start Menu

At the left of the **Taskbar** is the **Start** button. Clicking the **Start** button opens the **Start Menu** which can be used to "run" any program installed on the computer. The **Start Menu** can also be used to search for information, access your private files and folders, find help, and control your computer's settings.

Activity:

1. From the *Windows* **Desktop**, click the **Start** button. The **Start Menu** appears.

> Note: The shortcuts that appear on the left of the **Start Menu** change depending on the programs you have used most recently. Your most recently used files can be viewed in **My Recent Documents**.

2. Notice the buttons on the right of the **Start Menu**. These provide fast access to your private folders and allow you to access computer settings and find additional help and support. You will find out more about these in the following exercises.

> Note: The **Shut Down** button (which may also be labelled **Turn Off Computer**) can be used to turn off or restart your computer.

3. Click **All Programs** towards the bottom of the left area of the **Start Menu**. A list containing all programs installed on your computer is shown.

4. Click the **Start** button again to close the **Start Menu**. Alternatively, simply click away from the **Start Menu** to close it.

2.5 Working with Windows

Windows are rectangular areas of the screen within which you interact with programs, adjust computer settings and manage files and folders. Many windows can be open at a time and each can perform a variety of different, simultaneous tasks.

Windows appear on the **Desktop** and can be dragged around to any position and size you like. Once opened, a window can be **maximized** (filling the whole screen), **minimized** (appearing only as a button on the **Taskbar**), or **restored** (to any size in-between).

Activity:

1. Click the **Start** button, and then click **My Computer** from the right of the **Start Menu**.

2. The **My Computer** view is opened in a window. This view shows any and all storage devices currently connected to your computer (you may see a different set of icons).

> **Note:** This type of window is known as a **Windows Explorer** window. It allows you to navigate through the folders on your computer. The **Address Bar** shows the current folder name that is on view in the window.

> **Note:** If your window does not appear as shown above, click the **View** menu and select **Tiles**. Then expand the **Toolbars** group and make sure **Standard Buttons** and **Address Bar** are both selected (shown with a tick).

> Note: Above the **Address Bar** is the **Toolbar**. This is a row of buttons that allows you to perform simple tasks such as searching for files or changing the current view. You will learn more about these in a later exercise.

3. Notice the three **Window Control Buttons** at the top right of the window. These are **Minimize**, ![minimize icon], **Maximize**, ![maximize icon], and **Close**, ![close icon].

4. The **Maximize** button increases the size of the window to the maximum size available. If the **My Computer** window is not maximized already, click the **Maximize** button now.

> Note: If the window is maximized, the **Maximize** button is replaced by the **Restore Down** button, ![restore icon]. This restores the window to its last (non-maximized) size.

5. Notice that the window now fills the screen. Click the **Restore Down** button, ![restore icon], to reduce the size of the window.

6. The **Minimize** button hides a window completely, leaving only its button on the **Taskbar**. Click the **Minimize** button, ![minimize icon], on the **My Computer** window now.

7. When a window is minimized, the program or task inside the window continues to run. The **My Computer** window can be restored by clicking its **Taskbar** button. Do that now.

8. Move the mouse pointer over the **Title Bar** of the **My Computer** window. Click and drag the window to a new location anywhere else on the screen.

> Note: You can double click a window's **Title Bar** to **Maximize** or **Minimize** it.

9. The size of the window can also be changed. Move the mouse pointer over the right edge of the window until the pointer changes to a double headed arrow.

10. Click and drag to increase or decrease the width of the window. The same technique can be applied to increase or decrease the size of the window in all four directions.

11. The size of a window can be changed in two directions at once. Place the mouse pointer over the bottom right corner of the window so that it changes to a two headed diagonal arrow.

12. Click and drag to increase or decrease the size of the window.

> **Note:** If more than one window is open at a time they will overlap. The active window will always appear on top.

13. Click the **Start** button and then click **My Documents** from the right of the **Start Menu**. A second window is opened which shows your personal documents. Drag the **My Documents** window so that it appears on top of the **My Computer** window (if it is not already – you may also need to restore down if the window appears maximised).

14. Notice that there are now two **Windows Explorer** buttons on the **Taskbar**. Select **My Computer** to activate that window and bring it to the front.

15. The **My Computer** window now appears on top of the **My Documents** window. Click the **Title Bar** of **My Documents** to bring that window to the top again.

> **Note:** You can also move between active windows by holding down the <**Alt**> key and pressing <**Tab**>.

16. Click the **Close** button, ❎, to close the **My Documents** window. Then close the **My Computer** window.

2.6 Logging Off

If you use a computer in a public place, or if you share your computer with others, you must always log off when you finish your work. This does not shut the computer down completely but simply ends your session and allows other people to log on afterwards. Logging off closes any open windows or running programs. Importantly, anyone who tries to use the computer after you have left will not be able to gain access to your private files.

Activity:

1. Click the **Start** button and then the **Log Off** button, . The **Log Off Windows** dialog box appears.

---

2. From the options that appear, click **Log off**. You are logged out of *Windows* and returned to the login screen.

3. Log back in to *Windows* again.

4. Click the **Start** button and then the **Shut Down** button, ![Shut Down]. The **Shut Down Windows** dialog box appears.

5. Click the drop-down box below the prompt **What do you want the computer to do?** Examine the options available: **Log off**, **Shut down** and **Restart**. When turning off your computer you should always use the **Shut Down** option.

Note: Selecting **Stand By**, if available, will put your computer into a low-power "sleep" mode. Your computer is still on, but the screen and some internal components are switched off. This is useful when you are using a laptop and need to conserve energy. Pressing a key or clicking the mouse will *quickly* wake the computer up.

Note: Some computers have a **Hibernate** option available too. Selecting this will put your computer into a sleeping state again but will also turn the computer off.

---

6. Click **Cancel** to return to *Windows* without shutting down.

Note: If you are only leaving your computer for a few minutes you can simply lock it rather than log off. To do this hold down <▦> and press <**L**>. The computer will be locked and you will need to enter your password again to gain access.

2.7 Files and Folders

At home, in education and at work it is always very important to be well organised. If you don't keep a tidy desk and filing system you can never find anything when you need it. The same applies to the files that you store on your computer.

Files are small packages of information, and in *Windows* all of your files are kept in **folders** (which may also contain other **subfolders**). A file or folder in *Windows* appears as an icon with its name printed next to or underneath it (depending on the type of view selected). When you double click the icon the file or folder opens and its contents are displayed.

Activity:

1. From the **Start Menu**, open **My Documents**. The **My Documents** folder view opens in a **Windows Explorer** window.

---

2. The data files for this book can be found in your **My Documents** folder. The folder **DATA FILES** will therefore appear in the list.

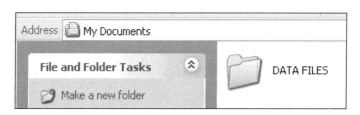

3. Double click the **DATA FILES** folder icon to open that folder and view its contents. Notice that the **path** in the **Address Bar** changes to show that you are now within the **DATA FILES** folder.

> **Note:** A **path** is the name given to the unique location of a file in a computer system. It describes the route you must take through the folder system to find a file. Each folder in the path is generally separated by a backslash symbol, ****.

4. Double click the **Functional Skills ICT** folder to view the subfolders within. Finally, double click **Section 2** to view the data files for this section. 18 items are displayed.

5. On the **Toolbar**, click the **Views** button, [icon], and select **Details**. This is one of 5 window views that you can select and shows the files in alphabetic order with file size, type, and date information.

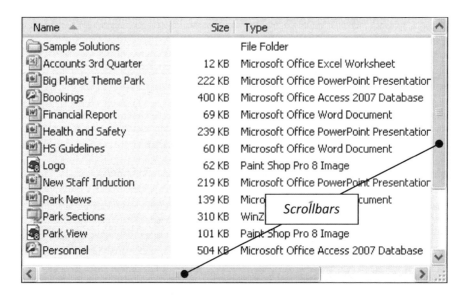

> **Note:** If **scrollbars** appear on the right and bottom of the window then there is too much data to show in the space available. Click and drag these up/down or left/right to view more of the window's contents.

6. Click the **Views** button and select **Thumbnails**. The files are displayed in a grid with large icons showing a preview of each file's contents.

7. Examine the various other views available, and then finally select **Details**.

8. Display the **File** menu and select **New | Folder**. A new folder appears at the bottom of the file list and you are prompted to enter a name.

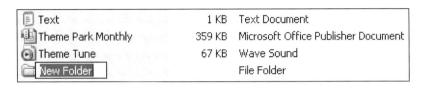

9. Type in the name **Reports** and press <**Enter**>.

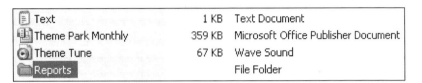

> **Note:** It is important that you give folders sensible, meaningful names so that you (or others) can readily identify their contents later. It also makes searching for files and folders a great deal easier.

10. Using the same technique, create 4 more new folders called **Publications**, **Presentations**, **Image Library** and **Databases**.

11. Double click to open the **Presentations** folder and then create two subfolders within it called **Training** and **Marketing**.

> **Note:** Files that are related to one another, or belong in the same logical group as each other, should be stored together in the same folder.

12. To return to the previous folder, click the **Back** button located to the left of the **Toolbar**. This can be used to move back up the folder structure one folder at a time.

Back/Forward Buttons

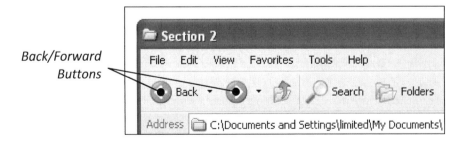

> **Note:** Similarly, the **Forward** button can be used to return to the last **subfolder** visited.

13. Click the **Up** button, , on the **Toolbar**. You are taken directly to the folder above the current one (known as a folder's **parent**).

14. Return to the **Section 2** data files folder, and leave it open for the next exercise.

2.8 Copying Files and Folders

There are many reasons why you might want to create a **copy** of a file or a folder. For example, you may want to create a copy of your data for backup purposes, to place on an external storage device so that you can take it elsewhere, or to use as a starting point for new data.

Activity:

1. With the **My Documents** window open and the contents of the **Section 2** data files folder on view, click <u>once</u> on the file **Financial Report**.

2. Display the **Edit** menu and select **Copy**. The file is copied and placed in memory.

> Note: You can also use **<Ctrl C>** to copy and **<Ctrl P>** to paste files and folders.

3. Display the **Edit** menu and select **Paste**. The copied file is pasted into the current folder (at the bottom of the file list).

Text	1 KB	Text Document
Theme Park Monthly	359 KB	Microsoft Office Publisher Document
Theme Tune	67 KB	Wave Sound
Copy of Financial Report	69 KB	Microsoft Office Word Document

> Note: When a file is copied and pasted to the same folder, **Copy of** is automatically added to the start of the file name. It is not possible to have two files with exactly the same name in the same *Windows* folder.

> Note: Any changes made to the copied file will not affect the original.

4. Create a new folder called **Copies**.

5. Using the **Edit** menu, copy the file **Bookings**.

6. Open the **Copies** folder and, using the **Edit** menu again, **Paste** the copied file. Notice that the file retains the same file name.

7. Click the **Back** button once to return to the **Section 2** folder.

8. Select the file **Logo** by clicking it once. Holding down the **<Ctrl>** key, drag the file over the **Copies** folder. Notice that the mouse pointer changes to the **Copy to** cursor.

9. Release the mouse button to drop a copy of the file into the **Copies** folder, and then release the **<Ctrl>** key. Open the **Copies** folder to find the copied file.

10. Click the **Back** button once to return to the **Section 2** folder.

> Note: Notice the **Explorer Bar** on the left of the window. This can also be used to perform simple tasks and explore the folder structure of your computer.

11. Click the **Folders** button, 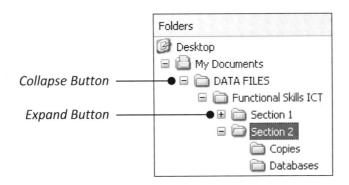, on the **Toolbar** to display the **Navigation Pane**.

> Note: The **Navigation Pane** also allows you to access and explore the folder structure of other computers on your network.

12. The **Section 2** folder should currently be selected. Select the **Copies** subfolder in the **Navigation Pane** (under **Section 2**). The contents of that folder are displayed.

> Note: The contents of the selected folder in the **Navigation Pane** are shown in the main window view.

13. Notice that the subfolder **Presentations** has an **Expand** button, ⊞, to the left of it. This indicates that the folder contains subfolders. Click the **Expand** button now to expand the folder and see the subfolders within.

14. The **Expand** button changes to a **Collapse** button, ⊟. Click it to hide the subfolders again.

15. Select the **Section 2** parent folder to view its contents.

16. Hold down <**Ctrl**> and drag the file **Health and Safety** to the **Copies** folder on the **Navigation Pane**. Release the mouse to copy the file, and then release the <**Ctrl**> key.

17. On the **Navigation Pane** click **Copies** underneath the **Section 2** folder. The contents of that folder now appear in the main view panel.

> Note: Using this technique, files and folders can be copied between different windows on your computer or to and from removable media devices such as memory sticks or writable CDs and DVDs. If your computer is networked to other computers it is also easy to copy objects between them. However, be aware that all devices have a limited size and can only hold a finite amount of data.

18. Select the **Section 2** folder in the **Navigation Pane** and leave the window open.

2.9 Moving Files and Folders

It is good practice at home, in education and at work to keep your electronic files well organised. This usually involves grouping related files into appropriately named folders so that you can quickly find information when you need it.

Activity:

1. With the **Section 2** data files window open from the previous exercise, click <u>once</u> on the document file **Financial Report** (<u>not</u> the copy that you created earlier).

2. Display the **Edit** menu and select **Cut**. The file is cut and placed in memory (notice that the cut file now appears faded).

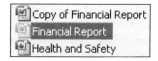

3. Open the folder **Reports** and select **Paste** from the **Edit** menu. The file is moved from the original folder to this one.

4. Return to the **Section 2** folder to confirm that **Financial Report** is no longer present.

5. Use the same technique to move the **Accounts 3rd Quarter** file to the **Reports** folder.

> **Note:** If you move a file to a location where a file with the same name already exists, you will be given the option to **replace** the existing file in the destination folder or cancel the move.

6. Drag and drop the **Bookings** database file onto the **Databases** folder to move it.

> **Note:** To select more than one file at a time, hold down <**Ctrl**> and click each file. To select a range of files, hold down <**Shift**> and click the first and last file. To select all files in a folder, press <**Ctrl A**>.

7. Hold down the <**Ctrl**> key on your keyboard as you select the image files **Logo** and **Park View** together. Release the <**Ctrl**> key.

8. Drag either of the two selected files to the **Image Library** folder. When you release the mouse *both* of the files are moved.

9. Expand the **Presentations** folder again on the **Navigation Pane** to show the 2 subfolders **Marketing** and **Training**.

10. Drag the files **Big Planet Theme Park** and **Rumbling Rails** to the **Marketing** folder.

11. Next, drag the files **Health and Safety** and **New Staff Induction** to the **Training** folder. Check that all files have been moved correctly.

12. Move the following files to the **Publications** folder: **Park News**, **HS Guidelines** and **Theme Park Monthly**. Next, move the **Personnel** file to the **Databases** folder.

13. Create a new folder called **Media Files** and move the following files from the **Section 2** folder into it: **Theme Tune** and **Pirate's Cove**.

14. Great! All files are now well organised and will be much easier to find later. You will deal with any remaining files later in this section.

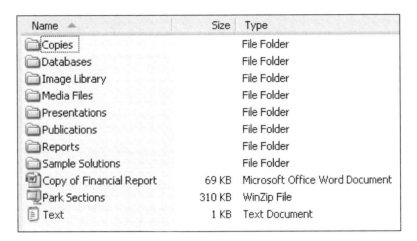

> **Note:** Folders can be moved using the same technique.

15. Leave the **Section 2** data files window open for the next exercise.

2.10 Renaming Files and Folders

From time to time you may need to change file and folder names as their contents change. Always try to give your files and folders descriptive names as this will let you know at a glance what they contain without needing to open them.

Activity:

1. With the **Section 2** data files window open from the previous exercise, click <u>once</u> on the document file **Copy of Financial Report**.

2. From the **File** menu click **Rename**. Notice that the file's name appears highlighted in a text box, ready for editing.

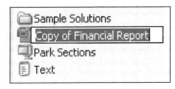

3. Enter **Budget Report** as the new file name and press <**Enter**>.

4. The file's name has been changed. Move it to the **Reports** folder.

5. Right click on the **Media Files** folder to display a drop-down menu.

> Note: Depending on the programs installed on your computer, you may see a different set of shortcut items.

> Note: Right-clicking an object in *Windows* usually displays a **context-sensitive menu** that can be used to perform the most common actions for that item. The menu is called context-sensitive as the items on it change depending on the object clicked.

6. Examine the options shown. There are a number of powerful file management shortcuts available here.

> Note: **Open** lets you open the selected folder in a new window. This is sometimes useful when moving files from folder to folder. **Create Shortcut**, as you will see later, lets you create a link to this folder that can be placed elsewhere.

7. For now, click **Rename** and then change the folder's name to **Sound and Video**. Press <**Enter**> to confirm the change.

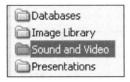

> Note: A very slow double click on a file or folder's name also lets you rename it.

8. Leave the **Section 2** data files window open for the next exercise.

2.11 Deleting Files and Folders

Files and folders can be **deleted** when they are no longer needed. This removes them from your computer and frees up space for other files and programs to use.

> **Note:** Deleting files and folders on your computer does not remove them straight away. Instead, they are moved to a special folder on the **Desktop** called the **Recycle Bin**. If you ever delete a file or folder accidentally they can always be found and restored from there.

Activity:

1. With the **Section 2** data files window open from the previous exercise, click once on the document file **Text**.

2. Press the <**Delete**> key on your keyboard. A prompt appears asking you to confirm that you want to delete this file. Click **Yes**.

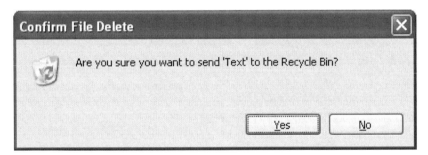

3. The file is moved to the **Recycle Bin**.

4. Display the **Edit** menu and select **Undo Delete**. Your last action is undone and the **Text** file reappears in the folder.

5. Right click once on the **Text** file and select **Delete** from the shortcut menu. At the prompt select **Yes** to move the file to the **Recycle Bin** again.

6. Next, select the **Copies** folder by clicking it once.

7. Display the **File** menu and select **Delete**. At the prompt, select **Yes** to move this folder and all of its contents to the **Recycle Bin**.

> **Note:** If you delete a folder, all of its contents will be deleted too.

8. Use the **Edit** menu to **Undo** the deletion.

9. Select the **Copies** folder again by clicking it once. Then press <**Delete**> and select **Yes** to move the folder to the **Recycle Bin** again.

10. Leave the **Section 2** data files window open for the next exercise.

2.12 The Recycle Bin

When files or folders are deleted they are not instantly removed from your computer. Instead they are placed in a special folder on the **Desktop** called the **Recycle Bin**. Until the **Recycle Bin** is emptied the contents can always be restored to their original locations.

> **Note:**   Once the **Recycle Bin** is emptied, the contents are permanently deleted and can no longer be recovered.

Activity:

1.   **Minimize** the **Section 2** data files window to return to the **Desktop** (or right click on the **Taskbar** and select **Show the Desktop**).

2.   Locate the **Recycle Bin** icon on the **Desktop**.

Recycle Bin

> **Note:**   Notice during this exercise that the icon for the **Recycle Bin** changes depending on whether or not it contains deleted items.

3.   Double click the **Recycle Bin** icon. The contents of the **Recycle Bin** are displayed in a new window.

> **Note:**   The current contents of your **Recycle Bin** will depend on the files and folders you have deleted.

4.   Locate and select the file **Text** that you deleted in the previous exercise. From the **File** menu, select **Restore**.

5.   The file is removed from the **Recycle Bin** and restored to its original location. Display the **Section 2** data files window to find the **Text** file has been replaced.

6.   Delete the **Text** file again and it is moved back into the **Recycle Bin**.

> **Note:**   Only files deleted from your own computer are placed in the **Recycle Bin**. Files deleted from external storage devices are deleted immediately, so be careful!

7. On the **Recycle Bin** window, display the **File** menu and select **Empty the Recycle Bin**. A prompt appears asking you to confirm the permanent deletion of all items in the folder.

8. If you are absolutely sure that you do not need any files currently contained in the **Recycle Bin** folder, select **Yes**. Otherwise select **No**.

9. Close the **Recycle Bin** window. If you deleted the contents of the **Recycle Bin** the **Desktop** icon will now appear empty.

Recycle Bin

> **Note:**   You can also empty the contents of the **Recycle Bin** by right-clicking its icon on the **Desktop** and selecting **Empty Recycle Bin**.

10. Leave the **Section 2** data files window open for the next exercise.

2.13 Zipped Folders

Files occupy space on your computer, which only has a limited amount of storage room available. To save space you can archive older files that you no longer use by moving them into one or more **compressed** folders. This process is known as **zipping**.

As you will see in *Section 8*, it is possible to share files via the Internet or by e-mail. Fortunately, zipping allows you to group multiple files into one smaller file which is much easier and quicker to send and receive over the Internet.

Activity:

1. With the **Section 2** data files window open from the previous exercise, click <u>once</u> on the document file **Park Sections**. This is a zipped file and appears with a zipped folder icon.

Park Sections
310 KB

> **Note:**   You can double click to open and view the contents of a zipped folder as you would any other folder in *Windows*. However, you cannot save any changes to the files contained within (unless you save them to a different location).

2. To work with the contents of this zipped folder, right click on it to display a shortcut menu. From the options displayed, select **Extract All**. The **Extraction Wizard** dialog box appears.

> **Note:**   You can also drag files and folders to and from a zipped folder.

3. Click **Next**. Notice that the directory path where the files will be extracted to matches the location of the zip file. Click **Next**.

4. After a moment the zipped files will be extracted and the final **Extraction Complete** screen will appear.

5. Make sure **Show extracted files** is <u>not</u> selected and then click **Finish**. Notice that a new folder, **Park Sections**, has now appeared.

6. Open the new **Park Sections** folder to reveal 9 files. You can now edit and work with these files as you would any other. Return to the **Section 2** folder.

7. The **Image Library** folder currently contains two files. To "zip up" this folder and its contents, right click on the folder icon and select **Send To | Compressed (zipped) Folder**.

8. After a moment, the zipped folder **Image Library** appears. You could now share this zipped folder and all of its contents with other people much more easily.

> **Note:** A zipped folder is actually a file like any other. That is why a zipped folder and a normal folder can share the same name.

9. Delete the **Image Library** and **Park Sections** folders, leaving the zipped files.

10. Close the **Section 2** data files window.

2.14 Starting and Closing Programs

All programs available in *Windows* can be started using the **Start** button on the **Taskbar**. Clicking this displays the **Start Menu** that contains a list of all programs available to you. Some simple programs such as a **Calculator** and **Notepad** are provided with *Windows*. However, more complex and powerful software such as *Microsoft Office* needs to be obtained on CD or via a web download and **installed** manually.

Note: When you **install** a program, all of the files needed to run it are automatically copied to the correct folders on your computer and the program is "registered" with *Windows*. Nearly all programs that you obtain on CD or via a web download have to be installed before they can be used.

Activity:

1. Click the **Start** button once and then select **All Programs** to display the list of all programs that are currently installed on your computer.

2. Click the **Accessories** folder once to open it, and then click once on **Calculator** to start the **Calculator** program. The **Start Menu** closes automatically.

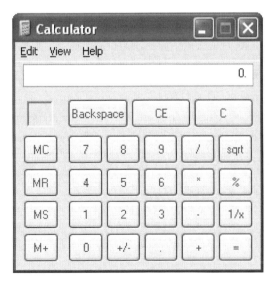

3. The **Calculator** program starts in its own window. This useful tool is ideal for working out simple calculations – try it yourself.

4. Click the **Minimize** button, . The program is minimised and appears as a button on the **Taskbar**. Although not visible, the program is still running in the background.

5. Use the **Start Menu** to start a second instance of the **Calculator** program. There are now two **Calculators** running which appear as separate items on the **Taskbar**. Each of these programs can be used completely independently.

Calculator	Calculator

6. From the **Accessories** folder in the **Start Menu**, start the **Notepad** program. This useful tool allows you to create basic text files – give it a try.

> Note: Some programs such as antivirus software will start automatically when you turn your computer on. Others can be started as and when needed.

7. When you are finished, click the **Notepad** program's **Close** button, ☒. If you are prompted to save any changes that you have made, select **No**. The program is closed and is no longer running.

8. Close both instances of the **Calculator** program.

9. Next, explore some of the other programs installed on your computer by yourself. Don't be afraid to experiment and start programs that are available in the **Start Menu** – this is perfectly safe and will never cause any unwanted damage to your computer.

> Note: Why not try the fun **Paint** and **WordPad** programs found in **Accessories**, or the useful **Windows Media Player** that can be used to create and view your own music and video libraries?

10. When you are finished, close any open programs and return to your **Desktop**.

2.15 Introducing Microsoft Office

Microsoft Office is a collection of very powerful computer programs that are used by businesses and individuals around the world. Installed on most *Windows* computers, the package contains a number of well known programs such as *Word, Excel, PowerPoint, Publisher, Access,* and *Outlook*.

Activity:

1. Click the **Start** button, and then select **All Programs** to display a list of all the programs that are currently installed on your computer.

2. Click the **Microsoft Office** folder once to open it (this folder may be labelled slightly differently depending on how *Office* was installed). A list of programs appears.

Application	Description
Word	A word processing program for creating documents.
Excel	A program for creating spreadsheets.
Access	A program for creating databases.
PowerPoint	A program for creating and giving presentations.
Publisher	A desktop publishing program for creating publications.
Outlook	An e-mail, calendar and task management program.

Note: You will learn how to use each of these programs in the sections that follow.

3. Locate and click once on **Microsoft Office Word 2007** to start the program. After a moment, the program's **user interface** will appear.

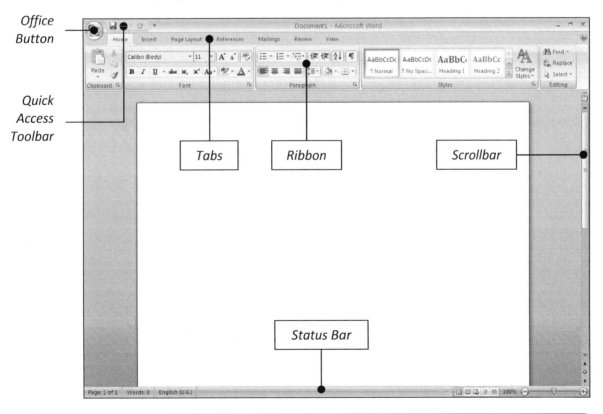

Note: If any **dialog boxes** "pop up" (short messages that require user input), always read the message text provided and consider your actions before responding.

4. Familiarise yourself with the various parts of the *Microsoft Word* window. Nearly all programs in the *Microsoft Office* collection use the same basic screen layout:

Quick Access Toolbar	Commands which you use most often are placed here, such as **Save**, **Undo** and **Redo**,
Ribbon	The **Ribbon** is a collection of program commands that appears across the top of most *Office* programs. Commands are placed into related groups so that they are easier to find.
Tabs	Each tab, when clicked, shows a different set of program commands on the **Ribbon**. Depending on what you are doing, other tabs may also temporarily appear here.
Office Button	The **Office Button** shows a number of commands to control file opening, saving and closing. Printing and help features are also available here.
Scrollbars	Scrollbars allow you to move around a page of information that is too big to fit on your screen.
Status Bar	Useful program information and notifications appear here.

> **Note:** Notice that the name of the program and the file you are working on are shown at the top of the program window; in this case **Document 1 - Microsoft Word**.

5. Examine the **Ribbon**. The **Home** tab is currently selected and a number of program commands are shown.

Home tab ———
Font group ———

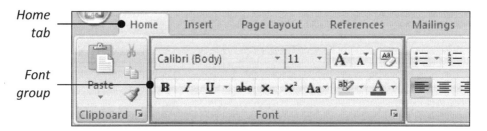

6. Locate the **Font** group and, without clicking, place your mouse pointer over the **Bold** button, **B**. After a moment, a **ToolTip** will appear explaining the use of that button.

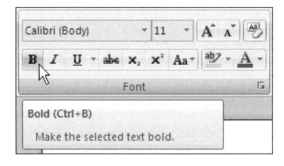

> **Note:** **ToolTips** are really useful for finding out the purpose of a program command. Most buttons that appear on the **Ribbon** will feature a **ToolTip** that describes their use.

7. Click the **Insert** tab on the **Ribbon**. A number of program commands for inserting items into the on-screen document appears, again arranged into related groups.

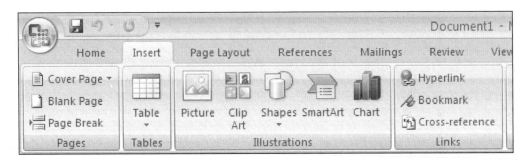

> **Note:** You will find that many *Microsoft Office* programs share the same **Ribbon** tabs. The **Ribbon** will also stay on screen at all times, but can be minimised by right-clicking anywhere on the selected tab and selecting **Minimize the Ribbon**.

8. Click the special **Office Button** to reveal a number of program features for saving, opening, printing, protecting and creating new files. Click the **Office Button** again to return without making any changes.

9. To close *Microsoft Word*, click once on the program's **Close** button, ☒.

10. If you are prompted to save any changes that you have made, select **No**. The program is closed and is no longer running.

11. Use the **Start Menu** to start each of the other *Microsoft Office* applications: *Excel*, *PowerPoint*, *Publisher*, *Access*, and *Outlook*. Familiarise yourself with the screen layout of each application.

12. When you are finished, close any open programs and return to your **Desktop**.

2.16 Opening and Closing Files

Saved files can be opened in one of two ways: you can start a compatible program and use its **Open** command to locate a file, or you can simply double click a file in **Windows Explorer** to open it in its default program. In general, files should only be opened in the program that created them.

Activity:

1. Use the **Start Menu** to start *Microsoft Word*. When the program window appears, click the **Office Button** and select **Open**.

2. The **Open** dialog box appears which shows a **Windows Explorer** view of your **My Documents** folder. Locate the data files for this section.

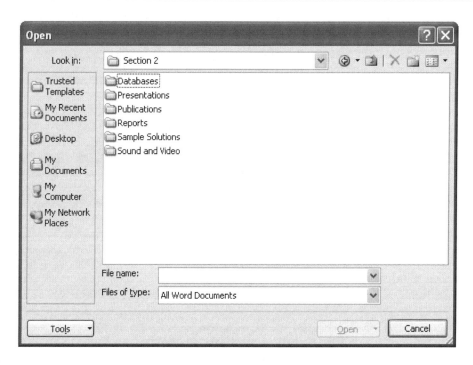

3. Open the **Publications** folder and click once to select **Park News**.

> **Note:** Notice the drop-down button labelled **All Word Documents**. This can be used to show only certain types of files (e.g. *Word* documents).

4. Click the **Open** button. The **Park News** document is opened and displayed on-screen, ready for editing. It is a short newsletter describing a new ride at the theme park.

5. Display the **Office Button** and select **Close**. The document is now closed again.

> **Note:** The technique described here can be used to open and close files in nearly all *Windows* programs (although the **Office Button** may be labelled **File**). Files can also be opened by double clicking them in **Windows Explorer**, as you will see later.

6. Leave *Word* open for the next exercise.

2.17 Creating and Saving Files

To start a new file in *Windows* (e.g. a document, spreadsheet, presentation, publication or database), you must first choose the program best suited to create that type of file (e.g. *Word, Excel, PowerPoint, Publisher* or *Access*).

In this exercise you will create and save a *Word* document. The technique described can be used to create and save files of different types in nearly all other *Windows* programs.

Activity:

1. Using *Microsoft Word*, display the **Office Button** and select **New**.

2. A list of possible document types appears. With **Blank document** selected, click the **Create** button found towards the bottom right side of the window.

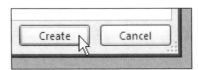

3. A new *Microsoft Word* document is created. At the moment this file only exists in your computer's memory and will be lost when your computer is turned off. To save the document as a file so that you can use it later, display the **Office Button** and select **Save**.

> Note: You should save your work regularly in case of problems (e.g. a computer crash).

4. As this document has not yet been saved, the **Save As** dialog box appears which shows a **Windows Explorer** view of your **My Documents** folder. Locate the **Section 2** data files.

5. Notice the text in the **File name** box. Change this to **new document**.

> Note: Notice the **Save as type** drop-down box. This can be used to save a file in a different format so that it can be opened in other programs.

6. Click **Save**. The **Save As** dialog box is closed and the document is saved (notice the file name has now appeared on the **Title Bar**).

> Note: Saving the document again will overwrite the contents of the last saved file. You will not be prompted to enter another file name. If you wish to save the file with a different file name, use **Save As** instead.

7. Display the **Office Button** and select **Prepare | Properties**. Notice the file properties which describe the currently open file appear temporarily across the top of the window. You can change these values if you wish.

8. Close *Microsoft Word* and the open file is closed automatically. Open the **My Documents** folder and locate your new saved file in the **Section 2** folder.

> Note: Right-clicking an empty area in **Windows Explorer** and selecting **New** allows you to create a variety of new, empty files at any time (e.g. *Word* documents, *Excel* worksheets, *PowerPoint* presentations).

9. Leave the **My Documents** window open for the next exercise.

2.18 Finding Files

Over time you will create and save a lot of files. Unfortunately, trying to find a specific item amongst all of these files can sometimes be like trying to find a needle in a haystack. Luckily, the *Windows* search features are on hand to help.

Activity:

1. With the **Section 2** data files window open, click the **Search** button, 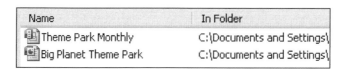, on the Toolbar. The **Search Companion** pane appears on the **Explorer Bar**.

2. Select **All files and folders** and enter the keywords **theme park** in the first text box.

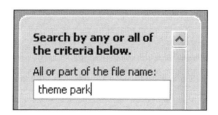

3. Click the **Search** button and *Windows* searches the current folder (and any subfolders) for file names matching the search text. The results are displayed in the main window view.

Name	In Folder
Theme Park Monthly	C:\Documents and Settings\
Big Planet Theme Park	C:\Documents and Settings\

> **Note:** The *Windows* search feature is not a replacement for a good, well-designed and meaningfully labelled folder structure.

4. Double click the first entry in the search results list, **Theme Park Monthly**. *Windows* recognises that this file is a **publication** and starts the program *Microsoft Publisher*.

5. This file contains a short monthly newsletter for staff at the theme park. Close *Publisher*.

6. Click the **Back** button on the **Search Companion** pane. Then, remove the text from the first text box and place it in the second. Click **Search** again.

7. *Windows* now searches for files *containing* the search text. Many more files are found.

8. Double click **HS Guidelines**. *Windows* recognises that this file is a **document** and starts *Microsoft Word*. Confirm the search text exists in the document, and then close *Word*.

9. To clear the search results, click the **Back** button on the **Toolbar**. The contents of the **Section 2** data files folder reappear.

10. Click the **Search** button again on the **Toolbar** to hide the **Search Companion** pane, and leave the **Section 2** data files window open for the next exercise.

2.19 Shortcuts

A **shortcut** is simply a link to a file, folder, external device or program stored on your computer (or any other networked location). They are most commonly used to place links to files, folders and programs on your **Desktop** or **Start Menu**.

Activity:

1. With the **Section 2** data files window open from the previous exercise, right click on the **Reports** folder and select **Create Shortcut**.

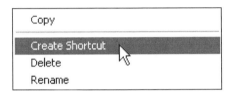

2. A shortcut is created in the same folder. Notice the shortcut icon, 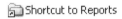.

3. Double click **Shortcut to Reports**. The **Reports** folder is opened.

4. Right click on **Financial Report** and select **Create Shortcut**. A new shortcut for that file is created in the same folder.

Shortcut to Financial Report

> **Note:** You can rename or delete a shortcut without affecting the item that it links to. You can also move a shortcut or its destination file to another location and the link will still work.

5. Double click **Shortcut to Financial Report**. The document is opened in *Microsoft Word*.

6. Close *Word*.

7. With **Shortcut to Financial Report** selected, display the **File** menu and select **Delete**. At the **Confirm File Delete** prompt, click **Yes**. The shortcut is removed but the original file remains unaffected.

8. Right click on **Financial Report** again and select **Send To | Desktop (create shortcut)**.

9. Close the **Section 2** data file window to find a new shortcut icon has been placed on the **Desktop**.

Shortcut to Financial Report

10. Double click the **Shortcut to Financial Report** icon. The linked document is opened again in *Word*. Close *Word*.

11. Right click the new **Shortcut to Financial Report** icon and **Delete** it.

2.20 Control Panel

The *Windows* **Control Panel** contains tools that control how the *Windows* environment looks and performs. For example, the sound volume, screen resolution, date, time, and background picture can all be changed from here.

Any changes made on the **Control Panel** are saved until changed again, and any changes made will still be in effect after closing and restarting *Windows*.

Activity:

1. Click the **Start** button and, from the list on the right, select **Control Panel**.

2. The **Control Panel** window opens and a number of setting "categories" are displayed.

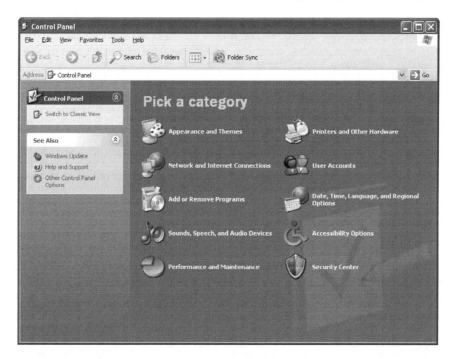

> **Note:**   If the **Control Panel** does not appear as shown above, click **Switch to Category View** on the **Explorer Bar**.

3. Examine the various option categories available on this screen:

Category	Description
Appearance and Themes	Change the way *Windows* looks, from desktop backgrounds to text colours and sizes.
Network and Internet Connections	Share files and change how your computer connects to a local network or to the Internet.

Add or Remove Programs	Manage the programs that are installed on your computer, or remove them altogether.
Sounds, Speech, and Audio Devices	Adjust your system's volume settings and change the default sounds that *Windows* makes.
Performance and Maintenance	Improve the speed (and battery life) of your computer by changing visual effects and power options. File backup and space saving options are also available.
Printers and Other Hardware	Add, remove and configure the hardware attached to your computer including mice, printers and keyboards.
User Accounts	Add or remove computer users and change account details, security levels and passwords.
Date, Time, Language, and Regional Options	Change your computer's date and time, and alter regional settings such as language and currency.
Accessibility Options	Useful settings to allow you to more easily access your computer if you are vision, hearing or mobility impaired.
Security Center	Adjust your computer's security settings including antivirus and firewall settings.

> Note: You can place your mouse pointer over a category title for a more detailed **ToolTip**.

> Note: Depending on your **User Account** type (accessible via **User Accounts**), you may be restricted from making significant changes to your computer. This is often the case when you are using a shared computer in a public place. As a rule, only the computer's **Administrator** can make changes which affect other users.

4.   Leave the **Control Panel** open. In the following exercises you will explore some of the categories described in more detail.

2.21 File Extensions

Nearly every file in *Windows* has a **file extension**; a short combination of letters that identifies a file's **type** (e.g. a *Word* document or *Excel* spreadsheet). Although file extensions are normally hidden in **Windows Explorer**, it is still important that you learn how to recognise them.

Activity:

1.   With the **Control Panel** open, click once on **Appearance and Themes**.

2.   A second list of system settings is displayed (you will learn more about these later). Select **Folder Options** to display the **Folder Options** dialog box.

3.   From here you can adjust a number of settings which control how files and folders are displayed in *Windows*. Display the **View** tab at the top of the dialog box and uncheck **Hide extensions for known file types** (if it is not unchecked already).

```
Hidden files and folders
    ⦿  Do not show hidden files and folders
    ○  Show hidden files and folders
    ☐  Hide extensions for known file types
    ☑  Hide protected operating system files (Recommended)
```

4.   Click **OK** to apply the change and close the dialog box.

> Note: Any display changes you make in the **Control Panel** will only affect you. Other users' settings will not be affected.

5.   Minimise the **Control Panel**, open your **My Documents** folder and navigate to the **Section 2** data files. Notice that the two zipped files created earlier now have **zip** file extensions.

        📁 Image Library.zip
        📁 Park Sections.zip

> Note: File extensions appear after a full stop in the file name. As such, if you change a file's name, make sure you do not accidentally change the file extension also.

6.   Open the **Reports** folder. There is one *Microsoft Excel* spreadsheet present with an **xlsx** file extension and two *Microsoft Word* documents with **docx** extensions.

7.   The table below describes a few of the more common file extensions that you might encounter. Explore the **Section 2** data files folder and notice the file extensions present.

Extension	File Type
docx/doc	*Microsoft Word* document
xlsx/xls	*Microsoft Excel* spreadsheet
pptx/ppt	*Microsoft PowerPoint* presentation
Accdb/mdb	*Microsoft Access* database
pub	*Microsoft Publisher* publication
txt	A plain text file
jpg/jpeg	A photo file
exe	A program file that will run when double clicked

8.   Close the data files window and use the **Control Panel** to **Hide extensions for known file types** again.

> Note: Of course, if you'd rather leave file extensions on, you are free to do so.

9.   Return to the **Control Panel's** main starting page by clicking the **Back** button on the window's **Toolbar**.

10. Leave the **Control Panel** window open for the next exercise.

2.22 Display Settings

The display quality of the information that you see on your computer screen – words, pictures, videos – is directly affected by your **screen resolution**. The higher your screen resolution the more crisp and clear your display becomes but the smaller everything appears. *Windows* will usually choose the best screen resolution for you automatically, but if you find this uncomfortable to work with you can manually choose a more appropriate setting.

If you continue to find it difficult to read text in *Windows* you can also adjust your computer's font sizes. A range of more advanced **Accessibility** features is also available to help those with low vision interact with and use a computer more effectively.

Activity:

1.   With the **Control Panel** open, click once on **Appearance and Themes** again.

2.   Examine the various options that appear to see what changes are possible.

> Note: Notice the settings available here to change your desktop background picture, theme colours (i.e. default text and window colours), and **Taskbar** and **Start Menu** options. Note also that the changes you make here will only affect you.

3.   Click once on **Display**. Select each tab at the top of the dialog box to view the changes that are possible. In particular, note the settings to change your computer's theme, desktop background picture and screen saver.

4.   Display the **Settings** tab. Then, drag the **Screen resolution** slider, ⬇, left and right to examine the various screen resolutions available. A preview is shown in the area above the slider.

> **Note:** At *Big Planet Theme Park* the computers use a resolution of 1024x768. This means that there are 1024 pixels (or single coloured dots) displayed in a grid across the screen and 768 down the screen.

5. Next, display the **Appearance** tab. Experiment changing the colours and default font sizes in *Windows* using the drop-down boxes available. The **Effects** and **Advanced** buttons also allow you to fine-tune your *Windows* display settings.

6. When you are finished, click **Cancel** to dismiss any changes that you have made.

7. Return to the **Control Panel's** main starting page by clicking the **Back** button.

8. Next, select **Accessibility Options** to view a number of settings for users with low vision or hearing. The **High Contrast** setting and **Magnifier** features are particularly useful.

9. Explore the various accessibility options available. When you are finished, return to the **Control Panel's** main starting page.

2.23 Sound Settings

Sound settings in *Windows* are grouped into two main categories: **Playback** and **Recording**. **Playback** controls how sounds are made by your computer, and **Recording** controls how sounds are captured by your computer.

Activity:

1. With the **Control Panel** open, click once on **Sounds, Speech, and Audio Devices**. Examine the various options that appear to see what changes are possible, and then select **Sounds and Audio Devices**.

2. The **Sounds and Audio Devices Properties** dialog box opens. Display each of the tabs and explore the various options that are available.

3. Return to the **Volume** tab and drag the **Device volume** slider, , left and right to increase or decrease your computer's playback volume.

> **Note:**   The **Mute** checkbox will stop all sound playback on your computer.

4. Click **Speaker Volume** to view speaker **levels**. You can adjust each individual speaker's playback volume here. Click **Cancel**.

> **Note:**   If the **Place volume icon in the taskbar** checkbox is ticked, a useful icon to adjust your computer's playback volume will appear in the **Notification Area** on the **Taskbar**, 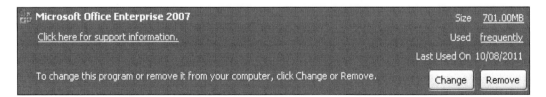. Click this icon once to quickly adjust sound levels.

5. Next, display the **Audio** tab and click **Volume** in the **Sound playback** group. The slides shown can be used to increase or decrease playback levels for individual types of audio.

> **Note:**   **Line In** is the port on your computer used for recording devices (e.g. microphones).

6. Close the volume control dialog box by clicking the **Close** button, ✖. Notice also that the **Sound recording** group has a similar **Volume** button for adjusting *recording* levels.

7. Click **Cancel** to close the **Sounds and Audio Devices Properties** dialog box without making changes. Then, return to the **Control Panel's** main starting page.

2.24   Uninstalling Programs

Unwanted programs can be removed from your computer by **uninstalling** them. This will delete the program completely and free up any storage space used. Note that any files that you created using the program will not be deleted.

Activity:

1. With the **Control Panel** open, click once on **Add or Remove Programs**. After a short wait, a list of all programs installed on your computer is displayed.

2. Select any one item and notice the options that appear on the right.

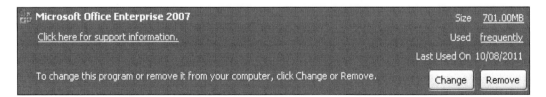

> **Note:**   Notice that the program's storage space and usage information are displayed. Depending on the item selected, **Change** may not appear.

3. If clicked, **Remove** will uninstall the selected program from your computer (do <u>not</u> do this now). The program will also be removed from your **Start Menu**.

> **Note:** If you experience any problems starting and using a program, the **Change** option (if present) can be used to reinstall the program and fix any issues.

4. Close the **Add or Remove Programs** dialog box by clicking the **Close** button, ☒. Leave the **Control Panel's** main starting page open for the next exercise.

2.25 Printers

Printers are a great way to produce hard copies of information stored on your computer. Using *Windows* it is easy to find, manage and use printer devices that are connected to both your own computer and to computers elsewhere on your network.

> **Note:** Think before you print! Unnecessary printing is a waste of resources and money.

Activity:

1. With the **Control Panel** open, select **Printers and Other Hardware**. From the second screen of options displayed, select **Printers and Faxes**.

2. The **Printers and Faxes** view appears showing all external connected devices and available printers.

> **Note:** A direct link to the **Printers and Faxes** view is available on the **Start Menu**.

> **Note:** Your view will show a different set of device and printer icons. Your default printer is shown with a tick symbol, ✔.

> **Note:** It is also possible to add a new printer to the selection available. Clicking **Add a printer** on the **Explorer Bar** starts the **Add Printer Wizard** which guides you through the process.

3.   If a printer is available, click once to select its icon. Notice that a number of additional options specific to that printer now appear on the **Explorer Bar**.

> Note: The default printer is the printer used when printing from a program. To choose a different printer as the default, right-click an icon and select **Set as Default Printer**.

4.   Click **See what's printing**. A window appears which lists all items that are currently waiting to be printed (this is likely to be empty). This is known as a **print queue**.

> Note: Items in a printer's queue can be **Paused**, **Restarted** or **Cancelled** using the **Document** menu. If a paper jam occurs on the printer, these settings can be used to restart the print after you have resolved the problem.

5.   Close the printer queue window by clicking the **Close** button, ⊠.

6.   To adjust the default settings for a printer, right click on the printer icon and select **Printing Preferences** from the shortcut menu that appears.

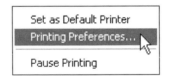

7.   Click each of the tabs at the top of the dialog box that appears to see which aspects of the printer's operation can be changed.

8.   When you are finished, click **Cancel** to close the dialog box without making any changes.

> Note: All external devices such as printers, mice, keyboards and storage devices need **driver software** in order to work. Drivers are small pieces of software that instruct *Windows* how to use a device and are usually found and installed automatically when you connect new hardware to your computer. If they are not, you can often find the software on a disc or website that accompanies the device.

9.   Close the **Printer and Faxes** window to return to the **Desktop**.

2.26 Program Crashes

Every once in a while a program will stop working when you are using it, often with little or no warning. In this case the program is said to have **crashed**. Fortunately this does not happen very often, but when it does it is very easy to close and then restart the program.

> Note: You should always save your work regularly to help avoid data loss as a result of program crashes.

Activity:

1. Using the **Start Menu**, start the **Calculator** program.

2. Assume this program has crashed and stopped working. When this happens the program will no longer respond to mouse clicks and key presses – it is said to be **frozen**. In many cases you will not be able to use the **Close** button to end the program.

> Note: *Windows* will often automatically detect a program that has stopped working and offer to close or restart it for you. In this case it is always worthwhile waiting a few minutes to see if the program starts working again on its own.

3. To force the program to close, press the key combination <**Ctrl Alt Del**>. From the options that appear, select **Task Manager**. The **Windows Task Manager** dialog box appears.

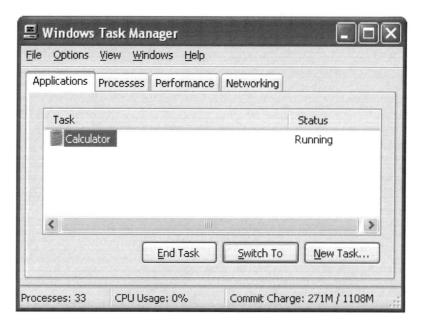

4. If it is not already selected, display the **Applications** tab to find the **Calculator** program running (other programs may appear here also).

5. Select **Calculator** from the list and click the **End Task** button. The **Calculator** program is closed immediately.

6. Close the **Windows Task Manager** to return to the **Desktop**.

2.27 Dealing with Errors

When you are using a computer you will often come across various error messages in dialog boxes. For example, they will be displayed when a program has stopped responding, storage devices are full, there's a paper jam in the printer, you've lost your Internet or network connection, or your computer has been threatened by a virus. Error messages are designed to grab your attention, explain what the problem is, and suggest possible solutions.

There are ways you can deal with problems when error messages appear; *Windows* generally gives some guidance in the message box text itself. For example, if you get a message that storage is full when you are saving work, delete any unwanted files and then try saving again – you could always save temporarily to another storage device while trying to fix the problem.

If you see an error message about a paper jam in your printer, try to clear the jam to remove the message. Sometimes paper can just be eased out of the printer. If a lost network connection message appears, check all of your wires are connected correctly and all external devices are switched on and working.

> Note: Many problems with your computer or external devices can be solved by simply turning them off and back on again. It's amazing how often this works!

Any messages about system security must always be read and the available options carefully considered before taking action. These include messages about your computer's antivirus and firewall software. It is never wise to simply ignore messages of this type.

2.28 Finding Help

If you encounter any problems using *Windows*, the built-in help system will usually answer any questions you have. You can access this by selecting **Help and Support** from the **Start Menu**.

> Note: If you have any problems with a specific piece of hardware or software, take a look in the manual or help files that come with it. These often contain a lot of useful information about how to deal with and correct common issues.

If you still don't know what action to take to deal with a problem, you should ask someone else who can help. Friends are always a source of good advice, but in some situations you may need to get expert help from your IT department or a help line. When you do this you will need to provide information to help the other person understand your problem; for example, they will need to know exactly what an error message says, what type of computer you are using, and which operating system and software versions you are running.

A technician may also try to talk you through the steps needed to resolve the problem. Follow their advice to the letter and, if you don't understand something, ask them to repeat the instructions. If you feel you don't have the skills needed to do what you are advised, then say so and find someone else who can take over and work through the instructions on your behalf.

2.29 Next Steps

Well done! You have now completed all of the exercises in this section. If you feel you are ready to test your knowledge and understanding of the topics covered, move on to the following **Develop Your Skills** activities. If there are any features of *Microsoft Windows* covered in this section that you are unsure about, you should revisit the appropriate exercises and try them again before moving on.

If you are interested in exploring some of *Microsoft Windows'* more powerful features, why don't you use the Internet to find out a little more about the following advanced topics.

Feature	Description
Sharing Folders	You can share specific folders for other people on your network to see and use. You can also share devices that are attached to your computer (e.g. printers).
Writing to CD/DVD	If your computer hardware supports it, files, music and videos can be copied to a CD or DVD (known as burning). This is very useful for backing up files or transporting large files to another computer.
External Devices	External storage devices such as USB memory sticks are really useful for storing your work and transferring files between computers.
Control Panel	Various control panel settings can help improve your experience of *Windows*. Explore the various settings that are available in the **Control Panel**.
Backup and Restore	Backing up is essential if you have important data stored on your computer that you cannot lose. Fortunately, *Windows* has a built-in **Backup and Restore** feature which makes this very easy to do.
Antivirus	Antivirus software protects your computer from malicious files that may enter and damage your system. If you open files on disc or you are connected to a network or the Internet then this type of software program is a must-have.
Windows Update	As problems are found with *Windows* and other *Microsoft* programs, the creators release updates to fix the errors. **Windows Update** can be set up to automatically download these updates for you.
Windows Firewall	The **Windows Firewall** prevents other people on a network from gaining access to your files and damaging your computer.
System Restore	If you have problems with *Windows* you can undo system-wide changes and revert to an earlier instance that worked.
Disk Cleanup	If your computer starts to run slowly or you run out of storage space, consider using the *Windows* **Disk Cleanup** and **Disk Defragmenter** tools to remove old files and increase performance.

At the end of every section you will get the chance to complete two full tasks without my assistance. This will help to reinforce learning and develop your skills. Don't forget to use the planning and review checklists at the back of the book to organise and evaluate your work.

> **Note:** Sample solutions for both tasks are provided in this section's data files folder.

Level 1: Creating a Folder Structure

In this task you will be asked to create a simple *Windows* folder structure for *Fiona*. You will need to use the ICT skills you have learned in this section to plan, develop and present an appropriate solution. You can ask for help from friends, colleagues or a teacher if you get stuck.

Level 1 Task

Starting soon, the reception desk team will handle all customer enquiries about the theme park's latest ride: *Rumbling Rails*. To allow us to respond to questions and requests for information quickly and efficiently, we first need to prepare a folder structure to store all of the information about the new ride.

The files won't arrive until next week, but we need to prepare by creating the folder structure as soon as possible. If I describe the types of files that are coming, would you create the folders for me?

Firstly, create a new folder called **Rumbling Rails**. Inside that folder create a structure of subfolders to accommodate files of the following types:

* *Promotional materials*, containing separate *leaflets, flyers* and *brochures*

* *Videos* of the new ride, separated into *small, medium* and *large* files

* *Pictures* of the ride, separated into *small, medium* and *large* files

* A range of documents containing information on ride *statistics*

Create this structure in the **Section 2** data files folder. Remember: the folder names need to be meaningful so that the relevant files can be found easily later on.

Level 2: File Management Theory

In this task you will be asked to consider three problems facing theme park staff. You will need to use the advanced ICT skills that you have learned in this section to recommend and present a suitable solution to each of the problems. Only level 2 students should attempt this task and it should be completed without help from others.

Level 2 Task

Zahra from *Pirate's Cove* has just called in to the office to request the park's **Health and Safety** presentation for new employees. This file is currently stored on your computer; how can she obtain a digital copy? You'll have to be quick as she's waiting for it.

Notes:

Julia from the *Laser Show* has telephoned the office with a problem. I sent her a CD containing a number of large image files, but for some reason she is unable to copy them to her computer. When she tries she receives a message about the destination device being full. Can you explain what she should do?

Notes:

I've been having problems with my printer lately, so *John* from the *IT Centre* has installed a lovely new one – it scans and copies too! However, whenever I try to print, the old one still appears as my default printer. Can you explain how I can change my computer's settings so that the new printer is selected by default?

Notes:

SECTION 3 | Microsoft Word

3 | Microsoft Word

Hi, my name's Priti...

I'm a member of the ride construction team here at *Big Planet Theme Park*. We've just finished building a brand new roller coaster called *Rumbling Rails* – a thrilling high speed train ride through rocky canyons and icy mountain passes!

My role in the park's construction team is to evaluate building plans and make sure environmental regulations are followed. Most of the time this involves using a computer to collect and analyse data on-site. However, it's also my job to communicate my findings to others in a variety of different ways. To do this I use the word processing application *Microsoft Word* to create professional reports and documents quickly and easily.

You have probably used *Microsoft Word* many times in your life already. If you've ever used a computer to write a letter, essay or short story then you will already know how to use basic word processing features. However, did you know that word processors are just as popular and useful in business? Indeed, people working in a variety of different professions use them all of the time to create a wide range of reports, memos, mailings and newsletters.

What you will learn:

In this section you will use the program *Microsoft Word* to help *Priti* complete a number of everyday tasks at *Big Planet Theme Park*. You will see how to use simple word processing techniques to design, create and edit professional documents for a variety of purposes.

Knowledge, skills and understanding:

* Use *Microsoft Word* to create and edit professional word-processed documents

* Learn how to use the best tools and features to solve a range of everyday problems

* Apply professional editing, formatting and layout techniques

Data files

Data files needed to complete the activities in this section are provided in the **Section 3** data files folder. Documents that you create or edit can be saved to the same folder.

3.1 Using Microsoft Word

One of the most common types of computer program in use today – at home, in education and at work – is the word processing application. This popular type of software enables you to produce professional, well-styled documents for many different purposes. Typical word processed documents you may create include:

* Letters and marketing/advertising "mail shots"

* Brochures, newsletters, books and documentation

* Reports, essays and memos

Microsoft Word is a word processing application that is an appropriate choice for any task that requires a largely text based solution, particularly if printed output is required. The entry and formatting of text is easily handled by such a program, as is the ability to include different types of object such as images and charts. Perhaps more important is the application's ability to present text professionally using a variety of alignment tools and tables.

> Note: Many of the simple text editing and formatting techniques taught in this section also apply to most other *Microsoft Office* programs.

Another important advantage of *Microsoft Word* is its widespread use; most people will have this program installed on their computer and will know how to use it. This makes it easy to send documents to others by e-mail, and if your solution needs to be changed by others (perhaps to update and reprint a newsletter) then it is highly likely they will be able to do so.

3.2 Inserting and Deleting Text

In a word processing application, any key pressed on an ICT device's keyboard appears in the document at the **insertion point** (where the **cursor** flashes). Each letter, number or symbol typed in is called a **character**.

Entering text into a document is easy|●——— *Insertion point or cursor*

The cursor can be moved to any place where text *already* exists by pointing and clicking (or by using the arrow keys on the keyboard). New text that you type is inserted at the cursor position, and text that is already there can be deleted using the <**Delete**> or <**Backspace**> keys.

> Note: The keyboard and mouse are known as **input devices** as they allow you to enter information into a computer or other ICT device. Monitors and printers are known as **output devices**.

> **Note:** The <**Delete**> key removes characters one at a time to the right of the cursor. The <**Backspace**> key removes characters one at a time to the left.

> **Note:** The layout of your keyboard may appear differently to that shown above

When the edge of the area you can type in is reached, the text automatically moves to the next line (this is called **word wrap**). You only need to press <**Enter**> to start a new paragraph or if you want to create a new line before you reach the end of the current one. To type a capital letter or a symbol at the top of a key, e.g. **%**, **£**, **@**, **?**, hold down the <**Shift**> key while typing it.

> **Note:** Only use the <**Caps Lock**> key if you are typing a lot of capitalised text.

Activity:

1. Start *Microsoft Word* and open the document **Progress Report** from the data files folder. *Priti* wants to send this simple document to the rest of her team, but it contains a number of small errors that must be corrected first.

2. Display the **View** tab on the **Ribbon** and locate the **Document Views** group. Make sure **Print Layout** view is selected.

> **Note:** There are 5 main ways to view a document in *Word*. The default **Print Layout** view shows your document as it will look when printed and is generally the best view to use. In this section it will be assumed that you are using **Print Layout** view.

3. To allow you to see more detail in a document, you can **zoom** in. On the **Status Bar** at the bottom right of the screen, click the **Zoom In** button to increase the zoom level to **110%**.

4. Click the **Zoom In** button four more times to increase the zoom level to **150%**. This does not change the size of the document, just your view of it.

5. From the **Zoom** group on the **View** tab, click the **100%** button to reset the zoom level to normal.

100% button —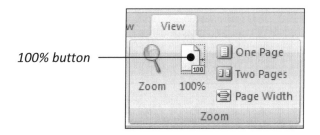

> Note: If you find it easier on your eyes, or if you simply want to see more detail, you can increase the zoom level in documents at any time during this section.

6. Click once with your mouse in the middle of the word **tested** on the first numbered line.

— in the process of being tested.

7. Characters to the left of the cursor are deleted by pressing the <**Backspace**> key, and characters to the right of the cursor are deleted using the <**Delete**> key. Delete the word **tested** using these key presses.

8. In its place type the word **trialled** instead.

9. There is an error in the report's title. Change **Rambling Rails** to **Rumbling Rails**.

10. Change the date to today's date.

11. On the second numbered line, remove the word **almost**.

12. In the last sentence, change the day of the meeting from **Thursday** to **Friday**.

13. From the **Quick Access Toolbar** at the top left of the screen, click **Undo**, ⮌. The last edit is undone and **Thursday** is replaced.

> Note: The **Undo** button is one of the most useful features in *Office*. It allows you to undo changes and correct mistakes simply and quickly by stepping back through each action that you have performed one change at a time.

14. From the **Quick Access Toolbar**, click **Redo**, ⮎. This repeats the last edit again and **Friday** reappears.

> Note: You can also use <**Ctrl Z**> to **Undo** actions and <**Ctrl Y**> to **Redo** actions.

15. Use the **Office Button** to save the document as **interim progress report**.

16. Leave the document open for the next exercise.

3.3 Finding and Replacing Text

The **Find** and **Replace** features in *Word* allow you to quickly search for and easily change specific pieces of text in your documents.

Activity:

1. The document **interim progress report** should still be open.

2. Display the **Home** tab and click the **Find** button, 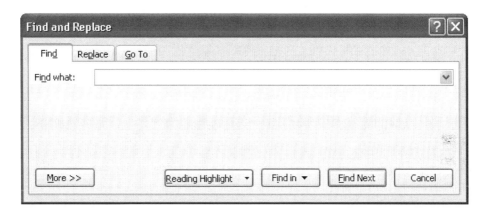, in the **Editing** group (not the small drop-down arrow). The **Find and Replace** dialog box appears and the cursor is shown flashing in the **Find what** box.

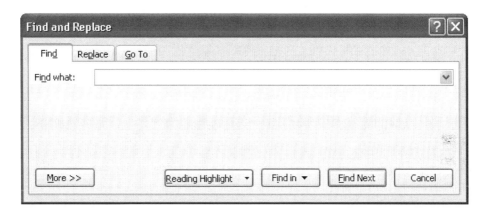

3. Type the word **advisor** and click **Find Next**. *Word* will search for and highlight the first instance of the word **advisor** *after* the cursor's current position.

4. Click **Find Next** again to locate the next instance of the word **advisor**. Continue to do this to locate all of the words that match your search criteria (four matches will be found). When the search is complete a message will appear informing you that **Word has finished searching the document**.

5. Click **OK**, and then click **Cancel** to close the **Find and Replace** dialog box.

6. Next, place the cursor at the start of the document (in front of the main title text).

> **Note:**   The keyboard shortcut <**Ctrl Home**> will take you to the start of a document.

7. From the **Editing** group, click **Replace**, . The **Find and Replace** dialog box appears again, but this time the **Replace** tab is selected.

8. The search text **advisor** will appear automatically in the **Find what** box (as it was the last search performed). If it does not, enter it now.

9. In the **Replace with** box, enter the word **expert** and then click the **Replace All** button. Each instance of the word **advisor** is replaced with the word **expert**.

10. A dialog box appears informing you that **4 replacements** have been made.

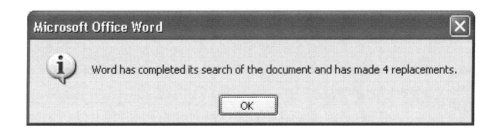

Note: The **Replace** button can be used to replace each occurrence of the search text one instance at a time. If you do not want to replace a specific match, you can use the **Find Next** button to skip to the next occurrence.

11. Click **OK** and then **Close** to dismiss the **Find and Replace** dialog box.

12. Save the document using the same file name and close it.

3.4 Basic Text Formatting

There are many text formatting tools available in *Microsoft Word* that you should already be familiar with. For example, you can make text **bold**, **italic** or **underlined**, you can adjust the **font type** and **size**, and you can apply a variety of **colours** to draw the reader's eye to certain important pieces of information. There is also specialised formatting that can be applied such as **superscript**, **subscript** and **double underline**.

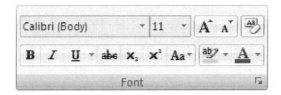

All text formatting options are available in the **Font** group on the **Home** tab.

Activity:

1. Open the file **Memo**. This practice document contains 16 plain lines of text, each of which needs to be correctly formatted.

2. Complete the document by formatting each line so that it matches its own description. At your level you should be able to apply the required formatting without any help.

> This line is underlined.
>
> *This line is bold, italic and underlined.*
>
> This line is double underlined.

Note: To format a specific piece of text you must first **select** it. To do this, use your mouse to click and drag from the start of the required text to the end.

> Note: Used properly, different text styles can help emphasise information and make it easier to read. It can also give your documents a more professional appearance. However, too many text styles and colours can have the reverse effect.

3.   Save the document as **memo complete** and close it.

3.5 Cut, Copy and Paste

The **cut**, **copy** and **paste** commands allow text to be moved around a document from one place to another quickly and easily. When you cut text, it is removed from its original location; when you copy it, the original is left untouched.

When cut or copied, text is placed in a temporary storage area known as the **Clipboard**. Up to 24 cut or copied items can be held on the **Clipboard** at any one time.

Activity:

1.   Open the document **Issues** which contains a list of outstanding tasks for the new *Rumbling Rails* ride.

2.   Make sure the **Clipboard** is visible. If it is not, display the **Home** tab and click the **Clipboard** dialog box launcher at the bottom of the **Clipboard** group.

3.   Because the **Clipboard** is shared between all *Microsoft Office* applications, there may already be some items stored on it. If so, click the **Clear All** button, .

4.   Click and drag to highlight the first sentence: **Name for ride to be decided**. Then, click the **Cut** button on the **Ribbon**, ✂.

5.   An entry for the cut text appears on the **Clipboard**.

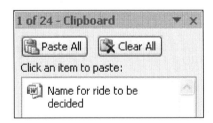

6.   Move the cursor to the end of the document and start a new line. Then, click the **Paste** button on the **Ribbon** to insert the cut text into the document at the cursor position (click the **Paste** button's icon, not the drop-down arrow).

7.   Next, select all of the sentence: **Test computer software**.

8.   Click the **Copy** button, 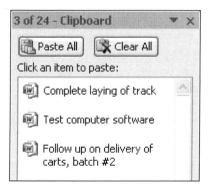. The copied text is placed on the **Clipboard** above the first item. Filling the **Clipboard** in this way is known as **Collect and Paste**.

9.   Create a new line at the end of the document and then click the first item on the **Clipboard** to paste that text. Notice how the original text is left untouched.

10. Use the **Clear All** button, | Clear All |, to clear the **Clipboard**.

11. Next, copy the first three items in the list one at a time.

12. Position the cursor at the end of the document, create a new line, and then click **Paste All**, | Paste All |, on the **Clipboard** task pane.

13. The three copied items are now pasted back into the document in the order they were added to the **Clipboard**. The spacing may need to be adjusted.

> Note: You can also use <**Ctrl X**> to **Cut**, <**Ctrl C**> to **Copy**, and <**Ctrl V**> to **Paste**.

14. Close the **Clipboard** and then close the document <u>without</u> saving.

3.6 Drag and Drop

The **drag and drop** technique speeds up the process of moving text from one location to another within a document. Once you have selected a piece of text, you can then simply click and drag it elsewhere.

Activity:

1.   Open the document **Issues** again, and select the first sentence in the text.

2.   Move your mouse pointer over the selected text. The pointer changes to an arrow.

3.   Click and hold down the mouse button and then drag the selected text down to the end of the document.

4.   As the text is being dragged, the cursor changes to 📋 and the **Status Bar** reads **Move to where?** A vertical line appears where the text will be inserted when you release the mouse button. Make sure this is at the start of the last line.

5.   Release the mouse button to drop the text. It is placed *before* the last line.

> Note: The **drag and drop** feature becomes **drag and copy** if the <**Ctrl**> key is held down as the text is being dragged. The cursor gains an extra icon, ⊞, and the **Status Bar** reads **Copy to Where?**

6.   Select the sentence that has just been moved (if it is not already selected). Holding down <**Ctrl**>, drag the text to the start of the very first line before releasing the mouse button.

7.   The text is copied to the beginning of the document (you may have to insert a space or start a new line). Check the end of the document for the same sentence.

8.   Practice moving and copying text within the document using this technique.

9.   When you are finished, close the document without saving.

3.7 Bullets and Numbering

Lines and paragraphs of text can automatically be **numbered** or **bulleted**. This can help to make points in a document clearer and improves the professional appearance of the text.

• Bullet 1	1. Number 1
• Bullet 2	2. Number 2
• Bullet 3	3. Number 3

If an item is added to or removed from a numbered list, then the remaining items are automatically renumbered.

Activity:

1.   Open the document **Issues** and select all of the text in the document.

> Note: To quickly select all of the text in a document, press <**Ctrl A**> on your keyboard.

2.   With the **Home** tab displayed, number the text by clicking the **Numbering** button, ▤, in the **Paragraph** group (click the **Numbering** button's icon, not the drop-down arrow).

3.   This is a useful technique for creating lists of items. Select and then delete line number **5** only (which refers to the loop the loop).

4. Notice how the remaining items are renumbered. Type **Test that track is safe** and press <**Enter**> to add a new numbered item.

5. Select all of the text again, and then click the **Numbering** button, ⊞. The automatic numbering is removed.

6. Click on the **Bullets** button, ⊞, to bullet the paragraphs instead. This is useful for creating a list of points where the sequence is not important.

7. Save the document as **issues bulleted** and close it.

3.8 Tab Stops

Tab stops are a really useful tool for precisely aligning text in a document (and are set by default every **1.27 cm**). Tabs are displayed on the ruler and only apply to text that has been selected or is yet to be typed.

> Note: It is always good practice to use tab stops to align text in your documents. You should <u>never</u> use spaces as this often looks very unprofessional.

Activity:

1. Start a new, blank document. On the **Home** tab, click the **Paragraph** group's dialog box launcher and click **Tabs** to display the **Tabs** dialog box.

2. Enter **1 cm** in the **Tab stop position** box. Check the **Alignment** is **Left** (you will see other alignment types in the next exercise), and then click **Set** to set the first tab.

3. Now enter **10** in the **Tab stop position** box (**cm** is assumed if you don't type it).

4. Click **Set** and then click **OK**.

> Note: Notice an **L** (Left) marker has now appeared on the ruler for each tab (if the ruler is not shown, display the **View** tab and check **Ruler** in the **Show/Hide** group).

5. Press the <**Tab**> key on your keyboard once to move to the first tab stop.

6. Type the word **Publication** and press <**Tab**> again to move to the next tab marker. Type **Price** and then press <**Enter**> to move to the next line.

7. Following the same technique, enter the following information as shown below:

Hospitality Today	**4.99**
Journal of Travel and Tourism	**5**
Theme Park Monthly	**3.75**
Construction Journal	**5.5**
Roller Coaster Review	**4**
Dream Spas Quarterly	**5.60**

8. You have now created a well-presented and professional-looking list of publications and prices. Save the document as **publication prices**.

9. Next, select all of the text in the document. Display the **Tabs** dialog box again and click **Clear All** to remove any existing tabs.

10. Click **OK**. Notice that the document has lost all of its tab stops on the ruler.

> Note: To quickly set new tabs, click at the required position on the ruler with your mouse.

11. With the entire document still selected, use the mouse to click on the ruler at approximately **0.5 cm** and **7 cm** to set two new tabs. Notice the effect.

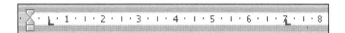

12. Save the document and close it.

13. Open the file **Coasters**. This file contains information about the types of roller coaster cars that are available to buy, but the two columns are too far apart...

14. Select the whole document and display the **Tabs** dialog box again.

15. Before the tabs can be changed, click **Clear All** to remove the original tabs.

16. Set a new tab by entering **4 cm** in the **Tab stop position** box. Click on **Set**.

17. Create another tab at **9 cm**, then click **OK** and notice the changes.

> Note: You can also change a tab's position by clicking and dragging the tab marker along the ruler to the required place.

18. With all of the document text still selected, click on the left tab stop at **4 cm** on the ruler and drag to **5 cm**. Release the mouse button. The first column will move.

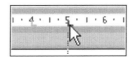

> Note: You can also remove a tab quickly by clicking and dragging its marker down, off and away from the ruler.

19. Click on the first tab stop and drag it down off the ruler. This deletes the first tab stop and the text automatically shifts to the next one.

20. Create a new tab stop at **3 cm** by clicking on the ruler.

21. Practice using the mouse and ruler to add, move and remove tab stops. When you are finished, close the document <u>without</u> saving.

3.9 Right, Center and Decimal Tabs

In the previous exercise you created a number of left tab stops. However, there are a number of other different types of tab, each of which lets you align text in a slightly different way. **Left**, **Centre**, **Right** and **Decimal** tabs are regularly used in common word processing tasks.

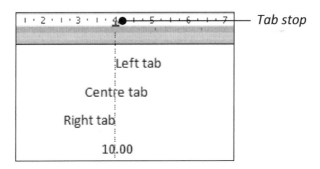

Activity:

1. Open the document **publication prices** which you created and saved earlier. Select the entire document's text and move the tab positions to **4 cm** and **11 cm**.

2. Select the **Home** tab and display the **Paragraph** dialog box and click **Tabs**. From the **Tabs** dialog box, select the **Tab stop position** at **4 cm**. Notice it is left aligned.

3. Click on **Center** from the **Alignment** options and then click **Set**.

4.   Repeat this procedure for the tab at **11 cm**, but make it **Right** aligned.

5.   Click **OK** and observe the effect of the new tab alignment.

6.   Experiment by changing the tabs into right, left and centre aligned tabs. When you are finished, close the document <u>without</u> saving.

7.   Next, open the document **Figures**. Notice that there is a left tab at approximately **4 cm**.

8.   Select all the text and remove the current tab by clicking and dragging it down off the ruler. Notice that each line of text returns to its default tab position of **1.27 cm**.

9.   You can also quickly create various tab stops directly on the ruler. Click the [L] button found to the left of the ruler to cycle through the available tab types.

> Note: The tabs alternate between the useful **Left**, [L], **Center**, [⊥], **Right**, [⅃], and **Decimal**, [⊥•] tab stops. The three other types are rarely used.

10.   Change the tab setting to **Right**, [⅃]. With all of the text still selected, click on the number **4** on the ruler (i.e. **4 cm**). Notice how the text is now right aligned against the tab stop.

11.   Remove the tab stop. Next, change the tab setting to **Decimal**, [⊥•], and click at **4 cm** on the ruler again. Notice how all the numbers line up around their decimal points.

12.   Save the document and close it.

3.10 Margins

Margins determine the distance between the text and the edges of the paper and are usually the same for the whole document. The top and bottom margins are reserved for features such as headers, footers and page numbering (which you will learn more about later).

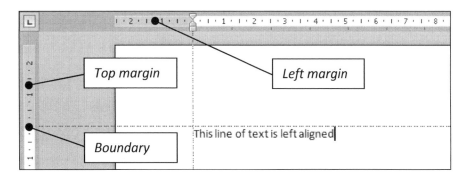

Activity:

1.   Open the document **Progress Report**.

2.   Display the **Page Layout** tab and click the **Margins** button. There are many options shown here, each of which applies a set of preset margins.

3. For more control over margin settings, select **Custom Margins** at the bottom of the menu. The **Page Setup** dialog box appears.

> Note: The **Top**, **Bottom**, **Left** and **Right** margins are, by default, set to **2.54 cm**. An extra side margin can also be added to allow space for binding (**Gutter** margin).

4. Increase the **Left** and **Right** margins to **6 cm** either by editing the numbers in the boxes or by using the up and down *spinners* (the small arrow buttons).

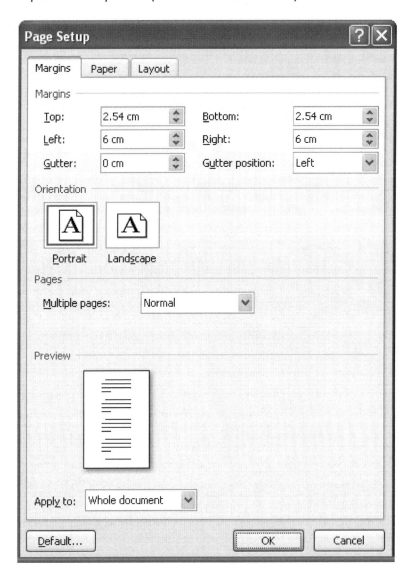

5. Click **OK**. Notice the effect this has on the document. There is now a **6 cm** space between each side of the text and the edges of the page.

> Note: You can also adjust margins by clicking and dragging the margin boundaries on the top and left rulers.

6. Move the mouse pointer over the **Top Margin** boundary on the left ruler. After a moment, it will become a double-headed arrow, ↕.

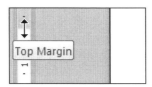

7. The dark area at the top of the ruler indicates the **Top Margin** space. Reduce this margin by dragging the boundary marker up until the margin is **2 cm** in height.

> Note: You can double click the margins on the ruler to view the **Page Setup** dialog box.

8. Now reduce the **Left Margin** by positioning the cursor over the margin boundary on the top ruler until it becomes a double-headed arrow, ↔. This will take some care as there are other markers here in virtually the same position. Drag the left margin to **2 cm**.

> Note: Try holding down <**Alt**> while dragging the margin boundaries to position them more precisely.

9. Click the **Margins** button on the **Ribbon** again and select **Normal**. The margins are reset.

10. Close **Progress Report** <u>without</u> saving the changes.

3.11 Paragraph Alignment

Paragraph **alignment** refers to the location where text appears on each line in relation to the margins. *Word* is capable of four types of text alignment: **Left**, **Centred**, **Right** and **Justified**. It is often a matter of preference which alignment you use, but justified text looks much neater for large paragraphs of text.

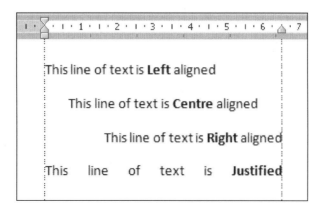

Activity:

1. Open the document **Letter**. All of the text in this document is left aligned, which is the default setting in *Word*.

2. However, this is not how most professional letters look – your address usually appears on the right and the subject line appears in the centre. Highlight the first 4 lines of the letter (the address of the *Big Planet Theme Park's* construction department).

> Note: Alignment is set by clicking one of the alignment buttons, ▤ ▤ ▤ ▤, which are found in the **Paragraph** group on the **Home** tab.

3. Click the **Align Text Right** button, ▤. The address is aligned against the right margin.

Construction Dept.

Big Planet Theme Park

Learnersville

LV1 1BP

4. Use the same technique to right align the date on the next line, and then make it **Bold**.

5. Highlight the line **Re: COPY OF INVOICE #CBS01234**. Centre align this text by clicking the **Center** button, ▤, and then apply **Bold** and **Underline**.

6. If only one paragraph is to be aligned, the cursor needs only to be placed in the paragraph for the effect to take place. Position the cursor anywhere within the main body of the letter (the paragraph starting "**I am writing...**").

7. Justify the text by clicking the **Justify** button, ▤. The text now fills the width of the page.

> Note: Notice how much clearer and professional the letter now appears. Although it only took a few clicks, the effect of alignment has a real impact on your documents.

8. Save the document as **letter final** and close it.

3.12 Indents

Indents are used to move one or more paragraphs of text away from the left or right margins. The indent markers are shown on the top ruler and can be moved in the same way as tab stops.

Left Indent ——  —— *Right Indent*

Activity:

1. Open the document **Agenda**. *Priti* created this simple document (which contains a list of topics to discuss at the next team meeting) and would now like to improve its layout.

2. Place the cursor in the first paragraph below the title **Monthly Meeting Agenda**, and then click the **Increase Indent** button, , in the **Paragraph** group. The entire paragraph is indented.

> Note: Similar to tab stops, the **Increase Indent** button creates indents at **1.27cm** intervals.

3. Notice the **Left Indent** marker on the top ruler now shows an indent at **1.27 cm**.

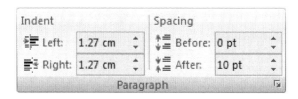

4. Click the **Increase Indent** button again. The indent is increased to **2.54 cm**.

5. Click the **Decrease Indent** button, to reduce the indent back to **1.27 cm**.

> Note: There are key presses for these functions also: to increase an indent press <**Ctrl M**> and to decrease an indent press <**Ctrl Shift M**>.

6. Display the **Page Layout** tab. In the **Paragraph** group, notice that the **Left Indent** setting is **1.27 cm**. Click once in the **Right Indent** box and enter **1.27 cm**. Press <**Enter**>.

Indent		Spacing	
⁜= Left:	1.27 cm ⇕	⬆= Before:	0 pt ⇕
⬛⁼ Right:	1.27 cm ⇕	⬇= After:	10 pt ⇕
	Paragraph		🗗

7. Examine the effect this has on the first paragraph. In particular, notice that the **Right Indent** marker on the ruler has moved inwards **1.27 cm**.

> Note: You can also drag the **Left** and **Right Indent** markers on the ruler. Try holding down <**Alt**> while dragging markers to position them more precisely.

8. Next, increase the **Left Indent** of the remaining list of items in the agenda to **2 cm**.

9. Save the document as **agenda final** and leave it open for the next exercise.

3.13 First Line and Hanging Indents

You may be wondering why the **Left Indent** marker appears differently to the **Right Indent** marker? The reason for this is that the left marker can be split into a **First Line Indent** and a **Hanging Indent**.

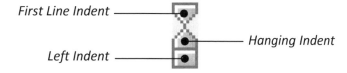

The **First Line Indent** indicates where the first line of each paragraph should start. The **Hanging Indent** indicates where each of the other lines should start.

Activity:

1. The **agenda final** document should still be open. Place the cursor in the first paragraph and then move your mouse pointer over the **First Line Indent** marker on the ruler.

2. Click and drag the indent to the **3 cm** mark. Notice that the first line of the paragraph is now indented further than the others.

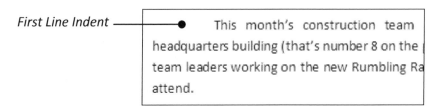

3. Next, move your mouse pointer over the **Hanging Indent** marker on the ruler.

4. Click and drag the indent to the **5 cm** mark. Notice that the first line of the paragraph is now indented less than the others.

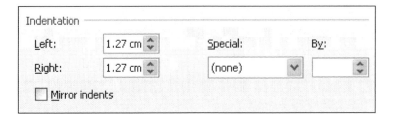

> Note: Dragging the **Left Indent** marker will move the **First Line** and **Hanging Indent** markers together. Hold <**Alt**> while dragging to position markers more precisely.

5. Click the **Paragraph** dialog box launcher. Precise indent settings can be set under the **Indentation** heading. Set the **Left** marker to **1.27 cm** and the **Special** to **(none)**.

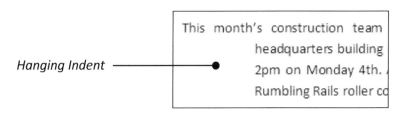

> Note: **Special** here can be used to set a **First Line** or **Hanging Indent**.

6. Click **OK** and the paragraph changes to a **Left Indent** and **Right Indent** of **1.27 cm**.

> Note: Applying bullets and numbering will automatically create a **First Line** and **Hanging Indent**. The first line will feature a bullet or number and then the text. All the remaining lines in the paragraph are indented to line up with only the text.

7.   Save the document with the same file name and close it.

3.14 Page Breaks and Formatting Marks

From time to time you may need to start a new page without the current page being full. This is known as inserting a **page break**.

Activity:

1.   Open the document **Staffing**. This file contains a brief, unformatted memo to the manager of the theme park regarding a number of important issues.

2.   Place the cursor <u>before</u> the heading text **Issues**. You can "force" a document onto two pages by inserting a page break. Display the **Insert** tab and, from the **Pages** group, select **Page Break**.

> Note: Page breaks can also be inserted by placing the cursor in the correct position and pressing <**Ctrl Enter**>.

3.   Scroll down and notice that the heading text **Issues** now starts on page 2.

> Note: The page break appears in your document as a hidden **formatting mark**. To see this and other hidden marks, click the **Show/Hide** button, ¶ , on the **Home** tab.

4.   Scroll back up to page 1 and display **Formatting Marks** by clicking the **Show/Hide** button in the **Paragraph** group. Notice that each line ends with a ¶ symbol – this is a **paragraph break** symbol and appears when you press <**Enter**> to start a new paragraph.

> Note: Formatting marks do not appear when you print a document.

5.   Notice the **Page Break** that you inserted earlier at the bottom of page 1.

6.   Click and drag to select the **Page Break** marker and then press <**Delete**> to remove it. The page break is deleted and the **Issues** header returns to page 1.

7.   Hide **Formatting Marks** again by clicking the **Show/Hide** button in the **Paragraph** group.

8.   Leave the document open for the next exercise.

3.15 Line and Paragraph Spacing

You can improve the appearance and readability of a document by changing line spacing – the white space that appears between lines of text. By default, line spacing is **1.15**. Other commonly used spacing is **Single**, **Double** and **1½**.

Activity:

1. The file **Staffing** should still be open from the previous exercise. Select the 5 paragraphs of text underneath the heading **Memo**.

2. In the **Paragraph** group, click the **Line spacing** button, ⬆☰⬇.

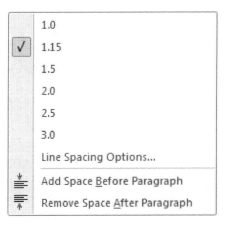

3. From the drop-down list that appears, select **2.0** (also known as **Double**) to change the line spacing for the document. Notice that the spacing between lines increases.

> Note: The spacing value refers to how much space is added below each line in a paragraph. For example, **2.0** means add space 2.0 times the height of the line.

4. Display the **Page Layout** tab. The **Paragraph** group contains controls to change the spacing before and after each paragraph (this is different from line spacing).

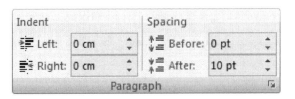

5. To leave space after the selected paragraphs, increase the value in the **After** box to **24 pt**. All selected paragraphs will now gain a **24 pt** space underneath the last line of text.

> Note: As with fonts, line spacing is measured in **points** (shortened to **pt**).

6. Launch the **Paragraph** dialog box. Notice that the settings which have been made are displayed under the **Spacing** heading.

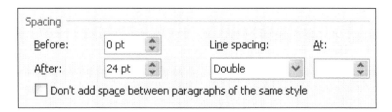

7.   Change the paragraph spacing **After** to **0 pt** and the spacing **Before** to **12 pt**. Change the **Line spacing** to **Single** (**1.0**) and then click **OK**. Notice the effect of these changes.

> Note: Spacing added after one paragraph and before the next will overlap.

8.   Save the document as **staffing complete** and close it.

3.16 Styles

For simple, short documents, the basic tools on the **Home** tab are more than sufficient for formatting text. However, for longer or more complex documents you need to create and use **styles**. Styles are specific combinations of font types, sizes and alignments which help ensure consistent formatting throughout a document. When applied, the selected text or current paragraph will adopt all of the style's format and alignment settings.

Activity:

1.   Open the document **Plan**. This file contains information on the future maintenance of the *Rumbling Rails* ride. Notice that there are a number of bold headers followed by a brief description in plain text.

2.   Display the **Home** tab and locate the **Styles** group. The options provided here allow you to apply new styles to the text in your documents.

3.   Notice that the style **Heading 1** is currently highlighted. This means that the cursor is placed in a paragraph of text which has the **Heading 1** style applied.

4.   Place the cursor on the second line of text containing the date; the style **Heading 2** is highlighted (you may need to click **More** to see this). Next, place the cursor on the third line containing the two lines of introductory text; the style **Normal** is highlighted.

> Note: The highlighted styles are built-in styles that were added when the document was created. It is common practice to use **Heading 1** for main titles, **Heading 2** for sub-titles, and so on. **Normal** is used for the main body text of a document.

5. With the cursor positioned in the third paragraph, select **Heading 1** from the **Styles** box. The text changes to match the **Heading 1** style.

6. Select **Normal** from the **Styles** box to restore the text's formatting.

> Note: Once you have applied a style it is very easy to change it. Changing a style will also change all the parts of your document that use it.

7. Open the **Styles** task pane by clicking the **Styles** launcher button.

8. Notice that **Normal** is currently selected. Place the cursor in the subheading text **Ride Improvements**. The style **Heading 3** is selected.

9. Move your mouse pointer over the selected style on the **Styles** task pane. Click once on the drop-down arrow that appears and then click **Modify**.

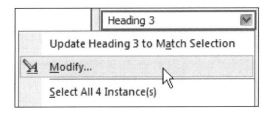

10. The **Modify Style** dialog box appears. From this dialog box you can change all formatting and alignment settings for the selected style.

11. Underneath the **Formatting** heading, change the **Font** to **Arial** and the size to **14**. Select **Underline** and a font colour of **Dark Blue**.

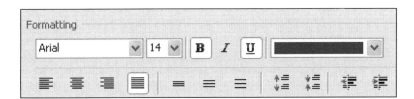

> Note: Options to alter **Paragraphs**, **Tabs** and **Borders** for the selected style can be found by clicking the **Format** button, Format ▾ , at the bottom of the dialog box.

12. Click **OK**. The style is updated and all paragraphs that are based on it are changed.

13. Use this technique to change the **Normal** style to use the font **Times New Roman** size **20**.

> Note: Styles can be based on other styles. If you change the original style, any style based on it will change too.

14. There are a number of built-in style sets that can be used to give your documents a professional look. From the **Styles** group, click the **Change Styles** button. From the submenu that appears, click **Style Set**.

15. Move your mouse over each of the style sets shown and the result of applying each will be previewed in the document.

16. Finally, click **Modern** to apply that style set. This replaces the formatting options for each of the built-in styles (and any text based on them will be updated).

> Note: Completely new styles can be created by clicking the **New Style** button, ⏣, on the **Styles** task pane and then specifying font formatting and alignment settings.

17. Close the **Styles** task pane.

18. Save the document as **maintenance plan** and close it.

3.17 Creating a Table

Word's **Table** feature provides a really effective way of presenting data in a clear and easy to read format. Tables consist of **rows** (running from top to bottom) and **columns** (running from left to right) to create a number of **cells** that can contain text. The table can also be formatted to create a more professional, eye catching document.

	Monday	Tuesday	Wednesday	Thursday	Friday
Scaffolding	Mira	Atsu/Alan	Mira/Alan	Atsu	Mira
Train Install	Chen	Chen	Chen	Priti	Priti
System Test	Priti	Priti	Priti	Chen	Chen
Landscaping	Dave	Ali	Dave	Ali	Ali
Labouring	Atsu/Paul	Dave/Mira	Atsu/Paul	Dave/Mira	Atsu/Paul

Activity:

1. Start a new, blank document.

2. To create a new table, display the **Insert** tab and click the **Table** button. When the grid appears, click **Insert Table** at the bottom of the menu.

> Note: A table can also be created directly from the **Table** drop-down button by moving your mouse pointer over the required number of cells on the grid and clicking once.

3. The **Insert Table** dialog box appears.

4. Enter **6** in the **Number of columns** box and **6** in the **Number of rows** box (these numbers can be typed in directly or the up/down spinners can be used).

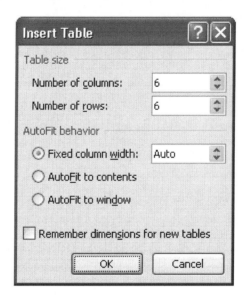

5. Click **OK** to create the table. It appears at the location of the cursor. Once a table has been created, it is simple to enter text and move around within it.

> Note: It is often easier to enter text into a table first and then format it later (i.e. add colour, adjust text size, correct column widths, etc).

6. The cursor should be flashing inside the first cell. If it is not, click once in the top left cell to place it.

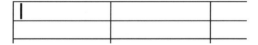

> Note: You can use the <**Tab**> key to move to the next cell in a table and <**Shift Tab**> to move backwards. When entering text, only use <**Enter**> when a new line is required within the same cell.

7. Using the <**Tab**> key to move between cells, enter the following text:

	Monday	Tuesday	Wednesday	Thursday	Friday
Scaffolding	Mira	Atsu/Alan	Mira/Alan	Atsu	Mira
Train Install	Chen	Chen	Chen	Priti	Priti
System Test	Priti	Priti	Priti	Chen	Chen
Landscaping	Dave	Ali	Dave	Ali	Ali
Labouring	Atsu/Paul	Dave/Mira	Atsu/Paul	Dave/Mira	Atsu/Paul

> Note: When the cursor is in the last cell of a row, pressing <**Tab**> will move the cursor to the first cell on the next row.

8. Save the document as **staff roster** and leave it open for the next exercise.

3.18 Move or Resize a Table

Once a table has been created, you can easily move it to a different position on the page and increase or decrease its size to suit your document.

Activity:

1. The document **staff roster** created in the previous exercise should still be open.

2. Rest the mouse pointer over the table until the **Table Move Handle**, ⊞, appears at the top left corner.

> Note: If the **Table Move Handle** does not appear, make sure **Print Layout** view is displayed by selecting the **View** tab and then clicking **Print Layout**. This view will show the document as it will appear on the printed page.

3. Now move the mouse over the **Table Move Handle** until a four-headed arrow appears.

4. You can now move the table anywhere on the page. Click and drag the **Table Move Handle** downward to move the table about half way down the page.

5. Rest the mouse pointer over the table again until the **Table Resize Handle**, ▫, appears at the bottom right corner. This allows you to resize the table to any size you like.

6. Now move the mouse pointer over the **Table Resize Handle** until a double headed arrow appears.

Ali	Ali
Dave/Mira	Atsu/Paul

7. Drag the mouse down a little until the table is about twice its original height.

8. Now use the **Table Resize Handle** to return the table to approximately its original size.

9. Use the **Table Move Handle** to move the table back to the top of the page again.

10. Leave the document open for the next exercise.

3.19 Selecting Cells

You need to be able to select table cells before you can do anything to them, just as a block of text must be selected before it can be formatted. Unfortunately, selecting cells can sometimes be a tricky and frustrating business, but there are a number of techniques to help you.

Note: Selecting the text inside of a cell is not the same as selecting the cell itself.

Activity:

1. Select the first cell containing the word **Scaffolding** by moving inside the left edge of the cell and clicking the left mouse button once when the selection arrow appears, ⬈.

2. The entire cell and its contents are now selected. Make the text bold by clicking the **Bold** button, ⃞ **B**, on the **Home** tab.

3. Move the mouse pointer over the inside left edge of the cell above and double click the left mouse button when the pointer changes to ⬈. The entire row is selected.

	Monday	Tuesday	Wednesday
Scaffolding	Mira	Atsu/Alan	Mira/Alan

4. Click the **Bold** button again to make all of the cells in the first row bold.

5. Next, move the mouse pointer just below the top edge of the first column until the selection arrow is displayed again. Click once to select the entire column.

Scaffolding
Train Install
System Test
Landscaping
Labouring

6. Click the **Bold** button. This first removes the **Bold** setting applied to **Scaffolding** earlier, so click again to make *all* of the cells in the first column bold.

7. Now move your mouse pointer over the cell containing the name **Mira**. Click and drag to select this cell and the 24 cells below and to the right.

	Monday	Tuesday	Wednesday	Thursday	Friday
Scaffolding	Mira	Atsu/Alan	Mira/Alan	Atsu	Mira
Train Install	Chen	Chen	Chen	Priti	Priti
System Test	Priti	Priti	Priti	Chen	Chen
Landscaping	Dave	Ali	Dave	Ali	Ali
Labouring	Atsu/Paul	Dave/Mira	Atsu/Paul	Dave/Mira	Atsu/Paul

8. Click the **Italic** button, ⃞ *I*, to make all of the text in the selected cells italic.

9. To select the entire table, move the mouse over the **Table Move Handle** and click once.

10. Next, use the **Font Color** button's drop-down arrow, **A** ▾, to change all of the text to **Dark Blue**. Leave the document open for the next exercise.

3.20 Cell Alignment and Direction

The contents of a cell can be aligned against the left, centre and right edges as well as the top, middle or bottom.

Activity:

1. With the table still selected from the previous exercise, display the **Layout** tab on the **Ribbon**. Notice in the **Alignment** group that the table's text is aligned to the **Top Left**, ▣.

2. Click **Align Bottom Right**, ▣, to see the difference.

3. Change the text to centre aligned by clicking **Align Center**, ▣.

4. Select the top row of the table only. To change the direction of the text click **Text Direction**. The text is rotated 90 degrees and the cell height is increased.

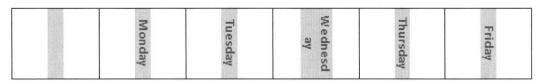

	Monday	Tuesday	Wednesday	Thursday	Friday

> **Note:** Changing the direction of text can often be a useful way of displaying lots of column headers in a small amount of space (notice that the icons in the **Alignment** group are also rotated). However, it's probably not suitable for this kind of table.

5. Continue to click the **Text Direction** button to cycle through the available alternatives. Stop when the text is horizontal again (as it was when it started).

6. Leave the document open for the next exercise.

3.21 Resizing Cells

Once you have created a table, it is very easy to resize individual cells or entire rows and columns. You can even automatically adjust rows and columns so that they are equal in size in order to produce a professional look to your finished tables.

Activity:

1. Notice that the height of the top row is now too high. Move the mouse pointer anywhere over the bottom edge of the topmost row (as shown below).

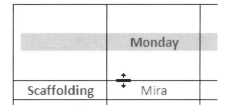

2. The mouse pointer becomes a double headed arrow, ⬍. Click and drag upwards to make the row approximately the same height as all of the others.

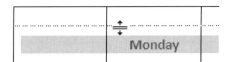

3. To resize the first column, move the mouse pointer anywhere over the leftmost vertical edge. The mouse pointer becomes a double headed arrow again, ↔.

4. Click and drag the border left a little way to increase the width of the column.

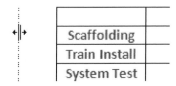

5. The leftmost column is now larger than the rest. To balance the table evenly select the entire table again.

6. Display the **Layout** tab and click **Distribute Columns**, ▦, from the **Cell Size** group. The columns are equally sized.

7. Click the **Distribute Rows** button also, ▤, to ensure that each row is the same height.

8. Position the table back in the middle of the page, and then save and close the document.

3.22 Merging and Splitting Cells

Sometimes you may need to create a table that contains cells that are bigger or smaller than others in the same table. You can do this by **merging** cells into a single cell or **splitting** cells into two or more smaller cells. Merging and splitting cells is often done to create documents such as invoices, timetables, forms, and so on.

Activity:

1. In a new blank document, create a table with **5** columns and **10** rows. Select the second and third cells by clicking and dragging.

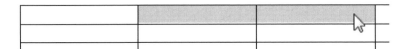

2. Display the **Layout** tab and click **Merge Cells** in the **Merge** group, ▦ Merge Cells. The cells are merged.

3. Next, merge the next two cells at the top right of the table. Then, merge all of the cells on the second row.

4. Merge cells **1** and **2** on rows **3** to **9**. This must be done one row at a time.

5. Merge cells **1** to **4** on the bottom row.

6. *Priti* needs to keep a record of building materials ordered for the new ride to send to the accounts department. Enter text into the table so that it matches the picture below.

Date	Name		Department	
Product		Price	Quantity	Total Price
Grand Total				

7. The accounts department has indicated that they need to see product reference numbers in the table. Position the cursor in the cell containing the text **Product** and click **Split Cells** from the **Merge** group on the **Layout** tab, ⊞ Split Cells .

8. Make sure **2** columns and **1** row are selected in the **Split Cells** dialog box and click **OK**.

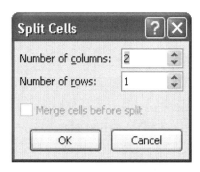

9. Enter **Ref.** in the cell to the right of **Product** and split the cells in the six rows below (you can split the remaining cells one row at a time or all at once).

Date	Name		Department	
Product	Ref.	Price	Quantity	Total Price
Grand Total				

10. This document is now perfect for keeping a record of future purchases. Save the document as **materials** and close it.

3.23 Deleting Cells

Once you have created a table it is very easy to remove individual cells, rows or columns.

Activity:

1. In a new blank document, create a table with **6** columns and **6** rows.

2. Select the entire second row. To delete this row, click the **Delete** button in the **Rows & Columns** group on the **Layout** tab.

3. From the drop-down menu that appears, select **Delete Rows**. The row is deleted.

4. Next, select the entire last column. From the **Delete** button's drop-down menu, select **Delete Columns**. The last column is removed.

5. Select the first two cells only. From the **Delete** button's drop-down menu, select **Delete Cells**. The **Delete Cells** dialog box appears.

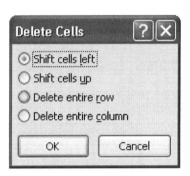

6. Before individual cells can be deleted, you first have to decide what will take their place. Select **Shift cells left** and click **OK**. The first two cells are deleted and the remaining cells on the row move to the left to take their place.

> Note: Selecting **Shift cells up** will move the cells directly below up to take the place of those deleted.

7. Select the entire table by clicking the **Table Move Handle**, ⊞.

8. From the **Delete** button's drop-down menu, select **Delete Table**. The entire table is removed.

9. Close the document <u>without</u> saving.

3.24 Gridlines, Borders and Shading

There are several effects that you can apply to tables to improve their look or to draw attention to certain parts of it. You can add **borders** to a table or individual rows, columns, or cells, and you can use **shading** to fill in the background of a table.

> **Note:**   Used properly, borders can emphasise information, make it easier to read, and can give your tables a more professional appearance. However, be careful not to go overboard and use too many styles and colours as this can have the reverse effect.

By default, tables in *Word* have a single, thin, black border around all cells. If you remove these, **gridlines** will continue to show the cell boundaries on the screen (but will not be printed).

Activity:

1. Open the document **materials** that you created earlier.

2. Select the entire table, and then click the **Borders** button drop-down arrow on the **Design** tab.

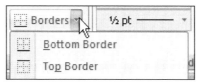

3. Select **Borders and Shading** from the bottom of the menu. The **Borders and Shading** dialog box appears.

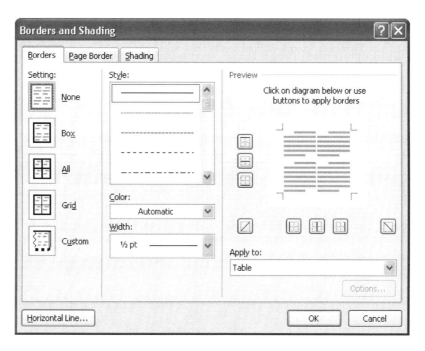

4. With the **Borders** tab displayed, select **None** from under **Setting** and then click
    OK. The table's borders are removed and faint dashed gridlines shown instead.

Date	Name	
Product	Ref.	Price

> Note: If gridlines are not shown, select **View Gridlines** on the **Layout** tab. These lines are
> for guidance only when working with tables and do not print.

5. Select the entire first row of the table.

6. Display the **Borders and Shading** dialog box again and select **Box** from under
    Setting.

7. From the **Style** box, select the first double line, ══════════.

8. From the **Color** drop-down box, select a dark blue colour. Then, from the **Width** drop-
    down box, select **¾ pt** (this setting represents the thickness of the line).

> Note: To apply a border to specific sides of a selected cell or table only, simply click on
> the table **Preview** where you want the chosen border settings to apply. A second
> click removes that border.

9. Click **OK**. The entire first row gains a dark blue border.

10. Select the second row. From the **Borders and Shading** dialog box, select the **Shading** tab.

11. From the **Fill** drop-down box, select a light blue colour and observe the effects in the
    Preview panel. Make sure **Clear** is selected under **Style** and then click **OK**.

> Note: **Clear** allows for a transparent solid colour. You can also add patterns to cells.

12. Continue to experiment with different table borders, line styles and shading options. Try
    to reproduce the following picture.

Date	Name		Department	
Product	Ref.	Price	Quantity	Total Price
Grand Total				

13. Save the document using the same name and close it.

3.25 Importing Objects

Various objects from other *Microsoft Office* applications can be imported into a document. For example, if you were producing a report you may want to include a chart or part of a spreadsheet that was created in *Excel*.

Activity:

1. Open the file **Update**, which contains a brief report on the *Rumbling Rails* ride. This document is incomplete and a number of items need to be imported from elsewhere. Place the cursor in the space underneath the paragraph starting "**The initial costs…**".

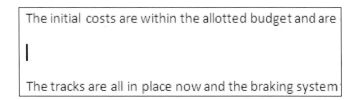

2. Display the **Insert** tab and click **Object**, 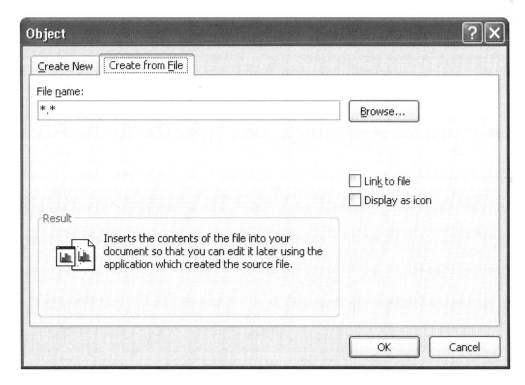, from the **Text** group. When the **Object** dialog box appears, display the **Create from File** tab.

3. To insert a chart created in *Excel*, click the **Browse** button at the right of the **File name** box. The **Browse** dialog box appears.

4. Locate the data folder for this section and select the **Initial Costs** file. Click **Insert**.

> Note: Notice the **Link to file** checkbox. If this is selected any changes made later to the imported file will also be shown in the *Word* document when it is reopened.

5. Select the **Link to file** checkbox and then click **OK**. The contents of the **Initial Costs** spreadsheet are imported (a chart).

> Note: Only the contents of the *default* worksheet are imported. If you need to import another part of a workbook, open it and make the relevant worksheet active and then resave the file. You can also copy and paste items between open files.

6. The imported chart is far too large and needs to be reduced in size. Click on the chart to select it and then drag a corner handle inward until it fits neatly on the page.

> Note: You will learn more about creating spreadsheets and charts in the next section.

7. Place the cursor below the paragraph starting "**Some technical statistics...**". Import the contents of the spreadsheet **Statistics** (a table).

> Note: To change the contents of an imported object you must first double click it. If the object was imported with **Link to file** selected it will open in its default program; if **Link to file** was not selected it will open as an embedded object in *Word*.

8. Select and then centre the table on the page.

> Note: Borders can be added to imported objects in the same way as tables.

9. Save the document as **update complete** and close it.

10. Next, try to open the **update complete** document again. You will be informed that the document contains links to other files.

11. Select **Yes** and any changes to the linked files will be reflected in this document. Leave the document open for the next exercise.

3.26 Inserting Pictures and Clip Art

To make your documents more interesting you can import pictures from files on your computer into a document. Various pictures are also available from the **Clip Art** library that is available online (**Clip Art** images are simple illustrations or photographs provided with *Microsoft Office*).

Activity:

1. Using the file **update complete**, position the cursor above the paragraph starting "**Some technical statistics...**".

2. Display the **Insert** tab and then click **Picture**. From the **Insert Picture** dialog box, locate the data files folder and select the file named **Photo**.

Picture

> **Note:** Make sure the **file type** drop-down box has **All Pictures** selected. Select **Large Icons** from the **Views** button to see a preview of the available pictures.

3. Click **Insert**. The image appears against the left margin, but it may be a little too small. Using a corner handle, click and drag outwards to make the picture about twice its original size. Centre the image in the middle of the paragraph.

> **Note:** The green handle at the top of the picture, ⌉, can be used to rotate an image.

4. The document is now complete. Save the changes and close it.

5. Next, open the document **Roller Coaster** (ignore any spelling mistakes for now).

6. Position the cursor at the beginning of the first paragraph under the heading **The thrill of the ride**.

The thrill of the ride

The excitement for the rider comes from the
on the body. When the coaster speeds up, th

7. Display the **Insert** tab and click the **Clip Art** button. The **Clip Art** pane appears at the right of the screen.

Clip
Art

8. Keyword searches are used to locate relevant **Clip Art** pictures. In the **Search for** box enter the keywords **roller coaster** and click **Go**. The results are displayed in the pane.

9. Click on any image that is relevant to place it in the document at the cursor's position.

10. If the imported picture is too large or too small, resize it using the corner handles, and then click away from the picture to deselect it.

The thrill of the ride

The excitement for the rider
gravity and acceleration on the body. When the coas

> **Note:** It is important to maintain the **proportions** of pictures and other objects such as charts when resizing them. The corner handles let you do this. However, if you use the other top, bottom or side handles, the image will be distorted.

11.   Select the **Clip Art** image again. The way text and images are laid out on the page is known as **text wrap**.

12.   Display the **Format** tab and click the **Text Wrapping** button, 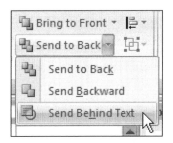, from the **Arrange** group.

13.   From the drop-down menu that appears, select **Tight**. Notice how the text now wraps around the **Clip Art** picture.

14.   With the image still selected, select **Square** wrapping. Notice the effect.

15.   Next, select **In Front of Text** wrapping. The picture appears *floating* above the text.

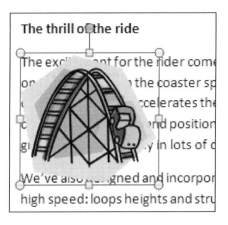

16.   Move the mouse pointer over the image until a four-headed arrow appears, ⟘. Click and drag the image into the middle of the page. The text underneath is not affected.

17.   From the **Arrange** group, drop down the **Send Backward** button and select **Send Behind Text**.

18.   The image appears behind the text. Click the drop-down arrow on the **Bring Forward** button and select **Bring In Front of Text** to place the picture in front of the text again.

19.   From **Text Wrapping**, select **In Line with Text** to restore the image to its original location.

> Note: When an image is placed "in-line" it will appear on the same line as the text around it and will move as you enter, edit and format that text.

20.   Close the **Clip Art** pane, save the document as **picture** and close it.

> **Note:**   A picture is worth a thousand words. Used properly, images and **Clip Art** can help support information in your document and give it a more professional appearance. However, too many or inappropriate pictures can have the reverse affect.

3.27 WordArt, Shapes and Text Boxes

Word has a powerful feature called **WordArt** which allows you to create impressive artwork automatically from the text in your document. This is particularly useful for creating headers for posters, flyers, and so on. There are various styles, shapes and colours to choose from.

You can also use *Word's* simple drawing features to add a number of basic shapes to your documents, and even place text inside floating boxes that can be placed anywhere you like.

Activity:

1.   Safety inspectors will be visiting *Rumbling Rails* in the next day or two. To direct them to the site office upon their arrival, an eye-catching notice is required for the ride's entrance gate. A simple A4 poster will be perfect.

2.   Start a new, blank document. On the first line enter the text **Rumbling Rails**.

3.   Select the new text, display the **Insert** tab and click **WordArt**, 4 WordArt , in the **Text** group. From the drop-down menu that appears, select any style that you believe looks the most striking.

4.   The **Edit WordArt Text** dialog box appears which can be used to change the selected text. Select a text **Size** of **48**, and click **OK** without editing the text to convert it to **WordArt**.

> **Note:**   Notice that the **WordArt Tools - Format** tab appears on the **Ribbon**. This can be used to apply a variety of **WordArt** styles and effects. As other *Microsoft Office* programs use **WordArt**, you will learn more about these features in later sections.

5.   Using the **Position** button, move the **WordArt** to the **Top Center** of the page.

> Note: Although useful for creating fancy headings for newsletters, flyers, and brochures, **WordArt** and shapes are rarely suitable for use in professional documents.

6. Display the **Insert** tab and click the **Shapes** button in the **Illustrations** group. From the drop-down menu that appears, examine the various shapes that you can select.

7. Under the **Block Arrows** heading, select **Right Arrow**.

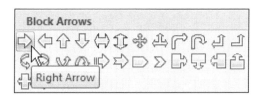

8. The mouse pointer changes to a crosshair, ╋. Underneath the **WordArt**, click and drag to create a shape that fills the width of the page between the margins.

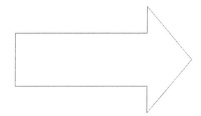

9. On the new **Drawing Tools - Format** tab that appears, select an interesting colour and style from the **Shape Styles** group.

10. Next, click the **Edit Text** button, , in the **Insert Shapes** group to add a text box to the new shape. Enter the text **This Way**.

11. Select the new text and then increase the **Font Size** to **72** and **Center** align it. Click away from the shape to deselect it.

12. Scroll down to the bottom of the page. Display the **Insert** tab again and, from the **Text** group, click **Text Box**. From the bottom of the drop-down menu, select **Draw Text Box**. The cursor changes to a crosshair again.

13. Using the rulers for reference, click and drag to create a text box approximately **8 cm** by **6 cm** in the middle of the page (it doesn't need to be exact). Type the following text into the text box:

    The Rumbling Rails ride is currently closed to the public. All official visitors must report to the site office.

14. Using the **Home** tab, **Center** align the text and increase the font size to **20**.

15. Place your mouse pointer over any edge of the text box until a four-headed arrow appears, and then click and drag the box so that it appears in a suitable position below the arrow shape. Resize it if necessary.

> Note: **WordArt**, shapes, text boxes and pictures can overlap. To control which object are in front of which, use the **Bring to Front** and **Send to Back** buttons.

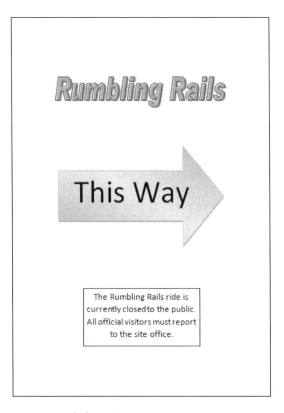

16.   Save the document as **poster** and close it.

3.28 Columns

Columns can be used to divide a page into two or more vertical sections. Once you fill the first column, text automatically flows into the second. This technique is really useful for creating documents such as newsletters or brochures.

Activity:

1.   Open the document **Newsletter**. This file contains basic information about the new *Rumbling Rails* ride.

2.   Display the **Page Layout** tab and click the **Columns** button, ⊞ Columns ▾ , in the **Page Setup** group. From the drop-down menu that appears, select **Two**.

3.   The page is now divided into two columns. The text reads down the first column and then flows into the second automatically. After the first paragraph of text, create a new line and insert the image **Photo** from the data files folder.

4.   Notice how the text in the first column has been pushed into the second column. Resize the picture to approximately twice its original size and **Center** align it in the first column, as shown on the following page.

high and will reach speeds of 80 miles per hour.

The ride is built entirely from steel and features a number of jaw-dropping falls,

> **Note:** Columns can be applied to an entire document or to specific parts of it. Once columns have been created they can be resized using the top ruler.

5. Similar to **Page Breaks**, you can also apply **Column Breaks** to force text into the next available column. Place the cursor before the subheading **Ride Features**.

6. From the **Page Layout** tab, click the **Breaks** drop-down button, Breaks ▾. From the submenu that appears, select **Column**. The remaining text is forced into the second column (notice that *Word* has automatically created a new page with columns).

7. Delete the column break. You may need to turn **Formatting Marks** on first, ¶.

8. Save the document as **newsletter complete** and leave it open for the next exercise.

3.29 Headers and Footers

Headers and **footers** can be added to a document and will appear at the top and bottom of each page. Although often the same across all pages in a document, they can also be set to appear differently on alternate pages. Special automatically updating **fields** such as the date, time and page number can also easily be added.

Activity:

1. Using the file **newsletter complete** saved in the previous exercise, select the **Insert** tab and click **Header**. From the submenu that appears, click **Edit Header** to reveal the header.

> **Note:**   Notice that the text in the main document becomes ghosted (and can't be directly edited). The **Header & Footer Tools - Design** tab also appears on the **Ribbon**.

2.   Enter the text **Press Release**.

3.   Locate the **Options** group on the **Header & Footer Tools - Design** tab and make sure that neither **Different First Page** nor **Different Odd & Even Pages** are checked.

> **Note:**   These useful settings allow you to create a different **Header** and **Footer** for the first page of a document, and then for each even and odd page afterwards.

4.   Click the **Go to Footer** button to switch to the footer.

5.   Press <**Tab**> to move to the centre tab stop (headers and footers have a number of tab stops added automatically). Enter the text **Rumbling Rails**.

6.   Press <**Tab**> again to move to the right tab stop and click **Page Number** from the **Header & Footer** group. Select **Current Position** and then choose **Plain Number**.

> **Note:**   The page number is inserted as a **field** which is automatically updated when you open the document or add a new page.

7.   Click **Close Header and Footer** on the right of the **Ribbon** to return to the main document view. Notice that the header and footer are now ghosted (and can't be edited directly).

8.   Create a **Column Break** before the heading **More Information** to force the text afterwards onto a new page. Notice that the second page also shows the same header and footer (and the page number has increased).

9.   Save the document with the same file name and leave it open for the next exercise.

3.30 Page Orientation and Printing

Page **orientation** simply refers to the direction in which a document is created and printed. It can be in **Portrait** (upright) or **Landscape** (sideways) mode.

Activity:

1. Normally, *Word* documents are created in **Portrait** mode. This is the default orientation.

2. To change the current document (**newsletter complete**) to **Landscape**, display the **Page Layout** tab and click the **Orientation** button in the **Page Setup** group.

3. Select **Landscape** from the options shown and the page is rotated 90 degrees (although the text is not).

> Note: For most professional uses you should always use **Portrait** mode to create documents. **Landscape** is useful for creative documents such as brochures.

4. Use the **Orientation** button to restore the page to **Portrait** mode.

5. Click the **Office Button** and expand **Print**. From the options that appear, select **Print Preview**. A preview of the current page as it will be printed is shown. From the **Preview** group click **Previous Page** to show the first page in the document.

6. Examine the print options on show and notice that you can change page orientation and margins from this screen also. Click **Print** to display the **Print** dialog box.

7. Enter **1** in the **Pages** box to print only the first page of the press release. Make sure **Number of copies** is set to **1** also so that only one copy of the page is printed.

8. Choose the printer you would like to print to from the printer **Name** drop-down button. All printers installed on your computer are visible here.

> **Note:** In a work or education environment you may have access to many printers. Try to find the name of the one closest to you. In some situations you may also be charged for printing so be careful what you print.

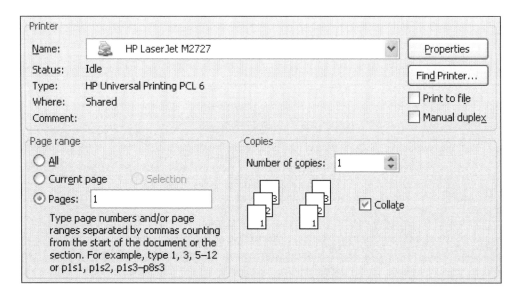

9. Click **OK** to print a copy of the newsletter on your chosen printer. Next, click **Close Print Preview** to return to the main document view.

10. Save and close the document.

3.31 Spelling and Grammar Checking

Word can check the spelling and grammar of any text-based documents that you open, and will even check new text as you type it. Words that are misspelled are shown with a wavy red line underneath them and grammatical errors are shown with a wavy green line underneath. *Word* makes suggestions to help you correct errors which can either be accepted or ignored.

> A speling error.
>
> A grammar errors.

Activity:

1. Open the document **Roller Coaster**. Wait a moment and spelling errors will appear underlined in red.

> **Note:** If red wavy lines do not appear below at least one word then the **Automatic Spelling & Grammar** feature is turned off. To turn it on, click the **Office Button** and select **Word Options**. Click the **Proofing** button and make sure **Check spelling as you type**, **Mark grammar errors as you type** and **Check grammar with spelling** are all selected. Click **OK**.

2.   The quickest way of correcting a small number of errors is by using the mouse. Place the mouse over the first item underlined in red, **plavce**, and click once with the right mouse button. A shortcut menu appears with a list of suggestions.

3.   Select **place** to correct the error.

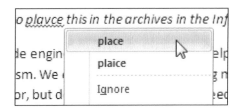

4.   When working with a document, a **Proofing** icon will be shown in the **Status Bar** indicating the current spelling status of the document. Find this now.

5.   Note that, if there are mistakes, , appears. If everything is correct, ![icon], appears.

6.   Locate the next error in the document. Notice that this one is not technically a spelling error but is a repeated word (**the the**). Right click the second word and select **Delete Repeated Word** from the shortcut menu that appears.

> Note: You could continue to correct errors in this way for the entire document. However, the **Spelling and Grammar** feature is far quicker for checking an entire document.

7.   Place the cursor at the beginning of the document.

8.   Display the **Review** tab and click the **Spelling & Grammar** button. The **Spelling and Grammar** dialog box appears.

ABC
Spelling & Grammar

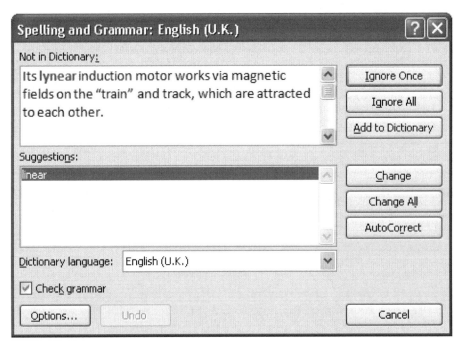

9.   The first spelling error is shown in the top area, **lynear**. Suggested alternatives are shown beneath. Errors can be ignored, changed or added to the dictionary.

10. Select the alternative **linear** (if it is not already selected) and click **Change**. The error is corrected in the document.

11. Work through the remainder of the document making any necessary corrections. A message appears when the check is complete.

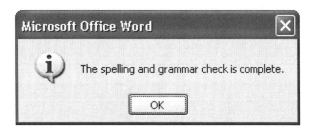

> Note: If the **Suggestions** box does not contain the required word you can type it into the top box directly to correct the error. Click **Change** to replace the document text.

12. Click **OK** and check that the **Status Bar** is no longer showing any proofing errors, .

13. Save the document as **roller coaster fixed** and then close it.

> Note: *Word's* spell checking feature only finds words that are not in its dictionary; it will not find mistakes such as **semi detached horse**. For this reason you should always proof read your documents after they have been spell-checked.

14. Open the document **Roller Coaster Grammar**.

15. A number of grammatical errors are underlined in green (it may take a few seconds for the errors to appear after the file is opened). Click the **Spelling & Grammar** button again on the **Review** tab.

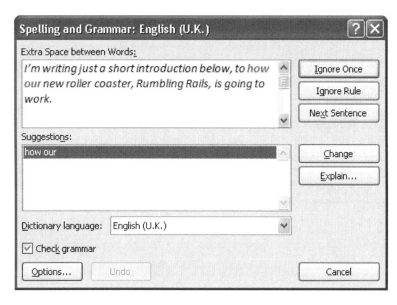

16. The first error is an extra space before **our**. Notice how the buttons at the right of the dialog box are slightly different to that shown when spelling is checked. Click **Change**.

17. The second error is the name of the *Rumbling Rails* ride. As this is correct, click **Ignore Once**. The third error is a **t** that should be uppercase. Click **Change** to accept the suggestion.

18. The next error is a little trickier in that a full stop has mistakenly been placed in the middle of a sentence. Click in the document text and remove the full stop (you may need to move the **Spelling and Grammar** dialog box out of the way first).

19. Click **Resume** on the **Spelling and Grammar** dialog box to continue the check, and then **OK** when the check is complete (the **Status Bar** should show no proofing errors,).

20. Save the document as **roller coaster grammar fixed** and then close it.

3.32 Templates

Templates are normal documents that have been saved in a special location to act a starting point for future documents. They are really useful for creating many documents of the same basic type (e.g. letters) as they have all the text and required styles, formatting and layout options set.

Activity:

1. Open the document **Outline**. This is a normal document which contains a basic outline for a letter but does not contain any specific details.

2. Click the **Office Button** and select **Save As**. From the **Save as type** drop-down box, select **Word Template**.

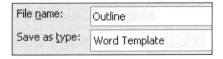

3. Make sure **Trusted Templates** is selected in the **Save As** dialog box's navigation panel.

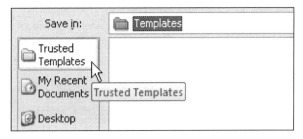

> Note: Documents created in *Word* have a **.docx** file extension (or **.doc** in older versions). *Word* **Templates** on the other hand have a **.dotx** (or **.dot**) extension.

4. Click **Save** and the template is saved. Close the **Outline** document.

5. Click the **Office Button** and select **New**. Under **Templates**, select **My templates**. Notice that **Outline.dotx** now appears in the **New** dialog box.

Outline

6. Select **Outline.dotx** and click **OK**. A new document is created based upon the **Outline** template created earlier.

> Note: There are a number of built-in templates available within *Word* (or downloadable from *Office Online*) which may be of use when creating new documents.

7. You have received a job application from **Miss Amos** for the role of **Engineer**. She lives at **32 Trent Street, Learnersville, LV2 3HJ**. Complete the letter by replacing the text in brackets with the real contact information for Miss Amos.

8. Save the document as **application** and close it.

> Note: Editing and saving this document will not affect the original template. If you need to change the template you must open it directly from the **Templates** folder.

3.33 Protecting Documents

Documents can be **password protected** or made **read-only** so that they cannot be opened by unauthorised people or mistakenly changed.

Activity:

1. Open the document **Sensitive**. This file contains employee information that you are required to keep private and confidential.

2. Click the **Office Button** and select **Prepare**. The options shown allow you to protect your document in a number of different ways.

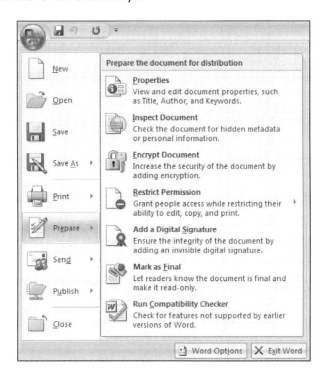

3. Click **Encrypt Document** to display the **Encrypt Document** dialog box. Enter the password **priti12345**.

4. Click **OK**. When prompted, enter the password again (this is to check that you entered it correctly first time) and then click **OK** again. The document is now password protected.

5. Close the document and save any changes.

6. Next, try to open the document **Sensitive** again. You are asked to enter a password in order to open the file. Enter the password **priti12345** and click **OK**.

Note: To remove the password protection from a document, display the **Encrypt Document** dialog box again, delete the password, and click **OK**.

7. To mark a document as **Final** and allow others to read it without making changes, click the **Office Button** and display the **Prepare** submenu again.

8. Select **Mark as Final** and click **OK**. Read the contents of the information dialog box that appears and then click **OK** to accept it.

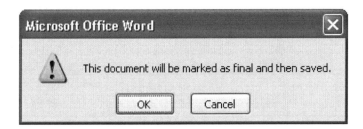

9. The document is now read-only. Notice that most of the editing features on the **Ribbon** have been disabled to discourage changes.

Note: You can still make changes to the document, but these changes must be saved as a different file.

10. Close the document and any other open documents without saving.

11. Leave *Word* open for the next exercise.

3.34 Taking Screenshots

Pressing the **Print Screen** key on your keyboard will take a snapshot picture of your entire screen's display and all of its contents. You can then paste this into a *Word* document in order to save or print it. This technique is really useful for gathering evidence of your work.

Activity:

1. Start a new, blank document.

2. Minimise *Word* so that only your *Windows* **Desktop** is visible.

3. Locate the <**Print Screen**> key on your keyboard. It is usually located towards the top right of the keyboard (and may be labelled slightly differently, e.g. <**Prt Scr**>).

4. Nothing appears to happen, but in fact a snapshot of your screen has been captured and placed in memory. Return to *Word*.

5. With the cursor flashing at the top left of your document, click the **Paste** button to insert the picture of your **Desktop**.

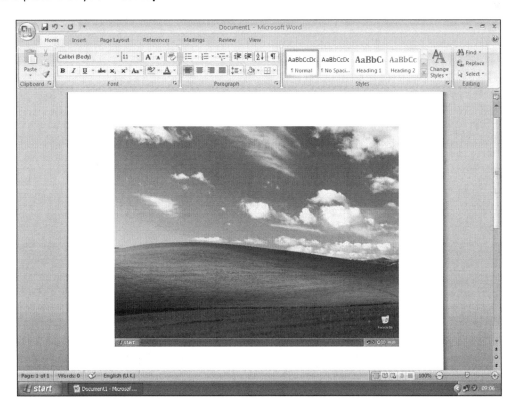

Note: Holding down the <**Alt**> key and pressing <**Print Screen**> will only capture the active window or dialog box.

6. Save the file as **screen capture** and close the document.

7. Close *Microsoft Word*.

3.35 Next Steps

Well done! You have now completed all of the exercises in this section. If you feel you are ready to test your knowledge and understanding of the topics covered, move on to the following **Develop Your Skills** activities. If there are any features of *Microsoft Word* that you are unsure about, you should revisit the appropriate exercises and try them again before moving on.

If you are interested in exploring some of *Microsoft Word's* more powerful features, why don't you use the Internet to find out a little more about the following advanced topics.

Feature	Description
References	*Word* can automatically create a **Table of Contents** and an **Index** page using a document's headers and keywords.
Sections	When certain pages or parts of a document are to be formatted differently from the rest, e.g. columns, page layout or page numbering, the document can be divided into sections. A document can have as many sections as required.
Mail Merge	*Word's* **Mail Merge** feature is used to combine a main document (a letter, for example) with a separate list containing names and addresses. These two files, when merged, create a personalised copy of the main document for everyone on the list. This is a really useful feature for creating letters and mail-shots for multiple recipients.
Styles	**Styles** are an extremely useful feature of *Word*. Build on the basic lessons learned in 3.16 and explore the various uses of styles and how they can help to improve your productivity.
Macros	A macro records keystrokes and menu selections and then plays them back exactly as they were recorded. A macro can be created so that frequently repeated tasks can be performed automatically.
Subdocuments	Large documents can be split up into many smaller documents called subdocuments which can be worked on independently. A **Master Document** is used to bring them all together in one place.
SmartArt	**SmartArt** lets you create diagrams from within *Word* using a variety of different layouts and visual styles. This feature is really useful for creating flow and relationship diagrams.
Hyperlinks	Hyperlinks and bookmarks allow readers of a document to jump to a specific place in the text (or to a file or web address) by clicking a single link or button.
Tracking	It is very common to have another person review and edit documents that you create. If a document has been set up to "track changes", any changes made to the document will be recorded. Once you get the document back you can either accept or reject each change.

At the end of every section you will get the chance to complete two full tasks without my assistance. This will help to reinforce learning and develop your skills. Don't forget to use the planning and review checklists at the back of the book to organise and evaluate your work.

> Note: Sample solutions for both tasks are provided in this section's data files folder.

Level 1: Rumbling Rails Mail Shot

In this task you will be asked to create a simple mail shot for *Priti*. You will need to use the ICT skills you have learned in this section to plan, develop and present an appropriate solution. You can ask for help from friends, colleagues or a teacher if you get stuck.

Level 1 Task

Did I tell you that our new *Rumbling Rails* roller coaster is a massive 100 metres high and will reach speeds of 80 miles per hour? It's now the biggest and best ride in the theme park, and to celebrate our "grand opening" we are planning to hold a party next week for park staff.

To advertise the event and inform all park employees about the new ride, I need you to design and produce a simple one page mail shot from scratch. It doesn't need to look too fancy, but it must be interesting and informative and include details on party times and ride opening dates. Information for the mail shot is available in the following files:

* **Rumbling Rails**   A document containing background information on the new ride and the grand opening party dates

* **Photo**   An image file containing a photograph of the new ride

* **Logo**   An image file containing the theme park's logo

Start by creating a new document and then add the contents of the **Rumbling Rails** file. Insert and arrange the **Photo** and **Logo** images as appropriate. Remember: the mail shot will be read by all park employees so it needs to look professional and be easy to read! When you are finished, save the document as **mail shot**.

Level 2: Financial Report

In this task you will be asked to create a detailed report for *Priti's* boss. You will need to use the advanced ICT skills that you have learned in this section to create a suitable solution (you may need to break the problem down into smaller parts first). Only level 2 students should attempt this task and it should be completed without help from others.

Level 2 Task

I've just received the following e-mail from *Monty Spangles*, the owner of the park:

I've not got much time so will you help me prepare the report? You will need to create a new, well-presented document for *Monty* that looks professional and is easy to read. Include a table showing the cost data in the **Final Costs** file. Unfortunately, I forgot to add **Maintenance** to the list which cost **£2500** – will you make sure this is included too?

To help *Monty* understand the contents of the document, describe the table of costs in one or two sentences. Also mention that the reason the cost of **Train components** has increased by approximately **£100,000** was due to the purchase of a third train (which will enter operation next month). If *Monty* has any questions about the report he can contact me on telephone extension **0456**.

Insert the **Logo** file so that the document meets the park's house style (all official *Big Planet Theme Park* documents must contain the park logo in the top right corner). When you are finished, save the document as **cost report**.

4 | Microsoft Excel

Hi, my name's Zak...

I'm a member of the engineering and maintenance department here at *Big Planet Theme Park*. My team and I are responsible for making sure that all of the rides are properly maintained and safe for visitors. Just imagine what would happen if the *Haunted Castle* ride broke down when people were half way through it!

My main role at the park is to reduce costly breakdowns and help develop ways to improve the overall safety and reliability of the rides. I have plenty of mechanical and engineering jobs to keep me busy, but I also spend a lot of time creating spreadsheets to manage my team's budget. We only have a small amount of money to spend, but if we invest it properly, the life of our rides will be extended and the park will save a lot of money in the long run.

To help me keep track of my team's spending, I use the program *Microsoft Excel*. Many professionals in various types of organisation use this program – it's really useful for working with numbers and performing calculations quickly and accurately. It also allows me to present complex data graphically, making it much easier to understand and communicate to others.

What you will learn:

In this section you will use the program *Microsoft Excel* to help *Zak* complete a number of everyday tasks at *Big Planet Theme Park*. You will see how to use simple spreadsheet techniques to enter, develop and organise numerical information for a variety of purposes.

Knowledge, skills and understanding:

   ✱   Use *Microsoft Excel* to create spreadsheets and manipulate numerical data

   ✱   Learn the best tools and features to solve a range of everyday problems

   ✱   Apply a variety of professional editing, formatting and layout techniques

Data files

Data files needed to complete the activities in this section are provided in the **Section 4** data files folder. Spreadsheets that you create or edit can be saved to the same folder.

4.1 Using Microsoft Excel

Microsoft Excel is most commonly used to work with figures and is a perfect choice of application for any task that involves numbers. Once a spreadsheet has been set up correctly, it can be used to perform a number of complex calculations quickly and accurately (and any results will be automatically updated when the data is changed). Typically, spreadsheets can be used to help with the following tasks:

* Maths problems, budgets and accounting

* Cash flows and forecasts

* Data analysis

A spreadsheet stores information in a grid of **cells**, which generally contain text, numbers or **formulas**. Cells are arranged in **rows** (across the screen) and **columns** (down the screen), forming a **worksheet**. One or more worksheets are together known as a **workbook**, the name *Excel* gives to a saved file.

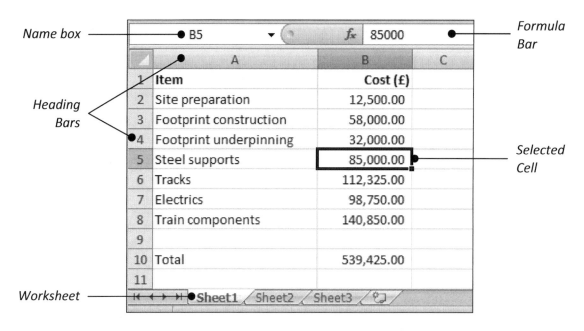

Notice the numbers running down the left side of the spreadsheet and the letters running across the top. These are called **Heading Bars** and are used to **reference** cells. In the picture above, the cell **B5** is currently selected (the location where **Column B** and **Row 5** intersect). This is highlighted on the **Heading Bars** and shown in the **Name** box.

> **Note:** When referring to a cell, the column letter <u>always</u> comes before the row number.

> **Note:** Although mainly used for working with numbers, people also use spreadsheets for creating and working with simple lists of data (e.g. product lists, stock lists, customer contact lists, etc).

Spreadsheets can also take basic data and present it in a variety of attractive graphs and charts. One important advantage of this is that the graphics created are much easier to understand at a glance. They can also be really useful for including in other documents or presentations.

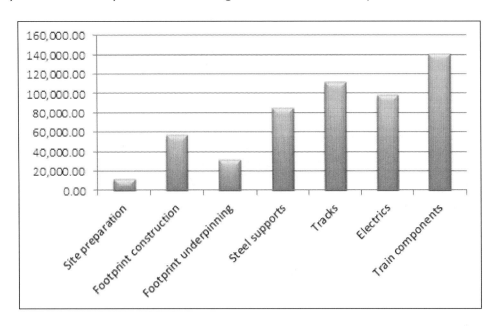

4.2 Creating a Spreadsheet

When creating a spreadsheet you should start on **Sheet1** (the default worksheet) and begin entering data in the top left corner. You should also add **labels** to the top of columns or the start of rows to help describe the contents of the worksheet.

It is <u>very</u> important to enter numbers correctly and accurately. If you make mistakes the spreadsheet will produce the wrong results.

Activity:

1. Start *Excel*. A blank workbook is created by default.

> Note: Notice that cell **A1** is currently selected (it is the **active** cell). The workbook contains three worksheets by default; **Sheet1**, **Sheet2**, **Sheet3**.

2. A label is entered into a cell by typing. Type **Maintenance checks week 7**.

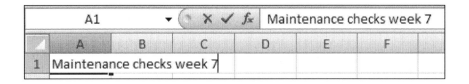

> Note: When entering text into a cell, notice that it also appears in the **Formula Bar**.

3. To complete the cell entry, press <**Enter**>. The active cell moves down to cell **A2**.

> **Note:** The text looks as though it also occupies cells **B1** and **C1**, but this is not the case. A label will expand and appear on top of other cells if – and only if – the other cells are empty. Cells containing numbers do not do this.

4. You can move to other cells by pointing and clicking or by using the arrow keys on your keyboard. Press the down arrow key, ↓, to move to cell **A3**, and then type **Staff**.

	A	B	C
1	Maintenance checks week 7		
2			
3	Staff		

5. Next, press → to move to cell **B3** (you do not need to press <**Enter**> to confirm an entry).

6. The worksheet that you are creating is to be used to record daily safety checks for the park's engineering and maintenance team. Enter data as shown below.

	A	B	C	D	E	F	G	H
1	Maintenance checks week 7							
2								
3	Staff	Mon	Tue	Wed	Thu	Fri	Sat	Sun
4	Aaron							
5	Adya							
6	Jack							
7	Sun							
8	Zak							

7. The actual maintenance figures now need to be entered. Move to cell **B4** by clicking it and then enter the number **16**. Enter the data below using whichever technique you like to move between cells (note that each employee has two days off).

	A	B	C	D	E	F	G	H
1	Maintenance checks week 7							
2								
3	Staff	Mon	Tue	Wed	Thu	Fri	Sat	Sun
4	Aaron	16	22	9	17	20		
5	Adya	21	16	19	15			12
6	Jack		19	15	14	17	11	
7	Sun			18	32	21	12	10
8	Zak	12	16			24	14	11

> **Note:** Notice that numbers appear right aligned by default. This helps you to tell at a glance which cells contain text and which cells contain numbers.

> **Note:** You can change a worksheet's name simply by double clicking the relevant tab at the bottom of the screen and typing a new title.

8.   Double click the current worksheet's title tab (**Sheet1**) and enter the title **Maintenance**.

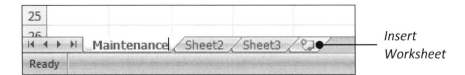

Insert Worksheet

9.   Press <**Enter**>. The worksheet has been renamed.

10. Click the **Sheet2** tab to display that worksheet. Click the **Maintenance** tab again to return to the first sheet.

> Note: To add a new worksheet to your workbook, click the **Insert Worksheet** button. It is a good idea to keep all relevant worksheets in the same workbook.

11. Display **Sheet2** again. From the **Cells** group on the **Home** tab, click the drop-down arrow on the **Delete** button and select **Delete Sheet**.

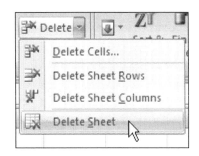

12. The worksheet is deleted and the next available sheet selected. Delete **Sheet3** also, leaving only the **Maintenance** worksheet remaining.

> Note: In the same way that you can protect documents in *Microsoft Word*, you can also protect workbooks in *Excel*. For instance, your spreadsheets can be password protected or marked as **Final** so that changes are discouraged.

13. Save the workbook as **maintenance** and then close it.

4.3 Resizing Columns and Rows

You may sometimes need to change column widths and row heights to better display the contents of cells and to make your spreadsheets easier to read. This is simply done by dragging the column or row boundaries on the relevant **Heading Bar**.

Activity:

1.   Open the workbook **Attendance**. This file contains information on visitor numbers to five specific *Haunted Castle* attractions. Unfortunately, it has been very poorly designed and many of the labels have been obscured.

2. Move your mouse pointer to the boundary line between column **A** and column **B** in the column **Heading Bar**. The pointer changes to a double-headed arrow, ⊹.

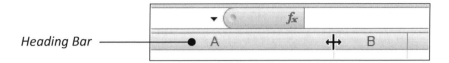

Heading Bar

3. Using click and drag, reduce the width of column **A** to approximately **20.00** (the column's width is shown in a **ToolTip** as you drag).

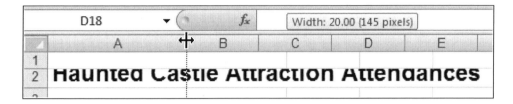

> **Note:** Width is measured in number of characters (20 will show 20 standard characters).

4. Using the same technique, increase the widths of columns **B**, **C**, **D** and **E** to **17.00**.

5. Row 2 is too small (in height) to contain the text contained in **A2**. Place the mouse pointer over the border between row 2 and 3 on the row **Heading Bar**, and using click and drag, increase the height of row **2** to approximately **24.00**.

> **Note:** For more precision, right click a column header and select **Column Width**. You can then enter a precise value. To adjust a row, right click and select **Row Height**.

> **Note:** Similar to *Microsoft Word*, *Excel* also has a **Zoom** feature on the **Status Bar** for zooming into worksheets.

6. Use the **Zoom Slider** on the **Status Bar** to increase the zoom level to **150%**.

7. Use the **Zoom Slider** to restore the zoom level to **100%**.

> **Note:** You can continue this section using any zoom level that you feel comfortable with.

8. Save the workbook as **visitors** and close it. You will use this file again later.

4.4 Basic Formulas

Formulas are used to calculate results from numbers entered in a spreadsheet. For example, formulas can be used to add a column or row of numbers together to obtain a total. If the data is changed, the formula will automatically recalculate the result.

Activity:

1. Click the **Office Button** and start a new, blank workbook.

2. In cell **B2** enter **34** and in cell **B3** enter **16.**

> Note: Although it is common practice to start creating spreadsheets from the upper left corner, you do not always need to start in cell **A1**. In fact, you can enter data in any cell that you like.

	A	B
1		
2		34
3		16

3. Make **B5** the active cell by clicking on it.

4. To add the contents of **B2** and **B3** together and display the result in **B5**, type in the formula **=b2+b3** and press **<Enter>**.

> Note: All formulas begin with an equals sign, =, followed by the calculation. Cell references are used so that results are recalculated if data in those cells change.

5. Cell **B5** now displays the result of adding cells **B2** and **B3** together (**50**).

6. Click cell **B5** and notice that the **Formula Bar** displays **=B2+B3**, the formula for this cell.

> Note: It is usually quicker to use the numeric keypad on the right of a standard keyboard for entering large amounts of numbers. However, you may need to activate the **Num Lock** feature on your keyboard first by pressing the **<Num Lock>** key (a light on your keyboard will appear when it is activated).

7. Click in cell **B3** and enter **26** to overwrite the original contents.

8. Press **<Enter>** and the formula updates **B5** to **60**, the new solution.

> Note: You will learn a lot more about formulas as you progress through this section.

9. Close the workbook <u>without</u> saving.

4.5 Mathematical Operators

The basic mathematical operators are **add**, **subtract**, **multiply** and **divide**. You will need to use these operators in your formulas to produce calculations (you have already used **add** in the previous exercise). However, the symbols for these operators on a keyboard are slightly different to those that you may be used to.

+	**Add**
-	**Subtract**
*	**Multiply**
/	**Divide**

These symbols appear twice on the keyboard; one set is placed around the main keyboard and the other set is placed on the numeric keypad. Many people find that the numeric keypad is easier to use because the keys are closer together and the <**Shift**> key is not needed.

Activity:

1.   Open the workbook **Operators**.

2.   Make **B6** the active cell by clicking on it, and then type in **=b4+b5**.

	A	B	C	D	E
1	Mathematical Operations				
2					
3	Number	Add	Subtract	Multiply	Divide
4	First	6	7	3	12
5	Second	3	4	5	4
6	Result	=b4+b5			

> Note: Notice that, as you type the formula, the referenced cells are highlighted on the worksheet. Lower case (small) letters will be automatically capitalised.

3.   Press <**Enter**>. This creates a formula to add the contents of cells **B4** and **B5**. The answer is displayed as **9**.

> Note: Have you noticed the pop-up menu that appears when you enter formulas? This is used to create more complex formulas which you will learn more about later.

4.   Click in cell **C6** and enter the formula to subtract the two numbers above, **=c4-c5**. Rather than press <**Enter**>, press the right arrow key, **→**. The answer is displayed as **3**.

5.   In cell **D6**, enter the formula to multiply the two numbers above, **=d4*d5**. The answer is displayed as **15**.

6.   In cell **E6**, enter the formula to divide the two numbers above, **=e4/e5**. Press <**Enter**> and the answer is displayed as **3**.

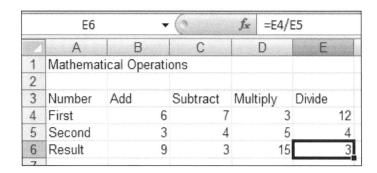

7.   Save the workbook as **operators complete** and close it.

4.6 Brackets

If more than one operator is used in a single formula, the order they appear is very important. For the four operators that you have seen so far, *Excel* performs calculations in this order: **Brackets**, **Division**, **Multiplication**, **Addition** and finally **Subtraction** (the **BODMAS** rule in maths). As brackets come first, they can be used to force *Excel* to perform calculations in a different order.

For example, in the formula **A1+A2/A3**, the value in cell **A2** would be divided by **A3** first and then added to **A1**. However, brackets can be used to make sure **A1** is added to **A2** first before being divided by **A3**, as the following formula shows: **(A1+A2)/A3**.

Activity:

1.   *Zak* has asked you to work out how many people are able to ride the *Haunted Castle's Black Hole* attraction at a time. Start a new, blank workbook.

2.   The *Black Hole* ride has two trains which always leave together. Each train has 10 cars and each car can hold a maximum of 4 passengers. Starting in **B2**, enter the following data (and increase the size of the columns so that the labels all fit).

A	B	C	D	E
1				
2	Passengers per car	Train 1 cars	Train 2 cars	Capacity
3	4	10	10	

3.   To work out how many people can ride the attraction – its *capacity* – the number of passengers per car must be multiplied by the total number of cars for both trains.

4.   Click on cell **E3** and type the formula **=b3*c3+d3**. Press **<Enter>** and the answer given is **50**. Unfortunately, this is wrong – but can you tell why?

5.   Due to the rules of **BODMAS**, the multiplication was carried out *before* the addition. Click on cell **E3** and press the **<Delete>** key to remove the formula.

6.   This time you will use brackets to make sure the addition occurs first. Type in the following formula instead: **=b3*(c3+d3)** and press **<Enter>**.

7. Check that the answer displayed is now **80**; passengers per car multiplied by the total number of cars.

Passengers per car	Train 1 cars	Train 2 cars	Capacity
4	10	10	80

Note: Brackets can also be placed inside of other brackets.

---

8. Good job. Save the workbook as **capacity** and close it.

4.7 Percentages

Percentage means "per hundred" and is a technique used frequently in business and everyday life to describe a fraction out of 100. It is always displayed with a percentage symbol, **%**. For example, **20%** is **20/100** as a fraction or **0.2** as a decimal. In the pie chart below, **20%** has been cut out leaving **80%** remaining.

In *Excel* there is a **Percent Style** button, %, that changes a decimal to a percentage automatically.

Activity:

1. For a report that *Zak* is creating, you have been asked to work out what percentage of special effects on the *Black Hole* ride are "pop-up ghosts".

2. Create a new, blank workbook. Starting in **B2**, enter the following data (resize any columns as necessary).

	A	B	C	D	E
1					
2		Pop-up Ghosts	All Special Effects	Percentage	
3		5	20		
4					

3. To display the number of pop-up ghosts as a percentage of all special effects, enter the formula **=B3/C3** into **D3**. Press **<Enter>**.

---

4. The result **0.25** appears as a decimal value. To format the answer as a percentage, first make sure **D3** is active.

5. With the **Home** tab displayed on the **Ribbon**, click the **Percent Style** button, %, in the **Number** group. The result changes to a percentage, showing that **25%** of all special effects are pop-up ghosts.

6. Change the value in **C3** to **27** and press <**Enter**>; notice that the percentage value changes automatically.

> Note: The **Percentage Style** button only shows percentages in whole numbers.

7. To display percentages to two decimal places, make the active cell **D3** and click the dialog box launcher on the **Number** group to display the **Format Cells** dialog box.

8. With **Percentage** selected under **Category**, change the value in the **Decimal places** box to **2** (notice the **Sample** area above which previews the percentage style).

9. Click **OK** to confirm the change. The percentage is now shown as **18.52%**.

10. Click **Undo**, ⟲, on the **Quick Access Toolbar** to undo this change. The percentage is shown rounded up to **19%** again.

> Note: **Undo** and **Redo** in *Excel* work in the same way as *Microsoft Word*.

11. Save the workbook as **ghost percentages** and close it.

4.8 Ranges

A **range** is a rectangular collection of cells. Just as single cells are identified by a cell reference, ranges are identified by the first and last cell in the selection. For example, the four cells **B2**, **B3**, **C2** and **C3** can be identified by the range **B2:C3**.

Ranges are selected by clicking and dragging to highlight a number of cells. Entire rows or columns can also be selected by clicking row or column headings.

Activity:

1. Start a new, blank workbook.

2. Move your mouse pointer over cell **B2**. Then, click and drag so that a range of four cells (two rows and two columns) is highlighted (as shown on the previous page).

3. Release the mouse button. Notice that the first cell in the range is white and the other cells are highlighted in blue. The first cell is the active cell.

4. More than one range can be selected at a time by holding down the **<Ctrl>** key while clicking and dragging. Press and hold **<Ctrl>** now and click and drag the range **C5:D6**. There should now be two separate ranges highlighted.

	A	B	C	D	E
1					
2					
3					
4					
5					
6					
7					

5. Click anywhere on the worksheet to remove the selected ranges. Next, click on **B** in the column **Heading Bar**. All of column **B** is now highlighted.

	A	B ↓	C	D
1				
2				
3				
4				

6. Click on **2** in the row **Heading Bar**. All of row **2** is now highlighted. Click and drag on the row **Heading Bar** to select the row headings from **5** to **7**. Three rows are now selected.

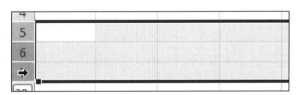

7. A range can also be selected by clicking the first and last cell while holding down the **<Shift>** key. Click on cell **B2**, hold **<Shift>**, and click on cell **F9**. The range **B2:F9** is selected.

8. A range can be extended (or reduced) by holding down the **<Shift>** key and clicking on another cell. Hold **<Shift>** and click on cell **G12**. The range is extended to **B2:G12**.

9. Select the cell **C5** and scroll across to column **Z**. While holding **<Shift>** click in cell **Z5**. The range **C5:Z5** is selected.

> **Note:**   Notice that after column **Z** the headings continue **AA**, **AB**, **AC**, **AD**, and so on.

10. Close the workbook <u>without</u> saving.

4.9 AutoSum

The most common calculation used in spreadsheets is simple addition. This calculation has been simplified by the creation of a **function** called **Sum**. Functions, which are built-in formulas, are covered in more detail later.

Activity:

1. Open the workbook **maintenance** that you saved earlier.

2. In cells **A9** and **I3**, enter the label **Total**.

3. Click on cell **B9**. The five cells above need to be added together to find the total. Enter the formula **=B4+B5+B6+B7+B8** and press **<Enter>**. The answer should be **49**.

> Note: *Why add cells that contain nothing?* Well, if numbers were placed in these cells at a later stage then the formula would still work, but a formula with cells missing from the range would not.

4. However, for large spreadsheets that contain hundreds of cells, creating a formula in this way is simply not practical. Fortunately there is a function called **SUM** that adds the contents of a range of cells.

> Note: The **SUM** function is so often used that there is a button for it on the **Ribbon**.

5. Select cell **C9**. In the **Editing** group on the **Home** tab, click the **Sum** button, $\boxed{\Sigma}$.

6. *Excel* automatically looks for nearby numbers to add. In this case only one number is found above. Click and drag to select the range **C4:C8** instead.

Mon	Tue	Wed	Thu	Fri
16	22	9	17	
21	16	19	15	
	19	15	14	
		18	32	
12	16			
49	=SUM(C4:C8)			
	SUM(**number1**, [number2], ...)			

7. Press **<Enter>** to place the answer **73** in cell **C9**. Select **C9** again and notice that the formula **=SUM(C4:C8)** appears in the **Formula Bar**.

8. Select cell **I4** and then click the **Sum** button, $\boxed{\Sigma}$. *Excel* finds numbers to the left and automatically sums the 7 cells **B4** to **H4**. Press **<Enter>**. The answer is **84**.

9. Formulas for the other cells will be added later by copying. Save the changes to the workbook and then close it.

> **Note:** **Sum** will automatically look up and down for numbers to sum first and then left to right. If the range it finds is wrong, simply click and drag to select a new one.

4.10 Fill Handle

Cells can be quickly filled with data by using the **Fill Handle**. This appears when the cursor is placed over the bottom right corner of an active cell. The **Fill Handle** is a very useful feature that is often used to quickly copy values or formulas into other cells.

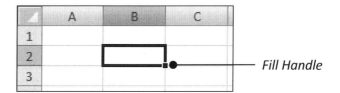

Fill Handle

Activity:

1.   Start a new, blank workbook and type your first name into cell **B2**.

2.   With cell **B2** selected, move your mouse pointer over the **Fill Handle**. The mouse pointer changes to a crosshair, **+**.

3.   Click and drag the **Fill Handle** across to cell **G2**.

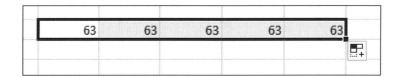

4.   Release the mouse and the text in **B2** is copied to all cells in the range **B2:G2**.

> **Note:**   It is only possible to drag in one direction, i.e. along a row or down a column.

5.   In **E4** enter **63**. Click and drag the **Fill Handle** of **E4** across to **I4**. The entry **63** is repeated.

63	63	63	63	63

6.   Click the **AutoFill Options** button, that has appeared towards the bottom right of the selected range. **Copy Cells** is currently selected which means that the value in **E4** has simply been copied to all other cells in the range.

7.   Select **Fill Series** instead to have *Excel* automatically increase the value of each cell in the range. This technique is very useful for quickly numbering cells.

> Note: The **AutoFill Options** button can also be used to copy (or ignore) the formatting in the source cell (i.e. the cell that is being copied).

8. Click the cell **E4** again. Hold <Ctrl> while dragging the **Fill Handle** to cell **E9**. Release the mouse button to fill the cells with increasing numbers up to **68** (holding <Ctrl> automatically applies **Fill Series**).

9. In **A11** enter **January**. Click and drag the **Fill Handle** of **A11** to **L11**. *Excel* recognises that the content of **A11** is a date, and then automatically applies **Fill Series** to the contents of each other cell in the selected range.

10. In **A13** enter **1st**. Click and drag the **Fill Handle** of **A13** down to **A23**. The automatic **Fill Series** applied is very useful when creating schedules, diaries and calendars.

11. Close the workbook <u>without</u> saving and then open the workbook **maintenance** that was saved earlier.

12. To save retyping the formulas in row **9** and column **I**, they can instead be copied using the **Fill Handle**. With cell **C9** selected, drag the **Fill Handle** across to **H9**.

12	16			24	14	11
49	73					+

13. When the mouse button is released, the formula contained in cell **C9** is copied to all other cells in the range **C9:H9**.

> Note: *Excel* automatically updates the cell references in each copied formula so that each calculation refers to the cells directly above. This is a very useful feature.

14. Click in cell **D9** and check the **Formula Bar** to see that the formula has been updated automatically to sum column **D** instead of column **C**.

15. To complete column **I** make the active cell **I4** and drag the fill handle down to **I8**. The completed spreadsheet should look the same as that shown below.

	A	B	C	D	E	F	G	H	I
1	Maintenance checks week 7								
2									
3	Staff	Mon	Tue	Wed	Thu	Fri	Sat	Sun	Total
4	Aaron	16	22	9	17	20			84
5	Adya	21	16	19	15			12	83
6	Jack		19	15	14	17	11		76
7	Sun			18	32	21	12	10	93
8	Zak	12	16			24	14	11	77
9	Total	49	73	61	78	82	37	33	

16. Save the workbook using the same file name and close it.

4.11 Editing Cells

You can change the contents of an individual cell by simply overwriting the text that is there. This is known as **In Cell Editing**. However, when a cell entry is long or complicated, the changes are sometimes best made by editing the data in the **Formula Bar**.

Activity:

1. Open the workbook **Train Cars**.

2. Click in cell **A7** and then click in the **Formula Bar**. The mode indicator on the **Status Bar** now shows the text **Edit**.

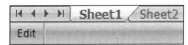

3. Use the <**Delete**> and <**Backspace**> keys to remove the label **Demon**. Enter the new label **Griffin** and press <**Enter**> to confirm the changes.

> Note: You can also click the **Enter** button, ✓, on the **Formula Bar** to accept the change.

4. Select cell **E7** which contains the value **23765**. Type **21254** to overwrite this value and then press <**Enter**> to confirm the change.

5. Select cell **E16** and overtype with the value **1200**. Instead of pressing <**Enter**> press <**Esc**>. The change is cancelled and the value in **E16** returns to **3500**.

> Note: You can also click the **Cancel** button, ✗, on the **Formula Bar** to cancel the change.

6. The **Kraken** car has been damaged and replaced by the **Harpy**. It has the same **Ref No.**, **Colour** and **Paint Code**, but its **Mileage** is **0**. Make those changes.

| 15 | Harpy | 14 | Red | 1800 | 0 |

> Note: When editing the contents of a cell, you can use the <**Home**> key to move the cursor to the start of the cell content and <**End**> to move the cursor to the end.

7. The **Vampire** car is getting old and has been taken out of action. Click on cell **A9** and then press the <**Delete**> key to remove the entry.

8. Click on cell **B9** and then click **Clear** from the **Editing** group, 🖉. Select **Clear All** from the drop-down list that appears.

9. Select the range **C9:E9** and press <**Delete**> to remove the contents of those three cells.

10. Save the workbook as **train cars updated** and close it. You will return to this later.

4.12 Cut, Copy and Paste

In the same way that you can cut, copy and paste text in *Microsoft Word*, you can also cut, copy and paste cells in *Excel*. You can cut and copy labels, values and formulas. Importantly, any formula that you copy to another location will be automatically adjusted so that it refers to the appropriate cells around it (this does not happen when you cut and paste a formula).

Activity:

1. Open the workbook **Breakdowns**. This spreadsheet contains an account of all ride failures that occurred last year in the *Haunted Castle*.

2. The label in cell **D10** is in the incorrect place. Select the cell and click **Cut**, , from the **Clipboard** group of the **Home** tab (you can also press <**Ctrl+X**>).

> **Note:** Unlike most other programs, the cut item is not removed immediately. Instead, an animated box is placed around it.

3. Select cell **B13** and click the **Paste** button from the **Clipboard** group (or press <**Ctrl+V**>). The cut cell is then moved to the new location.

> **Note:** Cut or copied cells are placed in a hidden area called the **Clipboard**, from where they can then be pasted back into the same worksheet, a different worksheet in the same workbook, or a completely different workbook altogether.

4. The result in **C10** needs to be in **B11**. Use cut and paste to move the formula in **C10** to the empty cell **B11**.

5. Copy the formula in **B11** using the **Copy** button, (or press <**Ctrl+C**>). Paste it into **C11**. *Excel* automatically adjusts the copied formula to reference the cells in the new column.

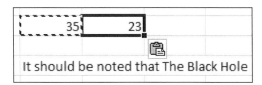

6. Select cell **D11** and click **Paste**. The formula is pasted a second time and updated again.

7. Select the range **E11:M11** and click **Paste**. The copied formula is pasted into all cells in the range and updated to reference the correct cells in each case.

8. Use this technique to copy the formula in cell **N5** to the range **N6:N9**.

9. Save the document as **breakdowns complete** and close it.

4.13   Checking Formulas

Spreadsheets aren't much use if the formulas within them contain errors. All formulas within worksheets should be checked thoroughly to make sure that you have entered them correctly and that they produce the expected results.

In some cases *Excel* will warn you that a formula is incorrect. If so, a formula error value starting with a **#** (hash) symbol is displayed in the relevant cell:

#NULL!	The ranges specified in your formula are incorrect
#DIV/0!	You tried to divide by 0 and this is not allowed
#VALUE!	You tried to apply a calculation with data of the wrong type
#REF!	Cell references are not valid or are missing
#NAME?	A part of the formula has been mistyped
#NUM!	The result created by a formula is too big
#N/A	A value referenced in your formula is missing
######	The result is too long to fit into a cell

Activity:

1. Open the workbook **Totals**. This spreadsheet shows the monthly number of visitors to the *Haunted Castle* in a six month period. Unfortunately, it also contains a number of errors which must be corrected before the results can be relied upon and used.

> **Note:** Notice the green triangles in the top left corner of some of the cells. These indicate that there is a possible error in the formulas for those cells.

2. Click once in cell **B5**. This cell contains the error **#VALUE!** indicating that the formula is using data of the wrong type.

3. Notice the **Trace Error** button that has appeared beside the selected cell, . Place your mouse pointer over this button without clicking to see a brief description of the error.

4. Double click in the cell. The formula for that cell is shown within the cell itself, with coloured borders indicating the ranges used in the calculation. This is a really useful way of checking the cells referenced by a formula. Can you tell what the error is?

5. The formula is trying to add the *label* in **A5** to the *value* in **B4**. Edit the formula so that it simply reads **=B4**. The error value disappears and **200** is shown in **B5**.

6. Next, click once in cell **H4** and read the brief description on the **Trace Error** button.

7. *Excel* has detected that the formula contains unrecognised text and has displayed the **#NAME?** error value in the cell. Can you see what the error is?

8. The function **SUM** has been spelled incorrectly. Correct this and press <**Enter**> to remove the error value.

9. The result appears as **0**, which is clearly not correct. Double click **H4** to see the range that the formula refers to.

Month 1	Month 2	Month 3	Month 4	Month 5	Month 6	Total
200	300	400	-100	150	500	=SUM(B7:G7)
200	300	700	600	750	750	SUM(number1,

10. The range **B7:G7** is not correct. You could edit the formula in the cell, but instead try dragging and dropping the blue range rectangle to the correct location, as shown below.

Month 1	Month 2	Month 3	Month 4	Month 5	Month 6	Total
200	300	400	-100	150	500	=SUM(B4:G4)
200	300	700	600	750	750	SUM(number1,

> **Note:**   You can also drag the corners of the rectangle to expand/contract a range.

11. Press <**Enter**> to confirm the change. The formula is now correct.

12. Next, click once in cell **I4** and read the brief description on the **Trace Error** button. *Excel* has detected that the formula is trying to divide by 0 and has displayed the **#DIV/0!** error.

13. Click the drop-down arrow on the **Trace Error** button and select **Edit in Formula Bar**. The formula should divide by **6** in order to get the monthly average – correct this now.

14. Press <**Enter**> to confirm the change. The average formula is now correct.

15. Although all of the errors that *Excel* warned you about have now been corrected, there are still a few errors remaining in this spreadsheet. Can you tell what they are?

16. Firstly, the cell **C5** should add the contents of **B5** and **C4**. Correct this now.

$$f_x \quad =B5+C4$$

17. Next, cell **G5** is a copy of **F5**. Correct this now.

> **Note:**   It is important to perform simple visual inspections on your spreadsheets to check that amounts tally and that the results of formulas are as expected.

18. The cumulative total in cell **G5** now matches the final total in **H4**, which is correct.

19. However, the value in **E4** does not make sense. You cannot have **-100** visitors. *Zak* informs you that this should have been **100**, so correct the error now. The spreadsheet is now complete and correct.

First Half Cumulative Totals								
	Month 1	Month 2	Month 3	Month 4	Month 5	Month 6	Total	Average per month
Number of Haunted Castle visitors	200	300	400	100	150	500	1650	275
Cumulative Total	200	500	900	1000	1150	1650		

Note: A useful feature of *Excel* is the **Error Checking** facility on the **Formulas** tab. This steps you through each error in a spreadsheet one at a time.

20. Save the workbook as **final totals** and close it.

4.14 Relative and Absolute Addressing

Normally the cell references that you use in your formulas are known as **relative** cell references; they can change depending on the position of the cell containing the formula. For example, if you copy the formula **B2+B3** in column **B** to column **C** it automatically becomes **C2+C3**.

However, you may sometimes wish to use a fixed cell address in a formula in order to refer to the same cell when the formula is copied. These are called **absolute** cell references. To make a cell reference **absolute**, you must use the **$** symbol.

Activity:

1. Start a new, blank workbook.

2. In cell **B2** enter **7** and in **B3** enter **8**. In cell **B4** create enter the formula **=B2+B3** to add the two numbers together.

3. Select cell **B4** and click the **Copy** button, . Move to cell **D8** and click **Paste**. The formula is copied and is automatically adjusted to reference the two cells directly above.

4. The result **0** is displayed. Enter **5** and **3** into cells **D6** and **D7** and the result is updated.

	A	B	C	D
1				
2		7		
3		8		
4		15		
5				
6				5
7				3
8				8

> **Note:**   The cell reference in **B4** is "relative" as it is automatically adjusted when copied elsewhere (in this instance, to cell **D8**). All formulas copied so far have been relative, whether using copy and paste or the **Fill Handle**. In fact, relative cell referencing is the default and most common way to reference cells in *Excel*.

5. Copy the formula in **D8** to **E8** and **F8**. Examine the copied formulas; these too have been automatically adjusted so that cell references are *relative* to their new location.

6. Close this workbook <u>without</u> saving.

7. Next, open the workbook **Parts** which contains the start of a tax calculation.

8. Select cell **C6** and enter the formula for **VAT** (**Price** multiplied by **VAT Rate**).

9. The result shown in cell **C6** is **£799.58**.

10. Select **B15** and enter the **VAT Rate** of **20%** (you can enter this as **0.20** or **20.00%**). Notice that the result in **C6** is updated.

11. Use the **Fill Handle** to copy the formula in **C6** to both **D6** and **E6**. The resulting **VAT** is zero.

£4,569.00	£6,408.00	£7,834.00
£913.80	£0.00	£0.00

12. Check the formulas in **D6** and **E6** to find the problem. It has been caused by relative addressing. The **VAT Rate** is in a fixed location but the formulas have been automatically adjusted to reference cells that are empty, e.g. the cells **C15** and **D15**.

13. In cell **C6**, enter the formula **=C5*B15**. The **$** symbols fix the row and column reference as absolute.

> **Note:**   If pointing and clicking on cell **B15**, pressing the function key <**F4**> automatically changes any formula references to absolute.

14. Use the **Fill Handle** to copy the formula in **C6** to both **D6** and **E6** again (overwriting the current contents). Check the formulas in **D6** and **E6** to see that they both refer to **B15**.

15. Complete the **Total Price** row by adding the **Price** and **VAT** together for each month. Cell **F7** should contain the final overall total **£22,573.20**.

16. Save the workbook as **parts complete** and close it.

4.15 Inserting Rows and Columns

When developing spreadsheets you will often need to create a new row or column within your data. Instead of starting again, rows or columns can simply be inserted. Columns are inserted to the left of the active cell and rows are inserted above.

Activity:

1. Open the workbook **visitors** that you saved earlier.

2. **The Viper**, an old ride that has recently been refurbished, is to be added to the statistics. Select all of column **E** by clicking the **Heading Bar** column title.

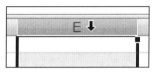

3. Click the **Insert** button, [Insert], in the **Cells** group on the **Home** tab. The **House of Wax** column is promoted to column **F** and a new column **E** is inserted.

4. Enter the label **The Viper** in cell **E4**. By default, the formatting is the same as the column to the left.

> Note: Notice that the formulas in column **G** have been automatically adjusted to include the new column. It is important to check that any formulas in your spreadsheets are correct after inserting new rows or columns.

5. Enter the attendance figures in column **E** as: **4000**, **2500**, **3000**, **2800**, **4200** and **5100**. The totals in column **G** are adjusted to include the new numbers.

6. Copy the formula from **D11** to **E11**. As the formula in **D11** contains relative cell references, they are automatically adjusted when copied to cell **E11**.

The Viper
4000
2500
3000
2800
4200
5100
21600

7. **Sunday** attendances also need to be included in the statistics. As an alternative to the **Insert** button, right click on row heading **11** to display a shortcut menu.

> Note: This shortcut menu approach can also be used to insert columns.

8. From the options available, select **Insert**. Row **11** is promoted to row **12** and a new row **11** is inserted. By default the formatting is the same as the row above.

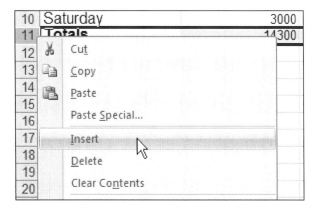

9. Enter **Sunday** in cell **A11** and enter the **Sunday** figures across the new row as: **2000**, **4000**, **1500**, **3000** and **2000**.

10. The formula in **G11** should be automatically inserted (if not copy the formula from **G10**).

11. Check the formula in cell **G11** has been copied from the row above and that the cell references have been adjusted correctly (**=SUM(B11:F11)**).

> Note: Cells can also be inserted at the location of the active cell (or range). By default, any existing data within or below the active cell will be moved down.

12. Save the workbook and leave it open for the next exercise.

4.16 Deleting Rows and Columns

Rows and columns can also be deleted easily if they are no longer required. The rows or columns immediately afterwards are then moved along to fill the space.

Activity:

1. The workbook **visitors** should still be open. *Zak* informs you that you no longer need to include the **Tower of Terror** and **House of Wax** columns.

2. Select the entire **Tower of Terror** column by clicking the **Heading Bar** for column **D**.

3. Click the **Delete** button, ⌐ Delete ▾ , in the **Cells** group on the **Home** tab. The **Tower of Terror** column is removed and the remaining columns move left to fill the space.

> Note: It is important to check that any formulas in your spreadsheets are correct after deleting rows or columns.

4. Right click on the **House of Wax** column header and select **Delete**.

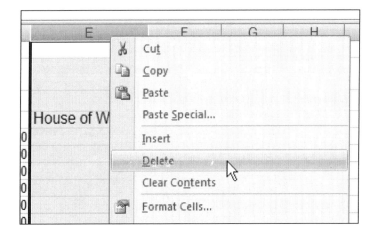

5. The column is removed. *Zak* has also informed you that the row for **Sunday** is not needed any longer. Select all of row **11**.

6. From the **Cells** group, click **Delete**. The row is deleted.

> Note: Cells containing formulas can be altered by deleting parts of a worksheet, resulting in **#REF** error values. In this case your formulas will need to be manually adjusted.

7. Save the workbook using the same file name and close it.

8. Open the workbook **train cars updated** that you saved earlier. Using whichever method you prefer, delete row **9** to tidy up the spreadsheet. *Zak* also informs you that column **D** is no longer needed; delete this column.

> Note: Entire rows and columns can be cut, copied and pasted. Copied rows and columns can also be inserted between others rows and columns.

9. Save the workbook using the same file name and close it.

4.17 Formatting Text

Formatting text can improve a spreadsheet's appearance and make it easier to read and use. Cell contents in a spreadsheet can be emphasised using bold, italic and underline, as well as changing the font type, size and colour.

> Note: Used properly, basic text formatting can highlight important information and give your spreadsheets a more professional appearance. However, too many different fonts and colours will often have the reverse affect.

Activity:

1. Open the workbook **visitors** and select cell **B4**. To make the text in the selected cell bold, click the **Bold** button, $\boxed{\textbf{B}}$, in the **Font** group.

2.   Click the **Italic** button, $\boxed{I}$, and then the **Underline** button, $\boxed{U}$, to italicise and underline the text.

Haunted Castle Attraction Attendances			
	Haunted Vault	The Black Hole	The Viper
Monday	2000	5000	
Tuesday	2200	5500	

> **Note:**   A range of selected cells can be formatted at the same time.

3.   To change the font type, click the drop-down button on the **Font** box.

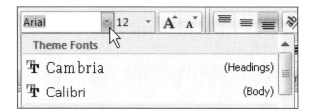

4.   Select **Calibri** from the list.

5.   The font size can be changed also by clicking the drop-down arrow on the **Font Size** box. Select cell **A2** and change the font size to **16 pt**. Change the **Font** again to **Calibri**.

6.   Another useful feature to make text stand out in spreadsheets is font colour. With **A2** still active, click on the **Font Color** drop-down arrow.

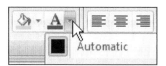

7.   Move your mouse pointer over any colour in the palette to see the change automatically previewed on the spreadsheet. Finally click a dark blue colour to select it.

> **Note:**   To copy the text formatting in a cell, the **Format Painter** tool can be used.

8.   Select cell **B4** again. From the **Clipboard** group, click the **Format Painter** button, $\boxed{\text{🖌}}$. Then move your mouse pointer over cell **C4**. Notice the mouse pointer changes to the **Format Painter** cursor, ⊕🖌.

9.   Click once to copy the formatting in cell **B4** to **C4**. Notice that the text content itself is not changed. Use the same technique to copy the formatting of cell **C4** to **D4**.

> **Note:**   You can also select a *range* of cells to apply the **Format Painter** tool to.

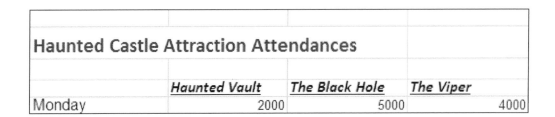

Haunted Castle Attraction Attendances			
	Haunted Vault	*The Black Hole*	*The Viper*
Monday	2000	5000	4000

> Note: The useful **Format Painter** tool is also available in other *Office* applications.

10. Insert an empty row above row **11** to separate the attendance data from the final totals. This spreadsheet now looks a lot more professional.

11. Save the workbook using the same file name and close it.

4.18 Cell Alignment

Alignment refers to the positioning of text or numbers within a cell. Content can be aligned to any side of a cell and can even be rotated to any angle you like.

Activity:

1. Open the workbook **maintenance** that you saved earlier and select the range **B3:H3**.

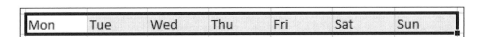

> Note: Cell alignment is set by clicking one of the alignment buttons in the **Alignment** group on the **Home** tab.

2. Click the **Center** button, to centre the labels horizontally. Click the **Align Text Right** button, and the labels are moved to the right.

3. Increase the height of row **3** to **60**. Notice that the contents are aligned to the bottom of the cell.

4. Click the **Middle Align** button, to centre the labels vertically. Click the **Center** button again, to centre the labels horizontally.

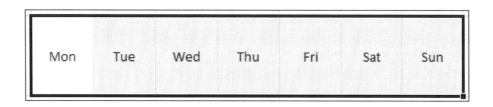

> **Note:** Similar to *Microsoft Word*, you can also **Indent** the contents of cells using the **Increase Indent** button, 📇, and **Decrease Indent** button, 📇.

5. Click the **Orientation** button, 🖊. From the drop-down list that appears, select **Angle Counterclockwise**. The text is rotated 45 degrees.

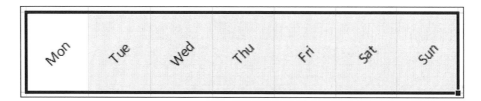

6. Click the **Orientation** button again and select **Rotate Text Up**. The text is rotated 90 degrees.

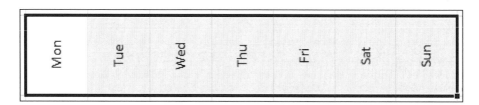

> **Note:** Rotated text is useful where cell widths are small. For more control over alignment, including merging cells and text wrapping, use the **Alignment** dialog box launcher.

7. Save the workbook and leave it open for the next exercise.

4.19 Borders and Shading

Borders are lines around the edges of cells. You can control the style and colour of lines used, and **shading** can be applied to add a background colour or pattern.

Activity:

1. Using the workbook **maintenance**, make sure the range **B3:H3** is still selected. Click on the **Borders** drop-down arrow in the **Font** group (not the icon button).

2. Select **All Borders** to add lines around and between the cells in the selected range. Click away from the selected range to view the results.

3. Click **Undo**, 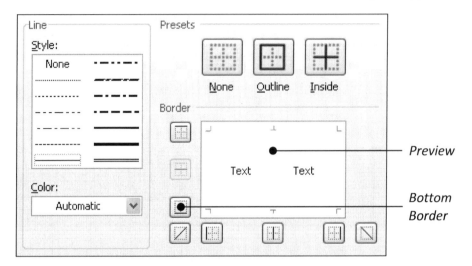, to remove the border. Then select the range **B3:H3** again.

4. Drop the **Borders** button and select **More Borders**. The **Format Cells** dialog box appears.

> Note: You must select a **Line Style** and **Color** before adding a border.

5. To apply a simple single border to the bottom of the selected row, click the **Bottom Border** button in the **Border** area. A line appears along the bottom of the **Preview** pane.

> Note: Notice the many line styles available under **Style**. The three **Presets** buttons can also be used to apply borders around and between cells quickly.

6. To apply the new border click **OK**. Click away from the selected range to view the results.

> Note: Borders can often be better seen if the worksheet's gridlines are hidden. To do this, select the **View** tab and uncheck **Gridlines** in the **Show/Hide** group. Be sure to check **Gridlines** again before continuing.

7. Shading is added to cell backgrounds using the **Fill Color** button in the **Font** group on the **Home** tab. Select the range **B3:H3** again.

8. Click the drop-down arrow on the **Fill Color** button, 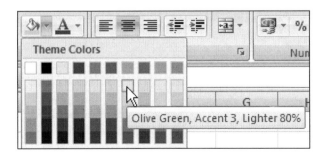, and select a light green colour.

> **Note:** It is often best to use light colours in cell backgrounds; too much colour can overpower the text and make it difficult to read.

9. Apply the same light green colour to the range **A4:A8** and apply a single black border on the right. The spreadsheet should look like that shown below.

	A	B	C	D	E	F	G	H	I
1	Maintenance checks week 7								
2									
3	Staff	Mon	Tue	Wed	Thu	Fri	Sat	Sun	Total
4	Aaron	16	22	9	17	20			84
5	Adya	21	16	19	15			12	83
6	Jack		19	15	14	17	11		76
7	Sun			18	32	21	12	10	93
8	Zak	12	16			24	14	11	77
9	Total	49	73	61	78	82	37	33	

> **Note:** You can reapply the most recent fill colour by clicking the **Fill Color** button.

10. Save the workbook and close it.

4.20 Formatting Numbers

Numbers can be formatted so that they are displayed in a variety of different ways, such as currency, percentages, fractions, etc. The most useful number formats available include:

General	No specific number format
Number	Plain number formats
Currency	Currency symbols and decimal places
Date	Various date formats
Time	Various time formats
Percentage	A value as a fraction of 100 (followed by %)
Fraction	Decimals expressed as fractions
Text	Text rather than a number (useful for labels)
Special	Telephone numbers, postcodes, etc.
Custom	Custom formats that you can design yourself

Activity:

1. Open the workbook **Time**. This is a simple timesheet that *Zak* has created for recording overtime, but many of the cells do not use the correct number format.

2. The **Hours Worked** cells should be displayed to one decimal place. Select the range **E10:E15**. From the **Cells** group on the **Home** tab, click the **Format** button, Format ▾.

3. From the drop-down menu that appears, select **Format Cells**. The **Format Cells** dialog box appears. Make sure the **Number** tab is displayed.

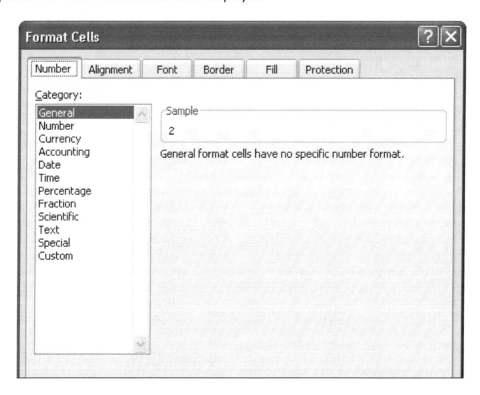

4. Click on each of the different types of number format shown in the **Category** list to see the various types and options available. Finally, select **Number**.

5. Check that the number of **Decimal places** is **1**.

> Note: Notice the **Sample** preview box. This shows the results of the chosen format if it was applied to the first number in the selected range.

6. Click **OK** to apply the chosen format. All the numbers in the selected range are now formatted to one decimal place.

> Note: There are buttons in the **Number** group on the **Ribbon** to **Increase Decimal** places, and **Decrease Decimal** places, . This is done one decimal place at a time.

7. Select the range **F10:F15**. Click the **Format** drop-down button and select **Format Cells** to display the **Format Cells** dialog box. This time select **Currency** from the **Category** list.

8. Make sure that **Decimal places** is set to **2**, and then make sure **£** is selected in the **Symbol** drop-down box. A preview is provided in the **Sample** box again.

9. Click **OK** to apply the chosen format. All the numbers in the selected range are now formatted to two decimal places and appear with a **£** symbol.

> Note: The **Number Format** drop-down menu in the **Number** group can be used to select new number formats quickly.

10. Apply the number format **Number** (to one decimal place) to cell **D17**. Then apply the currency format with a **£** symbol to cells **D19** and **D21** (to two decimal places).

> Note: When adjusting number formats, it is important to realise that the value in each cell is not changed. It is simply displayed in a different way.

11. With cell **D21** selected, notice that the **Formula Bar** says **10**, but the contents of the cell are displayed as **£10.00**.

12. Overtype the contents of cell **D21** with **9.50**. Press <**Enter**> and the value is automatically formatted as **£9.50**.

> Note: If cells display **#######** this means that the cell content is too big for the cell to display. Widening the effected columns will solve this problem.

13. Save the workbook as **timesheet** and leave it open for the next exercise.

4.21 Date and Time

In *Excel*, the date and time are stored as simple numbers that can be formatted to appear however you like. For example, the date is stored as a large number that represents the number of days since **1 January 1900**; however, this can be formatted so that it appears in a more recognisable form (e.g. **21 April 2011**).

Activity:

1. Using the workbook **timesheet**, select cell **D7**.

2. Enter today's date in the form **dd/mm/yyyy**. Press <**Enter**>.

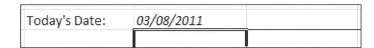

Today's Date:	*03/08/2011*	

3.   Select cell **D7** again. Notice in the **Number Format** drop-down menu that **Date** has been automatically selected by *Excel*.

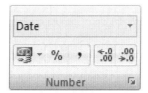

4.   Display the **Format Cells** dialog box. Examine each date format available within **Type**. When you are finished, select the **14 March 2001** format and click **OK**.

> **Note:**   The keyboard shortcut <**Ctrl ;**> can be used to quickly insert today's date.

5.   Select cell **F21** and enter the current time in the form **HH:MM**. Press <**Enter**>.

Last Updated:	14:30

6.   Select cell **F21** again. Display the **Format Cells** dialog box and select **Time** in the **Category** list. Examine each time format available within **Type**.

7.   When you are finished, select the format **13:30:55** and click **OK**.

> **Note:**   The keyboard shortcut <**Ctrl Shift ;**> can be used to quickly insert the current time.

Haunted Castle - Daily Overtime

Name:	Zak		
Today's Date:	03 August 2011		

Attraction	Hours Worked	Pay Accrued
The Haunted Vault	2.0	£19.00
The Black Hole	1.0	£9.50
The Tower of Terror	0.5	£4.75
The House of Wax	0.0	£0.00
Concessions	1.5	£14.25
Other:	2.0	£19.00

Total Hours:	7.0		
Total Overtime:	**£66.50**		
Hourly wage:	£9.50	Last Updated:	14:30:00

8.   Save the workbook using the same file name and close it.

4.22 Charts

Charts are used to show numerical information in a graphical way that is clear and easy to understand. There are many charts styles available in *Excel*, but the following list includes the five most popular types:

Column	The most commonly used chart in *Excel*, this displays shaded vertical columns that represent values in different categories.	
Line	Specific values are plotted on the chart and are connected by a line. This is useful for displaying how values change over time.	
Pie	Values are shown as slices of a circular "pie", which highlights the contribution that each value makes to the total. This is also a very common type of chart.	
Bar	Similar to a column chart, but the bars are shown horizontally across the page.	
XY Scatter	Specific values are simply plotted on the chart. Different sets of values can have different plot symbols.	

> **Note:** There are many layouts, styles and effects that can be applied to charts. For example, different themed colours or an impressive 3D effect can be applied.

Activity:

1.   Open the workbook **visitors** that you saved earlier. This spreadsheet contains information that *Zak* would like to include in a presentation. However, he would rather show this data as a chart so that it is easier for others to understand.

2.   Select the cell range **A4:B10**.

3.   Display the **Insert** tab and locate the **Charts** group. Many popular charts can be created using the buttons shown here.

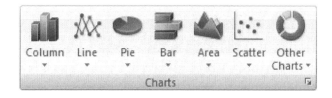

4.   To see all chart types available, click the **Other Charts** drop-down button and select **All Chart Types**. The **Insert Chart** dialog box appears.

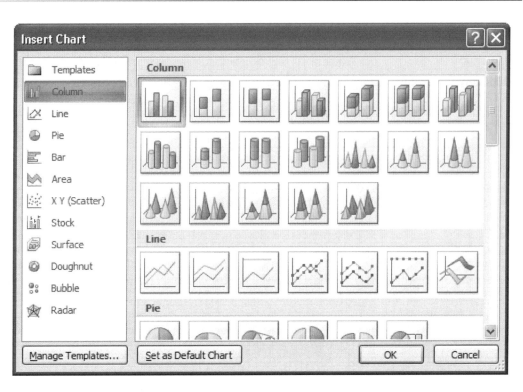

5. The **Column** category is selected by default. Select the first type of **Pie** chart instead from the list (there are many different variations of each chart to choose from).

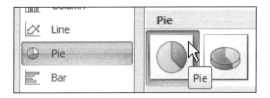

6. Click **OK**. A simple pie chart is created from the selected data and each value is shown as a slice of the pie. A **Legend** is automatically created to describe the contents of the chart.

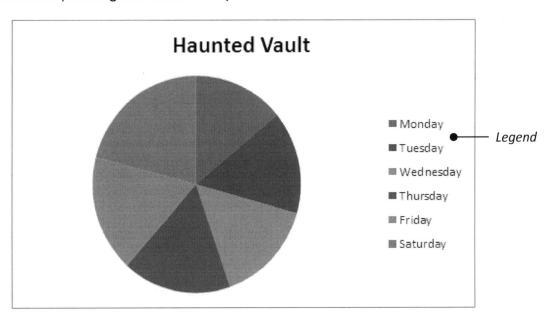

> Note: *Excel* automatically obtains chart and legend titles from data labels in the range.

7. Notice the **Chart Layouts** group on the **Chart Tools - Design** tab. Select each layout type in turn to automatically adjust the positioning of elements on the chart.

> Note: Each chart type has its own list of chart layouts. You can also reposition elements on a chart manually using drag and drop.

8. Locate the **Chart Styles** group on the **Design** tab. Select a variety of style types to automatically adjust the colours of the chart.

> Note: More **Chart Layouts** and **Chart Styles** can be accessed by clicking the **More** button, , found towards the bottom right corner of both groups.

9. When you have finished exploring the various **Chart Styles** and **Chart Layouts** on offer, click the **Change Chart Type** button in the **Type** group on the **Design** tab.

10. Select **Column** from the list of chart types available and then select the first column chart in the list (**Clustered Column**).

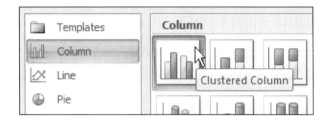

11. Click **OK**. The pie chart is replaced with a column chart.

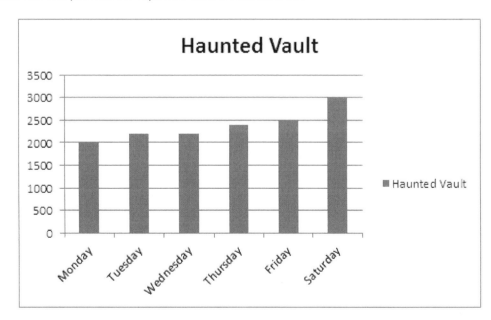

> Note: Your chart may appear differently depending on the chart styles selected earlier.

12. With the chart selected, press <**Delete**> on your keyboard to remove it.

13. Next, select the range **A4:D10**.

14. From the **Insert** tab, click the **Column** drop-down button in the **Charts** group and select the first chart type (**Clustered Column**). A column chart appears with all three rides shown as a separate bar.

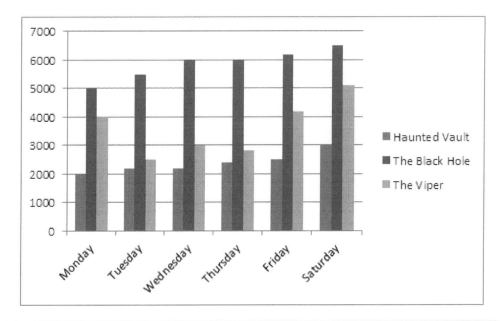

Note: As you can clearly see, **The Black Hole** ride is the most popular attraction, followed by **The Viper** and then **The Haunted Vault**. Notice how much easier it is to draw these conclusions by looking at a chart rather than the raw data.

15. Display the **Layout** tab and click **Chart Title** in the **Labels** group. From the options that appear, select **Above Chart**. Edit the chart title so that it reads **Haunted Castle Visitors**.

Note: Other options on the **Layout** tab allow you to add, edit and remove axis titles, gridlines, legends, and data labels.

16. Display the **Design** tab and click **Change Chart Type** again. Select the fourth column chart type on the top row (**3-D Clustered Column**).

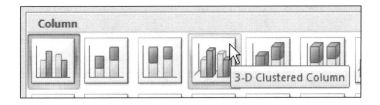

17. Click **OK**. The chart is transformed into a three-dimensional column chart.

Note: The **Move Chart** button on the **Design** tab can be used to move a selected chart to another sheet or workbook. You can also copy and paste charts into other *Microsoft Office* applications.

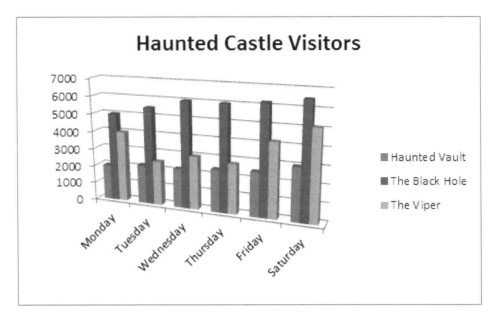

18. Using cut and paste, move the chart to **Sheet2** and change the title of the worksheet's tab to **Column Chart**. Position the chart in the middle of the sheet.

> Note: A chart can be manually moved or resized using the handles on the chart border.

19. Return to the **Attendances** worksheet and select the range **A4:D10** again.

20. Create a simple **Line** chart based on the selected range, and add an appropriate title of your choice. Move this chart to an empty worksheet renamed as **Line Chart**.

21. Perform the same steps to create a **Bar** and **X-Y Scatter** chart. Explore some of the other chart types and formatting options that are available.

> Note: Similar to *Microsoft Word*, the **Insert** tab can also be used to insert **Pictures**, **ClipArt**, **WordArt** and **Shapes** in *Excel*.

22. When you are finished, save the workbook as **visitor charts** and close it.

4.23 Page Setup

Page Setup allows you to modify how a worksheet will look when printed. It can be in **Portrait** (upright) or **Landscape** (sideways) mode. You can also adjust **scaling** and page **margins**.

Activity:

1. Open the workbook **Events** which contains a breakdown of turnover, spending and net profits for special events at the *Haunted Castle*.

2. Click the **Office Button**, expand **Print** and then select **Print Preview**. A preview of the first page as it will be printed is shown. Notice that the worksheet stretches over two pages.

3. To rotate the page so that all of the information will fit, click **Page Setup** and change the **Orientation** to **Landscape** on the dialog box that appears.

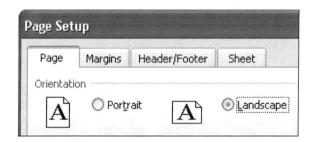

4. Click **OK** and notice that the page is rotated 90 degrees (although the contents of the workbook are not).

Note: The worksheet still covers two pages. To fit this on to one, there are two options available to you: **scale** the worksheet down on to one page or use the **Margins** tab to reduce the white space around the edges.

5. Display the **Page Setup** dialog box again and, under **Scaling**, select **Fit to**. Make sure **1 page(s) wide by 1 tall** are selected.

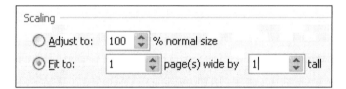

6. Click **OK**. The worksheet has now been scaled down a little so that it fits on to one page. This can be seen on the **Status Bar**.

7. Display the **Page Setup** dialog box again and select **Adjust to** under **Scaling**. Make sure **100% normal size** is selected to return the worksheet to its original size.

8. Next, select the **Margins** tab. Reduce both the **Left** and **Right** margins to **1.5**.

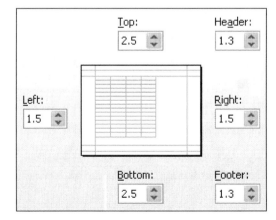

9. Click **OK**. The margins are reduced so that the worksheet fits on one page.

10. Click the **Print** button and select an appropriate printer from the **Name** drop-down box.

> Note: In some situations you may have access to more than one printer. Try to select and use the one closest to you. Remember that you may be charged for printing.

11. Click **OK** to print a copy of the current worksheet on your chosen printer. You will be automatically returned to the main worksheet view.

> Note: Notice that a dotted line has appeared on the worksheet. This is called the **Print Area** and indicates the boundaries of the cell range that will be printed.

12. Select the range **B5:G9**. From the **Page Layout** tab, click the **Print Area** button in the **Page Setup** group and select **Set Print Area**. The dotted line now surrounds this range.

23374	17980	19778	24273	26970	28768
4000	3000	6000	8000	8000	7000
0	0	2500	0	0	2000
320	350	450	320	450	350
2400	2400	2400	2400	2400	2400
2800	2500	2000	2000	2000	2000
9520	8250	13350	12720	12850	13750

> Note: You can click away from the selection to see the print area more clearly.

13. Display the **Print Preview** screen and examine the preview shown. Notice that only the cells within the custom **Print Area** will be printed. This technique is useful for printing parts of your worksheets.

4000	3000	6000	8000	8000	7000
0	0	2500	0	0	2000
320	350	450	320	450	350
2400	2400	2400	2400	2400	2400
2800	2500	2000	2000	2000	2000

> Note: **Margins** and **Orientation** settings are also available on the **Page Layout** tab.

14. Press <**Esc**> to return to the workbook.

15. From the **Page Layout** tab, click the **Print Area** drop-down button and select **Clear Print Area**. The custom **Print Area** is removed.

16. Save the workbook as **haunted castle events** and leave it open for the next exercise.

4.24 Headers and Footers

Headers and **footers** are lines of text at the top and bottom of every printed page. As with *Microsoft Word*, you can insert automatic **fields** such as page number, date and time.

Activity:

1. The workbook **haunted castle events** should still be open.

2. Display the **Insert** tab and click the **Header & Footer** button in the **Text** group.

3. The **Header** and **Footer** areas appear on the worksheet (and the **Header & Footer Tools - Design** tab appears on the **Ribbon**).

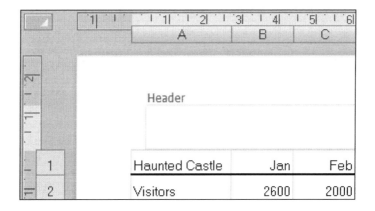

> Note: The **Header** and **Footer** areas contain three text boxes each: left, centre and right. Separate text can be entered in each one.

4. With the cursor flashing in the centre text box, click **Sheet Name** in the **Header & Footer Elements** group on the **Design** tab.

5. The text **&[Tab]** appears in the text box. This is known as a **Field** code and is updated automatically whenever your worksheet is opened or changed.

6. Click once in the left text box to move the cursor. Notice that the automatic **Field** in the centre box changes to **Events**. If you change the sheet name, this field will change too.

7. In the **Navigation** group, click **Go to Footer**. In the left text box, type your own name.

8. Move to the centre text box and click the **Current Date** button in the **Header & Footer Elements** group to insert today's date. The field **&[Date]** appears.

> Note: The **Header** and **Footer** drop-down buttons in the **Header & Footer** group can also be used to insert a number of predefined **field** codes.

9. Move to the right text box and click the **Page Number** button to insert another automatic field. The field **&[Page]** appears. Click away from the text box to see the effect.

10. Editing headers and footers automatically changes the worksheet view to **Page Layout**. In this view, rulers appear towards the top and left edges of the worksheet. Any margins, headers or footers can also be seen.

> Note: Similar to *Microsoft Word*, you can create a different header and footer for the first page and/or for every odd and even page afterwards.

11. Display the **View** tab and click **Normal** in **Workbook Views**. The margins and header/footer are hidden again.

12. Display the **Print Preview** screen and examine the preview shown. Notice the headers and footers and the updated **Fields**.

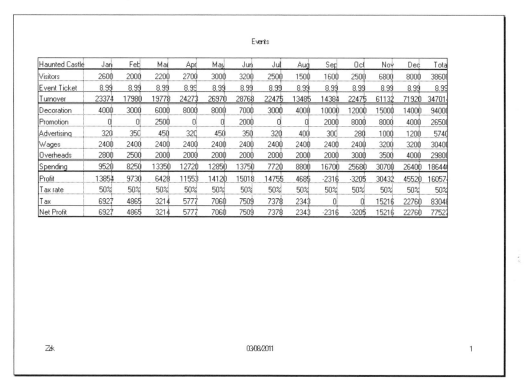

13. Save the workbook and leave it open for the next exercise.

4.25 Display and Print Formulas

When a cell contains a formula, the result of the formula rather than the formula itself is displayed in the cell. However, it is also possible to display the formulas in a worksheet rather than their results, which is very useful when checking for errors.

Activity:

1. The workbook **haunted castle events** should still be open.

---

2. To display all the formulas present in this worksheet, display the **Formulas** tab and click **Show Formulas** in the **Formula Auditing** group.

3. The formulas are displayed and the columns are widened to accommodate all of the cell contents.

=SUM(B5:B9)	=SUM(C5:C9)	=SUM(D5:D9)

4. If the formulas are to be printed, it is also a good idea to include the row and column **Heading Bars** also. Display the **Page Layout** tab and select **Print** in the **Sheet Options** group.

5. Display the **Print Preview** screen and notice that the **Heading Bars** are now also printed.

6. Return to the main view and hide the formulas using the keyboard shortcut <**Ctrl `**>.

7. Save the workbook using the same file name and leave it open for the next exercise.

4.26 Hide and Freeze Cells

When printing a workbook or showing it to others, you may find that you do not want to include particular rows or columns of data (e.g. those containing sensitive or personal information). If this is the case, it is very easy to temporarily hide them from view.

Alternatively, if you want to keep particular information on screen at all times (e.g. column and row header labels), you can freeze them in place. When scrolling through the data in a worksheet, the frozen cells will not move. An area that has been frozen in this way is known as a **Freeze Pane**.

Activity:

1. The workbook **haunted castle events** should still be open. *Zak* informs you that rows **8**, **12** and **13** contain sensitive data that should be hidden by default.

2. Select all of row **8** using the **Heading Bar**. Display the **Home** tab and click **Format** in the **Cells** group. From the drop-down menu that appears, click **Hide & Unhide | Hide Rows**.

7	Advertising	320	350
9	Overheads	2800	2500

3. Using click and drag, select rows **7** and **9** on the **Heading Bars**. From the **Format** drop-down menu click **Hide & Unhide | Unhide Rows**. Row 8 reappears.

> **Note:**   Columns can be hidden and displayed again using the same technique.

4. Hide row **8** again, followed by rows **12** and **13**. Notice that none of the results have been affected (hiding rows/columns does not affect any calculations).

5. Display the **View** tab and click the **Freeze Panes** button, ▦ Freeze Panes ▾, in the **Window** group. From the drop-down menu that appears, select **Freeze Top Row**.

6. The entire top row of the worksheet has now been frozen. Scroll down the workbook and notice that the top row remains on-screen at all times (a horizontal line marks the **Freeze Pane** boundary).

7. Click the **Freeze Panes** button and select **Freeze First Column**. Scroll right and notice that the first column also remains on-screen at all times.

> **Note:**   The **Freeze Panes** option on the **Freeze Panes** drop-down button can be used to freeze an entire area of a workbook above the active cell's row and to the left of the active cell's column.

8. Click the **Freeze Panes** button and select **Unfreeze Panes**. The frozen row and column are released.

9. Save the workbook using the same file name and close it.

4.27 Functions

Functions are common types of formula that are built into *Excel* to help save you time. There are various types of function available, but the following are used most often:

Statistical	AVERAGE, COUNT, MAX, MIN, STDEV, VAR
Financial	NPV, FV, PMT, RATE, IRR
Logical	IF, TRUE, FALSE
Math & Trig	MOD, SIN, LOG, SQRT
Text	LEFT, RIGHT, MID, LEN
Date & Time	DATE, NOW, TIME
Lookup & Reference	HLOOKUP, VLOOKUP, CHOOSE

Activity:

1. Create a new, blank worksheet.

2. Starting in cell **B3**, enter a column of numbers from **1** to **10** (you can type these manually or you can use the **Fill Handle**).

3.   To add the numbers together, enter the formula **=SUM(B3:B12)** into cell **B14**. Press <**Enter**>. The result **55** appears.

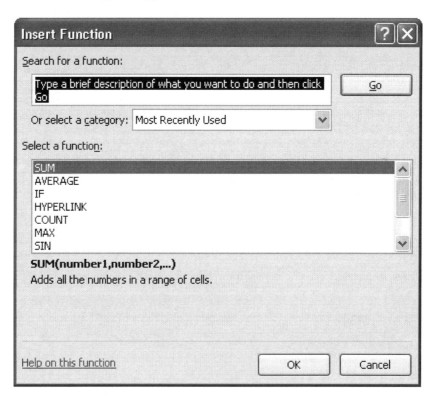

11	9
12	10
13	
14	55
15	
16	

4.   Move to cell **B15**. Type **=SUM(** and then use your mouse to select the range **B3:B12**. Finish the formula by pressing <**Enter**>. The result **55** appears again.

Note: It is very difficult to remember all of the functions built in to *Excel*. Luckily you don't need to – the **Insert Function** feature can be used instead.

5.   Select cell **B16**. On the **Formula Bar**, click the **Insert Function** button.

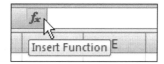

6.   The **Insert Function** dialog box appears.

Insert Function

Search for a function:

Type a brief description of what you want to do and then click Go   [Go]

Or select a category: Most Recently Used

Select a function:

SUM
AVERAGE
IF
HYPERLINK
COUNT
MAX
SIN

SUM(number1,number2,...)
Adds all the numbers in a range of cells.

Help on this function   OK   Cancel

Note: Functions can be found using the **Search for a function** text box or by selecting a category and then using the **Select a function** list.

7. From the category drop-down menu, select each category in turn to see all of the available functions – there are well over 200!

8. Select the category **Math & Trig**. From the **Select a function** list, find and select the function **SUM**. Notice the brief description of the function that appears towards the bottom of the dialog box.

> **SUM(number1,number2,...)**
> Adds all the numbers in a range of cells.

9. Click **OK**. The **Function Arguments** dialog box is displayed, prompting for a range of numbers to give to the function.

> Note: **Arguments** are simply the values that you give a function to work with. In the case of **SUM**, the arguments are a range of cell references containing numbers.

10. In the **Number1** box, delete the range that has been automatically found.

11. Next, click the **Collapse** button, ▦. This hides most of the dialog box and lets you select a range in the workbook by clicking and dragging.

12. Click and drag the range **B3:B12**. The range appears in the collapsed dialog box.

	A	B	C	D	E
1					
2					
3		1			
4		2			
5		3	Function Arguments		
6		4	B3:B12		
7		5			

13. Click the **Expand** button, ▦, to restore the **Function Arguments** dialog box again.

> Note: Notice that you can use the **SUM** function to add more than one range.

14. Click **OK**. The function is entered into the worksheet and the result is displayed.

> Note: Any of *Excel's* built-in functions can be applied using this method. In the next exercise you will get to use more complex functions.

15. Use the **Insert Function** dialog box to locate some of the functions described at the start of this exercise. The brief description text that appears below each one will describe their use in more detail.

16. When you ready to move on, close the worksheet <u>without</u> saving.

4.28 Statistical Functions

Statistical functions deal with analysing numerical data, from simple counting to more complex averaging. The most popular statistical functions include:

COUNT	Counts cells that only have numbers in them
COUNTA	Counts cells with any content
AVERAGE	Finds the simple average of a range of cells
MAX	Finds and displays the largest number in the selected range
MIN	Finds and displays the smallest number in the range
COUNTIF	Counts numeric items that match a set condition, e.g. the number of clients that owe more than £100

Activity:

1. Open the worksheet **Numbers**.

2. How many numbers would you say there are in column **B**? To find out move to cell **A102** and type **Count**.

3. Move to cell **B102** and click the **Insert Function** button, f_x. From the **Statistical** category, select **COUNT** and click **OK**.

> Note: When using a function, *Excel* tries to automatically find cells to work with. Nearby ranges that it finds are entered into the **Function Arguments** dialog box.

4. Delete the contents of **Value1** and enter the range **B1:B100** instead. Click **OK**.

5. This result **99** is displayed; the number of cells in the range that contain numbers. Scroll up to find a missing number in the range (cell **B56**).

6. Enter **23** in the empty cell and press <**Enter**>. Scroll back down to the bottom of the list to see that cell **B102** now reads **100**.

7. In cell **A103** type **Average**. Move to cell **B103** and click the **Insert Function** button, f_x.

8. From the **Statistical** category, select **AVERAGE** and click **OK**.

9. Enter the range **B1:B100** in the **Number1** box and click **OK**. This displays **50**, the average of the numbers in the specified range.

> Note: When the **Average** or **Count** functions are used, cells which are blank are ignored. However, cells containing zeros are included in the calculations.

10. Move back to the top of the worksheet and in cell **D11** type **Count**. In **D12** type **CountA**.

11. In **E11**, insert a function to count the number of numeric cells in the range **E1:E9**.

12. In **E12**, use the **CountA** function to count all of the cells in the range **E1:E9**.

| Count | 5 |
| CountA | 8 |

13. In cell **A104** enter the text **Max**. Move to **B104** and insert the function **Max** from the **Statistical** group. Enter the range **B1:B100** and click **OK**. This gives the maximum value present in the specified range (**123**).

14. In cell **A105** enter **Min** and in cell **B105** enter the function **=MIN(B1:B100)**.

> Note: Notice the box that appears underneath the cursor as you type a formula. This allows you to select a built-in function quickly as you type.

15. Click **OK**. This gives the smallest value (**1**).

16. Change the contents of cell **B100** to **201**. All the functions except **Count** change.

102	Count	100
103	Average	52
104	Max	201
105	Min	2

17. Save the workbook as **functions** and close it.

4.29 Sorting Data

Sometimes you may need to **sort** the contents of a spreadsheet so that related cells are grouped together or placed in a certain order. For example, you could rearrange the contents of a staff or product list alphabetically by name.

Activity:

1. Open the workbook **Temps**. This spreadsheet contains a list of temporary staff that have worked at the *Haunted Castle* in the past year.

2. Select any cell in column **A** that contains a name and, from the **Home** tab, click the **Sort & Filter** button in the **Editing** group. From the menu that appears, select **Sort A to Z**.

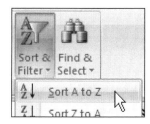

3.   The rows in the worksheet are reordered alphabetically using the contents of column **A**.

> Note: *Excel* automatically detects the type data and its range when sorting. However, if a range is selected first, only the contents of those cells will be sorted.

4.   Select a cell in column **B** containing a name and, from the **Sort & Filter** button, select **Sort Z to A**. The worksheet is reordered again by **Surname** in reverse alphabetical order.

5.   Select a cell in column **C** containing a number and click the **Sort & Filter** button. *Excel* recognises that the content of the selected cell is a number. Select **Sort Smallest to Largest** and the worksheet is reordered by increasing **Age**.

6.   You can also create more complex, custom sorts. Select any cell in the range **A5:D20** and display the **Data** tab. Click the **Sort** button in the **Sort & Filter** group.

7.   The **Sort** dialog box appears. Select **Column A** from the **Sort by** box and make sure **A to Z** is selected in **Order**.

> Note: If *Excel* is able to automatically detect the column headings in a worksheet, these will appear instead of **Column A**, **Column B**, and so on.

8.   Click **Add Level**, [Add Level], to add another level to the sort. In **Then by**, select **Column B** and again make sure **A to Z** is selected in **Order**.

> Note: It is very common to sort columns of data. However, if you need to sort by row instead, click the **Options** button and select the **Sort left to right** option.

9.   Click **OK** to perform the sort. The list is sorted on **First Name** *and then* **Surname**.

10.   Save the workbook as **temporary staff sorted** and close it.

4.30 Filtering Data

Filtering is a simple technique for selecting records that match certain conditions (these conditions are known as **criteria**). Only the records that match the criteria are displayed; records that do not match are hidden. When a list is filtered, the worksheet is said to be in **Filter Mode**.

Activity:

1.   Open the workbook **Research**. This spreadsheet contains the results of a recent visitor survey at the *Haunted Castle*. Select any cell in the range **A3:G3**.

2.   Display the **Data** tab and select **Filter** from the **Sort & Filter** group. The worksheet enters **Filter Mode** and drop-down arrows appear in the column headings in row **3**.

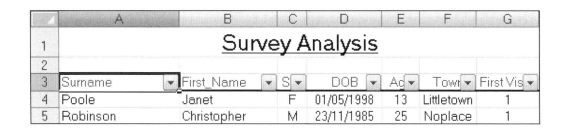

	A	B	C	D	E	F	G
1			Survey Analysis				
2							
3	Surname	First_Name	S	DOB	Ag	Town	First Vis
4	Poole	Janet	F	01/05/1998	13	Littletown	1
5	Robinson	Christopher	M	23/11/1985	25	Noplace	1

> **Note:** *Excel* automatically detects headers and then fills each drop-down filter list with values that can be found in that column.

3. Click the **Town** drop-down filter arrow, uncheck **Select All**, and click to select **Littletown**. Click **OK** and only the people from **Littletown** are displayed.

4. Using the **Town** filter arrow again, click **Select All** and **OK** to show the entire list.

5. To display all the males from **Noplace** who were visiting the park for the first time, select *only* **M** from **Sex**, **Noplace** from **Town**, and **1** from **First Visit**.

> **Note:** The drop-down arrows gain a filter symbol, [icon], if the column is currently filtered.

6. To redisplay the whole list quickly, click the **Filter** button on the **Ribbon** to exit **Filter Mode**. The worksheet returns to its normal state.

> **Note:** You can also apply custom search criteria for even more advanced filtering.

7. To only display visitors who are less than 50 years old, enter **Filter Mode** again and select **Number Filters** from the **Age** drop-down list.

8. Select **Less Than** from the submenu that appears and type **50** in the information box.

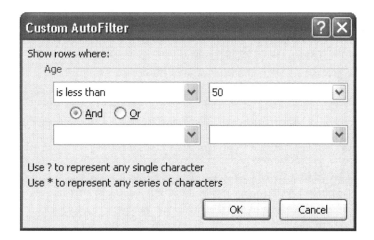

9. Click **OK** to filter the list. Only visitors under 50 years old are now displayed.

> **Note:** The number of records found, **151 out of 220**, is shown on the **Status Bar**.

10. To restore the list, click on the **Age** field drop-down. Then click **Select All** and **OK**.

11. Next, create a new filter to show only those people surveyed who are **50** years or *older*. You should locate **69** records.

12. Restore the full list and then create another filter to show only those people whose **Surname** begins with **B**. You should locate **22** records.

13. Restore the full list and then create another filter to show only those people who were born between **01/04/1979** and **01/04/1989** (**11** records). How many of these people were visiting the park for the first time? You should find only **2** records.

> Note: Other useful filters include **Top 10**, **Above Average**, **Below Average**, and a wide variety of date criteria. You can also create your own **Custom Filters**.

14. Close the workbook <u>without</u> saving.

4.31 Importing Data

Data can be imported into an *Excel* worksheet from a variety of external sources. In practice, however, it's usually far simpler to only import data contained in plain text files.

Text files must contain information separated (or **delimited**) by single characters such as tabs, spaces, or much more commonly, commas.

Activity:

1. Start a new, blank workbook. Display the **Data** tab and, from the **Get External Data** group, click **From Text**. The **Import Text File** dialog box appears.

2. Locate the data files folder for this section and import the file **Concession**.

> Note: The plain text file **Concession** is known as a **Comma Separated Values** file (**.csv**). Each value on a row is separated by a comma.

3. The **Text Import Wizard** appears. Notice that *Excel* has already recognised that the file contains data separated by characters.

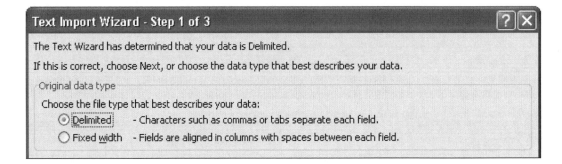

4. Click **Next** to move to **Step 2** of the wizard. Notice the **Data preview** at the bottom of the dialog box – this shows you the contents of the file that you are importing.

5. **Tab** is selected as the character which separates values. Change this to **Comma** and notice the effect in the **Data preview**.

Concession Sales					
	Popcorn	Drinks	Ice Cream	Candy Floss	Smoothies
Black Hole	23.45	340.59	450.45	101.34	34.67
House of Wax	29	609.34	670.98	340.56	56.89
Haunted Vault	134	67	456	2786.9	9.45

6. Click **Next**. The final screen of the wizard allows you to select which type of cell formatting you wish to apply to the new data. **General** is usually always best, so click **Finish**.

7. The **Import Data** dialog box appears prompting you to enter a cell reference into which the imported data will be inserted. Make sure that **Existing worksheet** is selected and enter cell **C5** (in practice you can import data into any starting cell that you like)

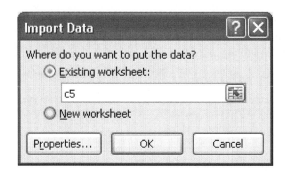

Note: The selected cell represents the top left corner of the imported data block.

8. Click **OK** and the data is imported. Each value that was separated by a comma in the original file is placed in its own cell.

	A	B	C	D	E	F	G	H
1								
2								
3								
4								
5			Concession Sales					
6				Popcorn	Drinks	Ice Cream	Candy Floss	Smoothies
7			Black Hole	23.45	340.59	450.45	101.34	34.67
8			House of Wax	29	609.34	670.98	340.56	56.89
9			Haunted Vault	134	67	456	2786.9	9.45
10			Tower of Terror	34.56	59	310	34.56	9.99
11			Viper	49.09	45.56	50	53.6	109.45

9. Save the workbook as **imported data** and close it.

10. Close *Excel*.

4.32 Next Steps

Well done! You have now completed all of the exercises in this section. If you feel you are ready to test your knowledge and understanding of the topics covered, move on to the following **Develop Your Skills** activities. If there are any features of *Microsoft Excel* that you are unsure about, you should revisit the appropriate exercises and try them again before moving on.

If you are interested in exploring some of *Microsoft Excel's* more powerful features, why don't you use the Internet to find out a little more about the following advanced topics.

Feature	Description
Templates	*Excel's* workbook templates work in generally the same way as *Word's* document templates. Any normal workbook can be saved as a template, allowing you to create a standard layout that can be used as a basis for future spreadsheets.
Formatting	*Excel* is capable of automatically formatting cells depending on their contents. This means that critical values which reach a specific value or level can be highlighted so that they stand out. This is called **Conditional Formatting**.
Goal Seek	**Goal Seek** allows you to perform "What If?" calculations on a worksheet. It can be used to help answer questions such as "What price do I charge to make a profit?" and "How many items do I need to sell to break even?"
Charts	There are many chart types available in *Excel*. Build on the basic lessons learned in 4.22 and explore the various layouts and styles on offer.
Tracking	It is very common to have another person review and edit spreadsheets that you create. If a workbook has been set up to "track changes", any changes made to a worksheet will be recorded. Once you get the updated workbook back, you can either accept or reject each change.
PivotTables	A **PivotTable** is a powerful feature of *Excel* that organises and then summarises large amounts of data. In many ways it is similar to the sorting and filtering features you have already seen in this section, but it allows for much more control over how the data is displayed.
Macros	A macro records keystrokes and menu selections and then plays them back exactly as they were recorded. A macro can be created so that frequently repeated tasks can be performed automatically.

At the end of every section you will get the chance to complete two full tasks without my assistance. This will help to reinforce learning and develop your skills. Don't forget to use the planning and review checklists at the back of the book to organise and evaluate your work.

> Note: Sample solutions for both tasks are provided in this section's data files folder.

Level 1: Haunted Castle Repair Log

In this task you will be asked to complete a simple spreadsheet for *Zak*. You will need to use the ICT skills you have learned in this section to plan, develop and present an appropriate solution. You can ask for help from friends, colleagues or a teacher if you get stuck.

Level 1 Task

My team and I often come across problems during our routine maintenance of rides. To fix these problems before a breakdown occurs, we usually need to buy and fit new parts. To allow us to keep track of spending and make sure we don't go over-budget, I plan to start keeping a monthly record of purchases in a spreadsheet.

I've made a start on creating this spreadsheet, but I need you to finish it for me. The information you will need is available in the following file:

✱   **Repair Log**   *Zak's* incomplete repair log spreadsheet

Start by opening *Zak's* spreadsheet, and then enter the most appropriate formulas to calculate results in the following columns:

F (Item Value * Quantity), **G** (Cost * VAT Rate), and **H** (Cost + VAT)

Enter a formula in cell **B24** to *count* the number of repairs, a formula in **B26** to *sum* the items in column **D**, and a formula in **B28** to *sum* the values in column **H**.

The spreadsheet also needs to look professional and be easy to read, so you should apply appropriate text and cell formatting. Add a more appropriate title to the spreadsheet so that it can be more easily identified, and then save the file as **final repair log**.

Level 2: Maintenance Report

In this task you will be asked to develop a spreadsheet and create a report for one of *Zak's* colleagues. You will need to use the advanced ICT skills that you have learned in this section to create a suitable solution (you may need to break the problem down into smaller parts first). Only level 2 students should attempt this task and it should be completed without help from others.

Level 2 Task

I've just received the following e-mail from one of my colleagues in the engineering and maintenance department.

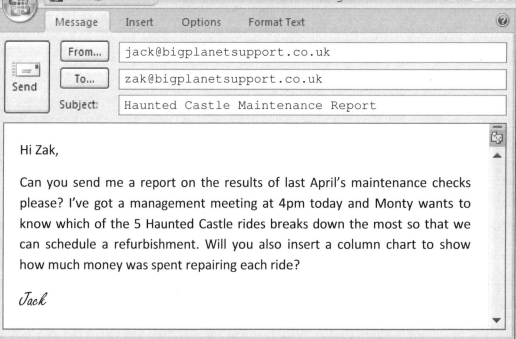

From... jack@bigplanetsupport.co.uk

To... zak@bigplanetsupport.co.uk

Subject: Haunted Castle Maintenance Report

Hi Zak,

Can you send me a report on the results of last April's maintenance checks please? I've got a management meeting at 4pm today and Monty wants to know which of the 5 Haunted Castle rides breaks down the most so that we can schedule a refurbishment. Will you also insert a column chart to show how much money was spent repairing each ride?

Jack

I need to head over to *The Viper* to repair a breakdown, so will you get this information together for *Jack*? I've made a start on the report in *Microsoft Word* but I've not included any figures yet. The information you will need is available in the following files:

❋ **Report** *Zak's* incomplete report document

❋ **April Checks** A file containing raw maintenance data for April

Start by opening *Zak's* report to see the types of information required to complete the document. Then use the most appropriate application to work out the necessary answers and create a chart. You may need to sort and filter the data that you have been given. The spreadsheet also needs to look professional and be easy to read, so you should apply appropriate text and cell formatting. Finally, save the document as **maintenance report**.

5 | Microsoft PowerPoint

I'm the head of ride design here at *Big Planet Theme Park*, and it's my job to create the blueprints for new rides and attractions. For my current project I've been asked to redesign *Demon of the Deep*, one of our older and less popular rides.

The *Demon of the Deep* log flume used to be one of the park's best attractions, but times and tastes change. It's now my responsibility to produce new ideas for improving the ride, from initial concepts and rough sketches through to fully developed models and working simulations. As I often work on my own, I need to manage my own time and stay focused to meet my deadlines.

I've already come up with a few new ideas to help improve the ride, and I plan to present these to park managers at a meeting in a few days time. To help me, I will use the application *Microsoft PowerPoint* to create a professional presentation quickly and easily. In fact, as you are here, maybe we can create the presentation together?

What you will learn:

In this section you will use the program *Microsoft PowerPoint* to help *Yan* design, create and edit a presentation. <u>IMPORTANT</u>: You will need to pay close attention and follow *all* of *Yan's* instructions carefully, as each exercise builds on the last to create a complete presentation.

Knowledge, skills and understanding:

✱   Use *Microsoft PowerPoint* to create and edit eye-catching presentations

✱   Apply a range of professional formatting and layout techniques

✱   Choose and display information that is relevant for the audience

✱   Select suitable animations and themes

Data files

Data files needed to complete the activities in this section are provided in the **Section 5** data files folder. Presentations that you create or edit can be saved to the same folder.

5.1   Using Microsoft PowerPoint

In both business and education, people are often asked to give a talk on a specific topic such as a new idea, product or service. People are also frequently required to present the results of their work or the findings of their research to other interested parties. To help lead the delivery of their talk, presentation software is used.

> **Note:**   It is a well known fact that most people do not enjoy public speaking. Fortunately, creating a slide show to accompany a presentation can really help. It can aid your memory and help get important points across to the audience.

Microsoft PowerPoint is an application that is an appropriate choice for any task that requires you to create, edit and give a presentation. It allows you to create a number of single **slides** containing key points on one or more topics. When combined in a sequence, the slides form a **slide show** that can be used to accompany your talk.

> **Note:**   Presentations are most often displayed using an overhead projector, monitor, or digital whiteboard. However, you can also use *PowerPoint* to save a slide show as a sequence of web pages or printed handouts.

The formatting of text and images is handled easily by *PowerPoint*, as is the ability to include different types of objects such as videos, music and charts. Perhaps more important is the application's ability to present information using a variety of professional text and background styles. To capture your audience's attention, a range of advanced animation effects can also be used to bring your presentation to life.

5.2   Creating a Presentation

PowerPoint features a variety of ready-made templates that you can use to create very impressive and professional presentations. However, it is recommended that you start from a blank template and focus on your presentation's content first. You can then apply formatting later.

Activity:

1.   Start *Microsoft PowerPoint*. A new blank presentation appears on the screen.

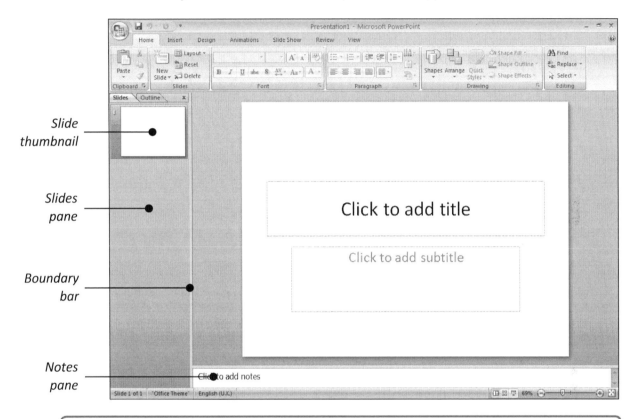

> **Note:**   You can also create a new **Blank presentation** using the **Office Button**.

2.   Examine the *PowerPoint* window. In particular, locate the familiar **Office Button**, **Ribbon**, **Status Bar**, **Quick Access Toolbar** and **Zoom** controls.

3.   Locate the **Slides** pane on the left of the window. This will display a small preview of all the slides in your presentation (known as **thumbnail** images). Clicking a thumbnail will open the full slide in the main editing window.

4.   Locate the **Notes** pane at the bottom of the window. This can be used to add notes to each slide which can be printed and used by a speaker during a presentation.

> **Note:**   The various panes can be resized or hidden by dragging their boundary bars.

5.   Leave the blank presentation open for the next exercise.

5.3 Slide Layouts

PowerPoint features a number of built-in slide layouts that can be used to quickly create new slides. Each layout features a slightly different arrangement of **placeholders** that you can use to enter your slide's content.

Activity:

1. Examine the layout of the single blank slide currently on-screen. This slide has a **Title Slide** layout (i.e. the slide is designed to be the first screen in a presentation).

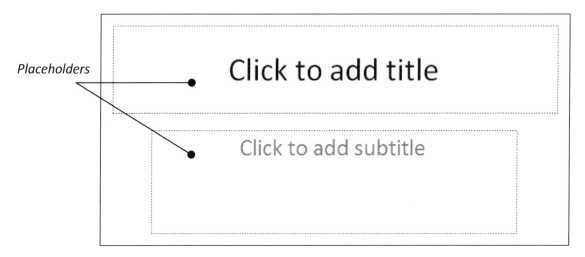

Placeholders

Click to add title

Click to add subtitle

> **Note:**   The default text that appears in the placeholders is used to prompt for information. This text will not appear when the slide show is viewed.

2. With the **Home** tab selected, click the **Layout** button, [Layout ▾], in the **Slides** group. A list of other slide layout types appears (notice that **Title Slide** is already selected).

3. Select **Title and Content** from the list. The current slide's layout is changed.

4. Select each of the remaining 7 slide layouts in turn and observe how each one affects the slide. Consider the possible uses for each of the layout types.

> **Note:**   The position of items on each slide layout can be changed using click and drag. To restore a slide back to its default layout, use the **Reset** button in the **Slides** group.

5. Return the current slide to its original **Title Slide** layout and leave the presentation open.

5.4 Adding and Removing Slides

New slides can easily be added to a presentation at any time using any slide layout you wish. It is also easy to remove any unwanted slides.

Activity:

1.   With the default blank presentation open on screen, click the **New Slide** button in the **Slides** group on the **Home** tab.

> **Note:**   Clicking the drop-down arrow on the **New Slide** button will let you add a new slide using any of the 9 available layout types.

2.   A new slide with **Title and Content** layout is created and added to the slide show. It appears on the **Slides** pane and is automatically selected.

3.   Use the drop-down arrow on the **New Slide** button to add a slide with **Two Content** layout. There are now 3 slides in the presentation.

> **Note:**   Notice that the slides are automatically numbered in the **Slides** pane.

4.   Using the **Slides** pane, click once on slide **1**. The slide thumbnail is selected and appears in the main editing window. Use the same technique to select slide **2**.

> **Note:**   To delete a slide, simply select it in the **Slides** pane and press <**Delete**>.

5.   Using the **Slides** pane, click once on slide **3**. Press the <**Delete**> key on your keyboard to remove the slide (leaving two slides remaining).

6.   Select slide **1** and leave it open for the next exercise.

5.5   Entering Text

Text can be added to a slide by simply clicking once within the boundaries of a placeholder and typing. The default "**Click to add...**" prompt will automatically disappear.

Activity:

1.   Slide **1** should currently be selected in the **Slides** pane. Click once in the placeholder box labelled **Click to add title**. The default prompt text disappears.

2.   Let's start creating the presentation for *Yan's* meeting. Enter the presentation title **Demon of the Deep**.

---

3.   Click in the second placeholder to add a **subtitle**, and then type **Redesign Ideas**. Notice that the first thumbnail on the **Slides** pane has been updated to reflect the changes.

> **Note:**   All of the standard text formatting options such as **Bold**, **Italic**, **Underline**, **Font** and **Font Size** are available on the **Home** tab in the **Font** group. Familiar text alignment options such as **Line Spacing** are also available in the **Paragraph** group.

4.   Display slide **2**, click once in the top placeholder and enter the text **Project Introduction**.

> **Note:**   In general, most *PowerPoint* slides should only contain brief bulleted points that help to emphasize key points in your presentation.

5.   Click once in the lower placeholder and enter the text **Demon of the Deep ride is getting old**. Notice that this slide layout automatically includes bulleted points. Press **<Enter>**.

6.   Enter the following key points, pressing **<Enter>** after each one.

Ride suffers from frequent breakdowns
Gives a bad impression of the park
Used to be very popular, but not any more
Too expensive to replace the ride
Needs a redesign to attract new visitors

7.   Save the presentation as **redesign** (in the data files folder for this section) and leave it open for the next exercise.

5.6   Running a Presentation

Once you have created one or more slides, you can run a presentation in **Slide Show** view. This will display the presentation as it will be seen by your audience, and is useful for testing that everything works and that the presentation appears as you expect.

Activity:

1.   Slide **2** should currently be selected in the **Slides** pane. Display the **Slide Show** tab and click **From Beginning** in the **Start Slide Show** group.

2.   The presentation runs and slide **1** fills the screen. Click your left mouse button once to move to the next slide (alternatively you can press **<Space>** or **<→>**). Click once more to reach the end of the slide show where a black screen appears.

3.   Press the **<Esc>** key on your keyboard to close the slide show. You can do this at any time during a presentation.

> **Note:**   You can also run a slide show from the currently selected slide by clicking **From Current Slide**. This option also appears on the right of the **Status Bar**, 🖵.

4.   Leave the presentation open.

5.7 Design Considerations

When creating a new presentation, special care needs to be taken when designing your slides. The following list briefly describes a number of important points that you should consider:

* Keep things simple. Don't include too much text or too many images on one slide

* Stick to key points and statements – avoid full sentences

* Don't mix and match too many fonts of different types and sizes

* Font sizes should be no smaller than 24 point for general text

* Use title case throughout a presentation and avoid block capitals

* Avoid dark text on dark backgrounds and light text on light backgrounds

* Sans serif fonts (e.g. Arial) are often easier to read that serif fonts (e.g. Times)

* Don't overdo distracting animations or slide transitions

* Use a consistent design theme for your entire presentation

Visual impact is almost everything in a presentation. In general, try not to use too many different colours, styles or effects in one presentation as the clarity of your message may be obscured. A simple, consistent design scheme is usually more effective.

> **Note:**   As a guide, 10 slides for a 20 minute talk is considered average. Also remember the "seven by seven rule", which recommends that each of your slides should have no more than 7 lines of text, and each line should contain no more than 7 words.

You should also be aware of the value of using pictures rather than too much text, and simple charts rather than complicated tables of figures. Always consider the emotional implications of certain colours too; reds are believed to be stimulating and representative of energy and danger, while blues are associated with calmness and stability. As some people have difficulty separating certain colour combinations (especially red-green), be careful when using these combinations to describe important information.

> **Note:**   Many businesses, schools, colleges and universities offer professional *PowerPoint* templates to their students and staff for use in formal presentations.

Furthermore, always consider the purpose of your presentation and design your slides accordingly. For example, a presentation to promote a company to potential investors will contain different information than one created to advertise a company to its customers. Furthermore, a presentation intended to run on a big screen in a large hall may need different design features to one which will run on a small screen in a meeting room.

5.8 Themes

It is important for a presentation to have a consistent design style across all of its slides. Although the same text formatting can be copied manually from slide to slide, *PowerPoint* offers several more effective methods to do this automatically. The quickest way is to apply a **theme** to the entire presentation.

> Note: A theme is a coordinated set of text styles, background colours and graphics.

Activity:

1.   The **redesign** presentation should still be open with slide **2** selected. At the moment, both of the slides in the presentation contain simple dark text on a white background. Fairly boring, wouldn't you say?

2.   Let's apply a theme to the presentation to make it more interesting. Display the **Design** tab and then examine the thumbnail theme previews that appear in the **Themes** group.

 — *More*

> Note: Placing your mouse pointer over a thumbnail will display a **ToolTip** containing the theme's name. The effect of selecting that theme is *previewed* on the selected slide. Notice that the default **Office Theme** is currently selected.

3.   Select the theme in the list named **Concourse**. Notice how the background colours, graphics, bullet points and text formatting on *all* slides in the presentation change.

4.   Select each of the themes currently shown to see their effect.

5.   Click the **More** drop-down arrow, to the right of the theme selection box to view more themes. Locate and select the theme called **Flow**.

> **Note:** If you are connected to the Internet, a range of additional themes is also available to download from **Office Online**.

6. The **Flow** theme is applied to the entire presentation. Examine both slides to see the effect.

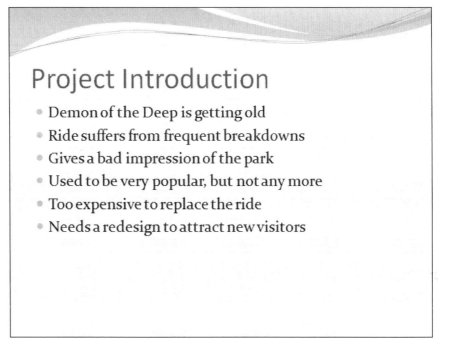

7. Save the presentation and leave it open for the next exercise.

5.9 Colour and Font Schemes

In addition to themes, you can also select a **colour** and **font scheme** for your presentation. These are sets of coordinated colours and fonts which set your presentation's default styles.

> **Note:** Changing schemes is useful when you like the basic design of a theme but not its colours or fonts. You can mix and match themes and colour/font schemes.

Activity:

1. The **redesign** presentation should still be open. Click **Colors**, , from the **Themes** group. The currently selected colour scheme is highlighted with a border.

2. Place your mouse pointer over a variety of colour schemes <u>without</u> clicking to preview each style on the selected slide. Notice that the background and text colours change.

3.   Select **Opulent** from the list, and then examine both slides in your presentation to see the effect. Experiment by selecting other colour schemes.

> Note: To customise the selected colour scheme, or create your own from scratch, select **Create New Theme Colors** from the **Colours** drop down list.

4.   When you are finished, click the **Colors** button and select **Flow** again from the list.

5.   Select slide **2** in the **Slides** pane and then click the **Fonts** drop-down button in the **Themes** group. The currently selected font scheme is highlighted.

> Note: Each font scheme features a *primary* font and a *secondary* font. Usually the primary font is used for titles and headings and the secondary font is used for bullets. Font schemes are useful for making sure that all of the fonts in a presentation are consistent across slides.

6.   Place your mouse pointer over a variety of font schemes <u>without</u> clicking to preview each style on the selected slide. Notice that both the header and bullet text changes.

> Note: To customise the selected font scheme, or create your own from scratch, select **Create New Theme Fonts** from the **Fonts** drop down list. You will find out more about font and colour schemes in the next section.

7.   Select **Office Classic** from the list. Examine both slides in your presentation to see the effect and notice that the title font is now **Arial** and the bullet font **Times New Roman**. These fonts were both defined in the selected font scheme.

8.   Experiment by selecting other font schemes. When you are finished, click the **Font** button and select **Flow** again from the list.

9.   Select slide **2** and leave it open for the next exercise.

5.10 Slide Master

To customise a selected theme and change the way fonts and designs appear on all slides in a presentation, you can edit the **Slide Master**. Changes to the slide master will affect all slides in a presentation (including any new slides added to it later).

> **Note:** A **Slide Master** is particularly useful if you want to change all text and bullet styles in a presentation, or if you want to add a graphic to every slide (e.g. a logo).

Activity:

1. The **redesign** presentation should still be open. Display the **View** tab and click **Slide Master** from the **Presentation Views** group.

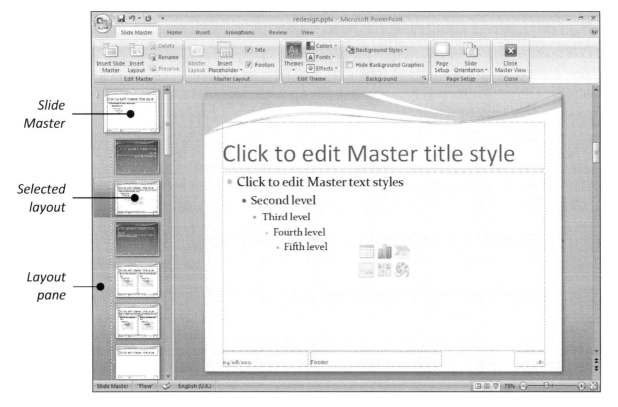

> **Note:** The **Slide Master** can be found at the top of the **Layout** pane. The slides under this allow you to customise individual slide layouts (e.g. **Title Slide**, **Title and Content**).

2. Click the **Slide Master** thumbnail in the **Layout** pane. Any changes made here to text or bullet styles will apply to every slide in the presentation.

> **Note:** If a **Layout** slide is selected in the **Layout** pane rather than the **Slide Master**, only slides of that type will be changed.

3. Click in the placeholder **Click to edit Master title style**. Simply place the cursor somewhere in the title text – do not select any words or characters.

4. With the cursor placed anywhere *inside* the text, display the **Home** tab and notice that the selected font is **Calibri**, size **50**. Change the size to **48**, apply **Bold** and **Centre** align.

5. Click once within the top bullet's text in the lower placeholder: **Click to edit Master text styles**, and then set the font to **Arial** and leave the size as **26**.

6. Click the **Line Spacing** button, ⬆⬇☰▾, and select **1.5** to increase the space between bullets.

7. Click within the next bullet's text: **Second Level**, and set the font to **Arial**, the style to **Italic**, and leave the size as **24**.

8. Set the **Third**, **Fourth** and **Fifth** levels to **Arial** size **18** (try selecting all three lines at once).

9. Click **Close Master View** from the **Slide Master** tab to see how the presentation has been changed. Save the presentation and leave it open for the next exercise.

5.11 Bullet Levels

When you add text to a slide, you need to be as brief and as concise as possible. Only important facts should be included in the form of **bullet points**. If you would like to expand on a bullet and add extra detail, you can add one or more minor bullets at a different **level** below.

* This is a level 1 bullet
  * This is a level 2 bullet
    * This is a level 3 bullet

There are several levels of bullet point available in *PowerPoint* which allow you to add minor details to major points.

> Note: The formatting of bullet points for the whole presentation can be set in **Slide Master View**. This also includes the bullet symbols.

Activity:

1. The **redesign** presentation should still be open. With slide **2** selected, use the **New Slide** button to add a new slide with **Title and Content** layout.

2. Add the slide title **Considerations** (notice that the new slide uses the defaults set up in the **Slide Master**). Next, add the following bullet points to the lower placeholder:

    Limited budget

    0.5 Million to spend on redesign

    Tight schedule

    Must complete ride redesign in 6 months

    Works must be done in winter season

    Ride must be environmentally friendly

> **Note:** When bullet points are first entered onto a slide, *PowerPoint* assumes they are **first level**. As such, all 6 bullets on the current slide are **level 1** bullets.

3. Place the cursor in the second bulleted line and click **Increase List Level**, ⬚, from the **Paragraph** group of the **Home** tab. The bullet's level is increased to **level 2**, making it a sub-point of the bullet directly above.

> **Note:** The second level bullet adopts the style set up earlier in the **Slide Master**.

4. The fourth and fifth bullets are really sub-points of the third bullet. Increase these to **level 2** also.

- Limited budget
    - *0.5 Million to spend on redesign*
- Tight schedule
    - *Must complete ride redesign in 6 months*
    - *Works must be done in winter season*
- Ride must be environmentally friendly

5. Leave the presentation open for the next exercise.

5.12 Bullet Symbols

You can change the symbols used for bullet points in your presentation. Although this can be done for each bullet individually, it is *far* easier to apply global changes using the **Slide Master**.

Activity:

1. With the **redesign** presentation open, display the **View** tab and click **Slide Master**.

2. The slide type **Title and Content Layout** is automatically selected. Select **Slide Master** from the top of the **Layout** pane instead.

3. Place the cursor in the first level of bulleted text. Display the **Home** tab and click the drop-down arrow on the **Bullets** button in the **Paragraph** group.

4. Examine the various bullet styles available (selecting **None** would remove the bullet symbol from this level of bullets).

> **Note:** Selecting **Bullets and Numbering** from the bottom of the drop-down menu will allow you to change the colour and size of the bullet or to use a custom image.

5. For now, from the list of bullet symbols that appear, select **Arrow Bullets**, 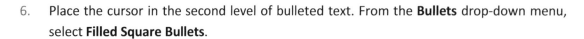.

6. Place the cursor in the second level of bulleted text. From the **Bullets** drop-down menu, select **Filled Square Bullets**.

7. Display the **Slide Master** tab and click **Close Master View** to see how the presentation has been changed.

8. Save the presentation and leave it open for the next exercise.

5.13 Rearranging Bullets

Once you have entered a number of bullets onto a slide, it is very easy to rearrange them into a different order using click and drag.

Activity:

1. The **redesign** presentation should still be open. With slide **3** selected, use the **New Slide** button to add a new slide with **Title and Content** layout.

2. Add the slide title **Initial Plan**. Next, add the following bullet points to the lower placeholder in the order shown:

> **Close the ride at the end of October**
> **Refill the ride with water and test for leaks**
> **Fit new ride features**
> **Drain the ride of water**
> **Remove old, unwanted ride parts**
> **Ride is ready in time for spring season**

3. Hold on! The order of events in this list is all wrong. Place your mouse pointer over the fourth bullet point symbol (**Drain the ride of water**). Notice that the pointer changes to a four way arrow.

⊕ Drain the ride of water

4. Using click and drag, move this bullet below the first line and into second place. Notice that a faint horizontal line appears between bullet points to indicate where the current bullet will be placed when dropped.

5. Use the same technique to reorder the remaining bullets into the correct order, as shown below:

> ➤ Close the ride at the end of October
>
> ➤ Drain the ride of water
>
> ➤ Remove old, unwanted ride parts
>
> ➤ Fit new ride features
>
> ➤ Refill the ride with water and test for leaks
>
> ➤ Ride is ready in time for spring season

> **Note:**   You can also **Cut**, **Copy** and **Paste** bullet points.

6. Save the presentation and leave it open for the next exercise.

5.14 Inserting Pictures and Clip Art

To make your presentations more interesting, you can insert pictures or diagrams stored on your computer onto a slide. Various illustrations are also available from the **Clip Art** library that is available at **Office Online**.

> **Note:**   When using a picture in your presentation, always make sure you have permission from the person who owns it. This does not apply to **Clip Art** from **Office Online**.

Activity:

1. The **redesign** presentation should still be open. With slide **4** selected, use the **New Slide** button to add a new slide with **Title and Content** layout. Add the slide title **First Ideas**.

> **Note:**   Have you noticed the faded icons in the centre of the slide? These can be used to quickly insert objects such as **Tables**, **Charts**, **Pictures** and **Clip Art**.

2. Click once in the lower placeholder and then display the **Insert** tab. From the **Illustrations** group, select **Picture**. The **Insert Picture** dialog box appears.

3. Locate the data files folder for this section and then select the **Sketch** image file. Click **Insert** to place the picture in the centre of the current slide.

> Note: Inserted objects can be repositioned using click and drag, resized using a corner handle, , or rotated using the green rotation handle, .

4. Feel free to resize and reposition the image as necessary to match the slide below.

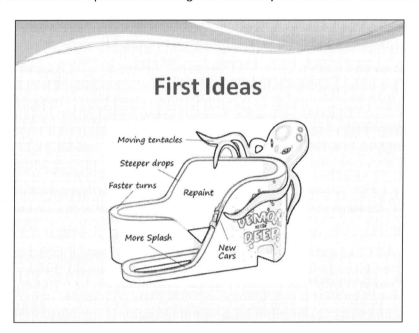

5. Next, display the **Insert** tab again and click **Clip Art** from the **Illustrations** group. The **Clip Art** task pane appears on the right of the screen.

6. Type **lightbulb** in the **Search for** box, and check that **All media file types** is selected in the **Results should be** box.

7. Click the **Go** button and, after a short delay, a list of **Clip Art** images matching the **lightbulb** keyword will be displayed.

8. Locate the **Clip Art** image shown below (you may need to scroll down), and click it once. The illustration is placed in the centre of the current slide.

9.   Resize the **Clip Art** image and position it to the right of the header text (**First Ideas**) as shown below.

10.   Close the **Clip Art** task pane and leave the presentation open for the next exercise.

> **Note:**   You can add a picture to a slide's background (including solid, gradient, texture and pattern fills) by clicking the **Background Styles** button on the **Design** tab and selecting **Format Background**.

5.15   Inserting Charts

A **chart** can be added to a slide to display complex data in a format that is more meaningful and easier to understand for your audience. The relevant information is entered into a spreadsheet which is then converted into a chart.

Activity:

1.   The **redesign** presentation should still be open. With slide **5** selected, use the **New Slide** button on the **Home** tab to add a new slide with a **Blank** layout.

2.   *Yan* would like to include a **Column Chart** on this slide containing all of the costs for the ride's redesign.

3.   Display the **Insert** tab and click **Chart** from the **Illustrations** group. The **Insert Chart** dialog box appears.

4.   The first **Column** chart is selected by default. This is ideal for use in *Yan's* presentation, so click **OK**. *Microsoft Excel* starts alongside the *PowerPoint* window.

> **Note:**   All of the chart types available in *Excel* are also available in *PowerPoint*.

5.   Replace the sample data in the *Excel* window with the information shown below.

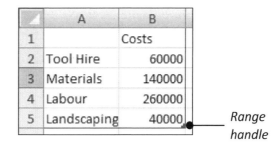

Range handle

> **Note:** The sample data range includes two extra columns. You will need to use the range handle to reduce the chart data range to include columns **A** and **B** <u>only</u>.

6.   Close *Excel*. The data range selected is now used to build a **Column** chart on the current *PowerPoint* slide. Click away from the chart to see how it will appear.

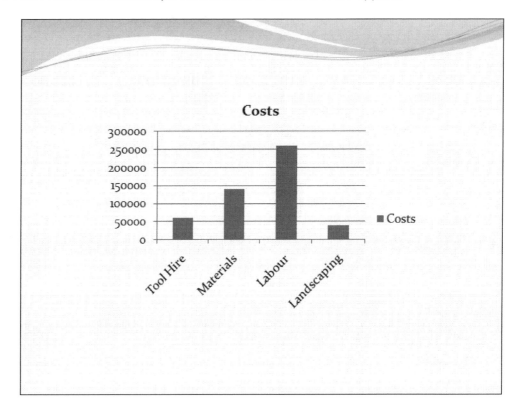

7.   Click the chart once to select it and notice the **Chart Tools** tabs appear on the **Ribbon**.

> **Note:** Once a chosen **Chart** type has been selected, you can change your mind and apply another using the **Change Chart Type** button on the **Chart Tools - Design** tab.

8.   Display the **Chart Tools - Design** tab now, and click the **Change Chart Type** button in the **Type** group. The **Change Chart Type** dialog box appears.

9.   Select the first **Pie Chart** and click **OK**. The chart is changed.

> **Note:** Like *Excel*, each chart type has its own list of **Chart Layouts** and **Chart Styles** to choose from (variations on the selected chart type). You can also reposition elements in a chart manually using drag and drop. Other options on the **Layout** tab allow you to add, edit and remove axis titles, gridlines, legends and data labels.

10.   Change the **Chart Type** and select the first **Bar Chart**, and then change the title of the chart to **Redesign Costs** (hint: you can right-click the chart's title and select **Edit Text**).

11.   Select the chart's **Legend**, ■ Costs , and press <**Delete**> to remove it.

12. By clicking and dragging the chart's border, move the chart down a little so that it is positioned better in the white space available (as shown below).

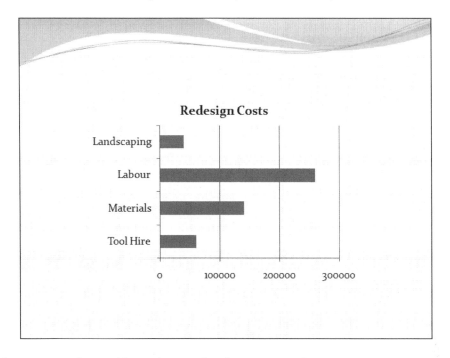

13. Save the presentation and leave it open for the next exercise.

5.16 Inserting WordArt

PowerPoint, like *Microsoft Word*, has a powerful feature called **WordArt** which allows you to create impressive artwork from the text on your slides. There are various styles, shapes and colours to choose from.

Activity:

1. The **redesign** presentation should still be open. With slide **6** selected, use the **New Slide** button on the **Home** tab to add a new slide with a **Blank** layout.

2. Display the **Insert** tab and select **WordArt** from the **Text** group. A drop-down menu appears containing a range of **WordArt** styles (notice that they reflect the presentation's chosen colour scheme). Select the first **WordArt** style in the list.

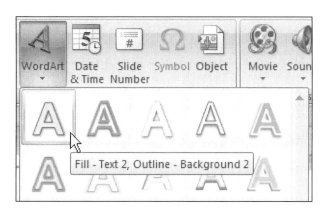

3. A **WordArt** box appears in the centre of the screen with the words **Your Text Here** already selected. Overtype this with the text **Any Questions?**

> Note: Once a chosen **WordArt** style has been selected, you can change your mind and apply another using the **WordArt Styles** selection box. Your text will be preserved.

4. Examine the various formatting features in the **WordArt Styles** group on the **Drawing Tools - Format** tab. These can be used to customise **WordArt** in a number of ways.

5. With all the **WordArt** text selected, click the **Text Fill** drop-down button and choose the first **Blue** colour from your chosen colour scheme's **Theme Colors**.

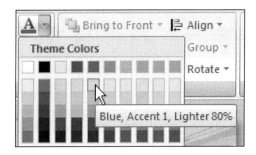

6. The **WordArt** text is filled with your chosen colour. Next, click the **Text Effects** button and examine the various effects that you can apply.

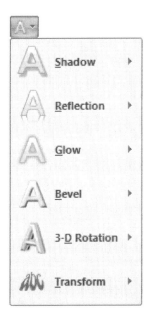

7. Move your mouse pointer over **Shadow**, and then select the first shadow style that appears (labelled with the **ToolTip: Offset Diagonal Bottom Right**).

8. Display the **Text Effects** button again, expand **Reflection** and select the first reflection style (labelled with the **ToolTip: Tight Reflection, touching**).

> Note: You can use **WordArt** and apply these effects in other *Microsoft Office* applications.

9. Click away from the **WordArt** to deselect it and observe the results.

10. Leave the presentation open for the next exercise.

5.17 Inserting Shapes and Text Boxes

PowerPoint offers a number of simple drawing features to add basic shapes to your slides. You can also place text inside floating boxes that can be positioned anywhere you like.

Activity:

1. The **redesign** presentation should still be open. With slide **7** selected, use the **New Slide** button on the **Home** tab to add a new slide with a **Title Only** layout.

2. *Yan* has decided that he would like to include a few interesting quotes from park visitors about the current *Demon of the Deep* ride. Add the slide title **Visitor Opinions**.

3. Display the **Insert** tab and click the **Shapes** drop-down button. Then, from the **Callouts** section, select the first shape, ⬜ (**Rectangular Callout**).

4. The mouse pointer changes to a crosshair, ✚. In the centre of the slide, click and drag to create a shape of any size.

5. With the new shape selected, display the **Drawing Tools - Format** tab and locate the **Size** group. By editing the values in the boxes, set the **Shape Height** to **4 cm** and the **Shape Width** to **6 cm**.

6. Using the **Copy** button on the **Home** tab, copy the new shape. Then use the **Paste** button to create two identical copies and arrange them below the slide title as shown below.

> **Note:** **WordArt**, shapes, text boxes and pictures can overlap. To control which object is in front of which, use the **Bring to Front** and **Send to Back** buttons.

---

7. Select the leftmost shape. Then type the first visitor quote: **"The ride is very old fashioned"**. The text appears in the middle of the shape. Use the **Font Size** drop-down button on the **Home** tab to increase the size of the text to **24**.

8. In the second box enter the text: **"It is really slow and boring"**. In the third box, enter: **"It is looking a little run down"**. Increase the **Font Size** to **24** for both shapes.

9. Next, display the **Insert** tab again and select **Text Box**. Click once below the three **Callout** shapes to create a text box, and then type the text: **Quotes collected by a survey on 01/06/2011**.

10. Reposition the text box neatly so that it appears in the middle of the slide underneath the shapes containing the visitor quotes.

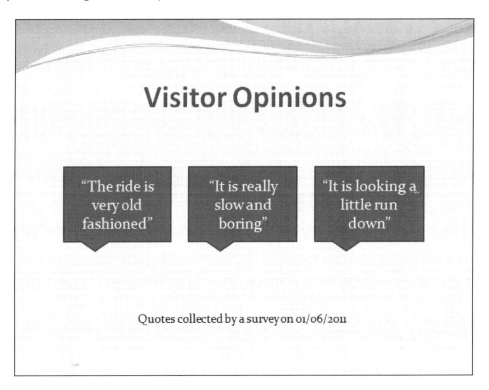

> Note: The **Align** button on the **Drawing Tools - Format** tab can be used to position shapes.

11. Save the presentation and leave it open for the next exercise.

5.18 Inserting Tables

PowerPoint allows you to insert well-designed tables (grids of cells containing text in rows and columns) that can be used to present data in a clear and easy to read format.

Activity:

1. The **redesign** presentation should still be open. With slide **8** selected, use the **New Slide** button on the **Home** tab to add a new slide with a **Title Only** layout.

2. *Yan* would like to include statistics on the drop in visitor numbers on the *Demon of the Deep* ride. Add the slide title **Visitor Numbers**.

3. Display the **Insert** tab and click **Table**. From the drop-down menu that appears, use the grid to select a table **3x5**.

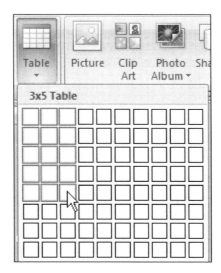

4. A new, blank table appears on the current slide.

> **Note:** Notice that the table matches the presentation's colour scheme. For advanced table options, select **Insert Table** from the **Table** drop-down button.

5. Enter the following data into the table. You can use the <**Tab**> key to move from cell to cell (<**Shift Tab**> can also be used to move back one cell).

Quarter/Year	2000	2010
Winter	123000	23000
Spring	89000	31000
Summer	49000	14000
Autumn	78000	11000

6. Move the table, by clicking and dragging its border, into the middle of the slide.

Quarter/Year	2000	2010
Winter	123000	23000
Spring	89000	31000
Summer	49000	14000
Autumn	78000	11000

7. Save the presentation and leave it open for the next exercise.

5.19 Inserting Videos and Audio

Videos and sounds (including music) can all be imported into *PowerPoint* and added to a slide. Various options allow you to control when and for how long the items are played.

Activity:

1. The **redesign** presentation should still be open. With slide **9** selected, use the **New Slide** button on the **Home** tab to add a new slide with a **Title Only** layout.

2. As visitors queue to ride the redesigned *Demon of the Deep* ride, TV screens will be used to display waiting times. *Yan* has created a new video that will **loop** (play continuously) in the background on all screens, and he would like to include this in his presentation.

3. Add the slide title **Waiting Screen**. Display the **Insert** tab and click the **Movie** button (not the button's drop-down arrow) from the **Media Clips** group. The **Insert Movie** dialog box appears.

4. Select the **Fish** video from the data files folder and click **OK**. Choose **When Clicked** when prompted and the video is placed in the centre of the current slide.

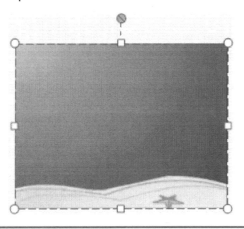

> **Note:** Notice that you can resize, rotate and reposition the video using its handles.

5. Click the **Preview** button in the **Play** group of the **Movie Tools - Options** tab to watch the short video. This video has no sound, but if it did you would also hear that now.

6. Display the **Picture Tools - Format** tab and, from the thumbnails shown in the **Picture Styles** group, select **Simple Frame, White** (you may need to expand the box using the **More** button to find this).

7. A border appears around the new video. Next, return to the **Movie Tools - Options** tab and examine the video playback settings available here.

8. From **Movie Options**, place a tick in the **Loop Until Stopped** checkbox.

9. Click the **Preview** button in the **Play** group to watch the short video again. It now runs in a continuous loop. Click the **Preview** button again to stop it.

10. From **Movie Options**, click the **Play Movie** drop-down button and select **Automatically**. The video will now start straight away when the slide appears in the presentation.

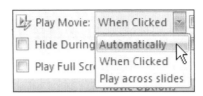

> **Note:** If **When Clicked** is left selected, the video will not play until it has been clicked using the mouse.

11. *Yan* also has a sound effect that he would like visitors to hear throughout the ride. Display the **Insert** tab and click the **Sound** button (not the button's drop-down arrow) from the **Media Clips** group. The **Insert Sound** dialog box appears.

12. Select the **Bubbles** sound file from the data files folder and click **OK**. Choose **When Clicked** when prompted and the sound clip is added to the slide as a small speaker icon.

> **Note:** You can drag the small speaker icon anywhere on or outside of the current slide. You can then click the icon during the presentation to hear the effect.

13. Display the **Sound Tools - Options** tab and examine the sound playback options available here. From **Sound Options**, place a tick in both the **Loop Until Stopped** and **Hide During Show** checkboxes.

> **Note:** When **Hide During Show** is selected, the small speaker icon will not appear and you will have no control over the sound during the presentation.

14. Click the **Play Sound** drop-down button and select **Automatically**. The sound clip will now also start straight away when the slide appears in the presentation.

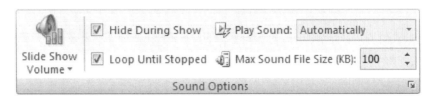

> **Note:** Notice also the option in the **Play Sound** drop-down to **Play across slides**. If this is selected, the sound file will play on all slides in a presentation.

15. Display the **Slide Show** tab and click **From Current Slide** in the **Start Slide Show** group to run the presentation from the current slide.

16. Observe the results, and then press <**Esc**> twice (once to stop the video and again to end the slide show).

17. Save the presentation and leave it open for the next exercise.

5.20 Objects on the Slide Master

Any objects such as text boxes, **Clip Art, WordArt,** pictures and shapes can be added to a presentation's **Slide Master**. They will then appear on every slide in the presentation.

Activity:

1. With the **redesign** presentation open, display the **View** tab and click **Slide Master**. Then, select **Slide Master** from the top of the **Layout** pane.

2. Using the **Picture** button on the **Insert** tab, insert the **Logo** image from the data files folder. It appears in the centre of the **Slide Master**.

3. On the **Picture Tools - Format** tab, click the **Align** drop-down button, and select **Align Bottom**.

4. Click the **Align** button again and select **Align Right**. The theme park logo now appears in the bottom right corner of the **Slide Master**.

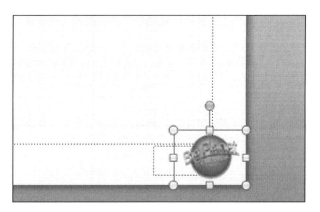

> Note: Notice that the logo appears on all **Layout** slides in the **Layout** pane. You can also hide the logo on specific slide layout types if required.

5. Display the **Slide Master** tab and select the **Title Slide Layout** slide in the **Layout** pane.

6. On the **Ribbon**, place a tick in the **Hide Background Graphics** checkbox in the **Background** group (this feature hides all background images). The background graphics disappear.

7. Click **Close Master View**. The theme park logo now appears in the bottom right corner of all slides apart from the first (which uses the **Title Slide** layout).

8. Save the presentation and leave it open for the next exercise.

5.21 Changing Slide Order

The order that slides appear in the **Slides** pane is the order that they will appear when a presentation is run. To change this order, individual slides can be moved elsewhere in the slide show sequence. To do this, it is recommended that you use *PowerPoint's* **Slide Sorter** view.

Activity:

1. With the **redesign** presentation open, display the **View** tab and click **Slide Sorter** from the **Presentation Views** group.

> **Note:**   The **Zoom** controls found to the right of the **Status Bar** can be used to resize the slide thumbnails displayed in **Slide Sorter** view.

2. If necessary, use the **Zoom** controls to select a zoom level that allows all 10 slide thumbnails to appear on the screen without needing to scroll.

3. *Yan* would like to move slide **8**, **Visitor Opinions**, between slides **2** and **3**. Click on slide **8** and drag the slide towards slide **2**. A vertical drop bar appears between slides to indicate where the current slide will be placed when dropped.

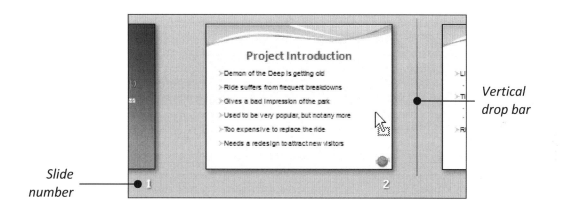

4. When the vertical drop bar appears between slides **2** and **3**, release the mouse. The **Visitor Opinions** slide is moved and becomes slide **3**.

> **Note:**   To delete a slide, right click its thumbnail and select **Delete Slide**.

5. Move slide **9**, **Visitor Numbers**, between slides **3** and **4**, and then move slide **10**, **Waiting Screen**, between slides **7** and **8**.

> **Note:**   Slides can also be moved using click and drag in the **Slides** pane in **Normal** view.

6. Switch back to **Normal** view using the button in the **Presentation Views** group.

7. Save the presentation and leave it open for the next exercise.

5.22 Applying Animation

Simple **animations** can very quickly be applied to objects on a slide so that they appear in a variety of fun and interesting ways. Use animation carefully, however, as too many fancy effects can be distracting for the audience.

Activity:

1.   Select slide **2** of the **redesign** presentation in **Normal** view.

2.   Select the title **Project Introduction**, and then display the **Animations** tab. From the **Animate** drop-down list in the **Animations** group, select **Fade**. A preview of the animation may briefly appear on the slide.

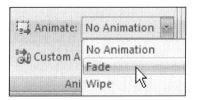

3.   Next, place the cursor anywhere in the bulleted list below the title and click the **Animate** drop-down button. From under **Fly In**, select **By 1st Level Paragraphs**.

4.   Display the **Slide Show** tab and click **From Current Slide** in the **Start Slide Show** group. The presentation runs from slide **2**.

5.   Click the mouse button once to activate the first animation: the title text fades in.

6.   Click again to activate the second animation: the first line of bulleted text flies in. Click again five more times to display each remaining line of text. Click once more to move on to slide **3** and then press <**Esc**> to end the show.

7.   Select slide **2** again and display the **Animations** tab. Place the cursor in the bulleted text and click the **Animate** drop-down button again. From the list of options available, select **All At Once** under **Fly In**.

8.   Run the slide show from the current slide again and observe the effects (use your mouse or keyboard to move the slide show forward). Press <**Esc**> when finished to end the show.

9.   Next, click **Custom Animation** in the **Animations** group to show the **Custom Animation** task pane. You can use this pane to fine tune the animations on the current slide.

> **Note:**   Notice the small numbers that have appeared to the left of both the title and bulleted list. These represent the sequence in which each animation will occur.

10.   Click the **Direction** drop-down button and select **From Right**. Then click the **Start** drop-down button and select **With Previous**. The bulleted list animation will now occur at the same time as the first title animation (notice the effect on the animation sequence).

> **Note:** The **Preview** button can be used to see effects on the slide without needing to run the slide show. The length of an animation can also be controlled using the options available in the **Speed** drop-down box.

11. Run the slide show from the current slide again and observe the effects (use your mouse or keyboard to move the slide show forward). Press **<Esc>** when finished to end the show.

12. Select slide **2** again and display the **Animations** tab. With the bulleted list selected, drop down the **Animate** button and select **No Animation**. Use this technique to remove the animation from the slide's title also.

> **Note:** An easy way to apply animation to all slides is to use the **Slide Master**.

13. Display the **View** tab and click **Slide Master**. Then, select **Slide Master** from the top of the **Layout** pane.

14. Select the title placeholder containing the text **Click to edit Master title style**. Then display the **Animations** tab and, from the list of animations in the **Animate** drop-down, select **Fade**.

15. From the **Custom Animation** task pane, drop-down the **Start** list and select **With Previous**. The effect will now happen immediately when the slide is shown during the presentation.

16. Change the **Speed** to **Fast** and then close the **Custom Animation** task pane.

17. Display the **Slide Master** tab and click **Close Slide Master**.

18. Run the slide show from the beginning and observe the effects (use your mouse or keyboard to move the slide show forward). All slide titles now fade in.

19. Press **<Esc>** when finished to end the show. Save the presentation and leave it open for the next exercise.

5.23 Applying Transitions

Transitions are special effects that appear when you move from slide to slide during a presentation. An impressive selection is available to choose from.

Activity:

1. Select slide **1** of the **redesign** presentation and then display the **Animations** tab on the **Ribbon**. Examine the various transition options that appear in the **Transition to This Slide** group.

2. From the list of transitions, select **Fade Smoothly** (as shown on the following page).

3. Run the presentation from this slide and observe the effect. Press <**Esc**> to end the slide show when you are finished.

4. Apply and then preview some of the other available transitions. The **More** button can be used to access a range of further transitions.

5. When you are finished, select **Wipe Right** (under the **Wipes** heading).

6. Next, click the **Apply To All** button, 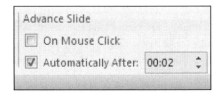, to apply this slide's transition effect to all other slides in the presentation.

> **Note:** You can apply a different transition effect to each slide. The time it takes for the transition effect to run can be changed using the **Transition Speed** box.

7. Run the presentation from the first slide and observe the effect. The **Wipe** transition appears between each slide. Press <**Esc**> to end the slide show when you are finished.

8. Save the presentation and leave it open for the next exercise.

5.24 Applying Timings

So far you have moved from slide to slide in a running presentation by clicking the mouse or using the keyboard. However, you can also set up your slides to advance automatically after a set amount of time. To do this, slide transitions must have **timings** applied.

> **Note:** This feature is particularly useful if you want your presentation to run unattended, for example as a promotional slide show in a public place.

Activity:

1. Select slide **1** of the **redesign** presentation, and then display the **Animations** tab.

2. In the **Transition to This Slide** group remove the tick from the **On Mouse Click** checkbox. Then, select the **Automatically After** checkbox and use the up spinner to set the delay to **2 seconds**.

3. The current slide will now automatically move on after two seconds. Click **Apply To All**.

4. The *entire* slide show will now advance automatically after 2 seconds has elapsed on each slide. View the show from the beginning and observe the effect.

> **Note:** As the slides are set to advance automatically, any animation effects will also be activated automatically.

5. Change to **Slide Sorter** view. Notice that the timings are displayed below each slide. The small star icon, ☆, indicates that there is a transition or animation effect applied.

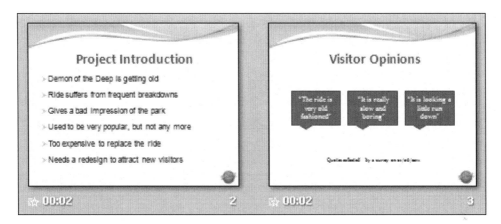

> **Note:** Often, an automatic show will be required to loop continuously, advancing from the last slide back to the first slide.

6. Display the **Slide Show** tab and click the **Set Up Slide Show** button in the **Set Up** group. The **Set Up Show** dialog box appears. Examine the options displayed.

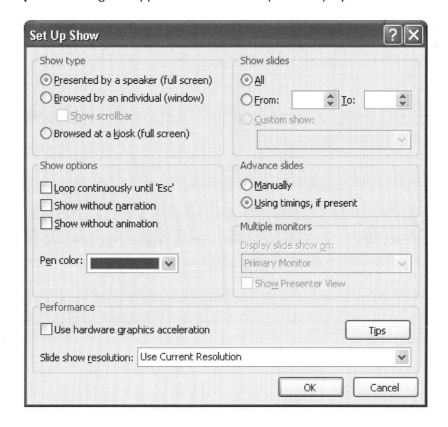

7.   Under **Show options**, select the checkbox to **Loop continuously until 'Esc'**. Click **OK**.

8.   View the slide show from the beginning. The slide show will now play automatically using the set timings to advance between slides. When slide **10** is reached, slide **1** is shown next. Click <**Esc**> at any time to end the show.

9.   *Yan* would like to control the presentation manually. With any slide selected, display the **Animations** tab and, in the **Transition to This Slide** group, remove the tick from the **Automatically After** checkbox. Then, select the **On Mouse Click** checkbox again.

10. Click **Apply To All** to use these timings on all slides. Next, use the **Set Up Show** dialog box to remove the tick from the **Loop continuously until 'Esc'** option. Click **OK**.

11. Return to **Normal** view, save the presentation and leave it open.

5.25 Speaker's Notes

To help a speaker deliver a presentation, notes can be added to each slide in a show. The notes do not appear during the presentation, but they can be printed or viewed on another screen.

Activity:

1.   Select slide **1** of the **redesign** presentation and make sure **Normal** view is currently selected. At the bottom of the main editing window is an area to add notes.

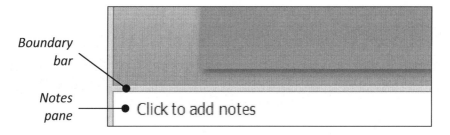

> Note: If the **Notes** pane is not visible or is too small, you can use the area's boundary bar to increase its size.

2.   Click once in the **Notes** pane (the default prompt text disappears). Enter the text: **Demon of the Deep is twenty years old and has broken down 16 times this year already!**

3.   From the **View** tab, change the view to **Notes Page**. The new note appears below the slide (and there is more room here to add and format note text).

4.   Scroll down to slide **6** (**Initial Plan**), click once in the notes area, and then add the following text: **Mention that October is the beginning of our low season and is an ideal time to close the ride.**

> Note: If necessary, use the **Zoom** controls on the **Status Bar** to zoom in to read the text.

5.   Return to **Normal** view, save the presentation and leave it open for the next exercise.

5.26 Spelling Check

PowerPoint's spelling check feature can check the spelling of all words on your slides, and will even check new text as you type it. Words that are misspelled are shown with a wavy red line underneath them. *PowerPoint* makes suggestions to help you correct errors which can either be accepted or ignored.

> **Note:**   The spell checker will only highlight words it does not have in its dictionary; it will not find incorrectly used words or grammar errors, e.g. **her** instead of **here**.

Activity:

1.   Select slide **1** of the **redesign** presentation and make sure **Normal** view is currently selected. Display the **Review** tab and click the **Spelling** button.

2.   *PowerPoint* will now automatically check your presentation. If any errors are found, the **Spelling** dialog box will appear.

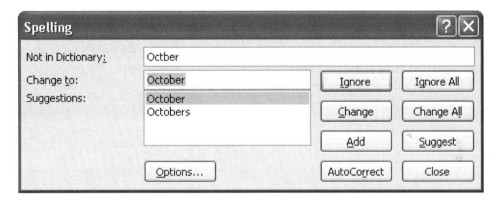

> **Note:**   The **Spelling** dialog box is similar to the familiar spell checking feature available in *Microsoft Word*. If an error is found, you can choose to **Ignore** it or **Change** the selected word to one of the **Suggestions** given.

3.   When no errors are present in the slide show, a message appears informing you that **The spelling check is complete**. Click **OK** to close it.

4.   Save the presentation and leave it open for the next exercise.

> **Note:**   Well done, you have now successfully created a presentation for *Yan* to use at his meeting in a few days time. The ability to follow complex instructions and work accurately is an important skill to learn in business. To check that you followed all of *Yan's* instructions correctly, a model solution is provided in the data files folder named **Sample Redesign**. Compare your final presentation against this solution.

5.27 Handouts and Notes

Slides can be printed in various ways, but the most useful formats allow you to create **Handouts** and **Notes Pages**. Handouts can be printed with several slides per sheet for an audience to follow as the presentation is running.

Activity:

1. Select slide **2** of the **redesign** presentation, click the **Office Button**, and then select **Print** from the options shown. The **Print** dialog box appears.

> **Note:**   Familiar settings such as printer selection, number of copies, print range and paper orientation are also available on this screen.

2. Notice that **Slides** is currently selected under **Print what**.

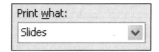

3. Click the drop-down button and select **Notes Pages**. A small slide thumbnail will now be printed – one per page – with any notes included below.

4. Click the **Preview** button, [Preview], to see how the print will appear, and then use the **Next Page** button in the **Preview** group to view the other slides.

5. Click **Print** to open the **Print** dialog box again, and then select **Handouts** under **Print what**. Change **Slides per page** to **3** and preview the print. Three small thumbnails are now shown on each page with space for audience members to take notes.

6. Click the **Close Print Preview** button to return to **Normal** view *without* printing. Save and close the presentation.

5.28 Templates

Templates are useful *PowerPoint* designs that can be used as a basis for new presentations. *PowerPoint* includes a small selection of built-in templates, but many more are available online.

> **Note:**   Some organisations recommend that employees use a specific template for all presentations. These will often reflect the business's corporate image and will include logos, backgrounds and fonts.

Although many templates look very impressive, you should ensure that any design theme you choose is suitable for the target audience. Sometimes less is more, and a simple design with large clear fonts is all that is required for a formal presentation.

Activity:

1. Click the **Office Button** and select **New** from the options shown. When the **New Presentation** dialog box appears, select **Installed Templates** and examine the various templates that are displayed.

2. Select **Quiz Show** from the list, and then click the **Create** button, [Create], found towards the bottom right of the dialog box. A new presentation is created based on the selected **Quiz Show** template.

3. Explore the various slides that are available and feel free to alter any default text (the original template will not be affected).

4. Run the presentation from the start. Notice that many basic designs, animations and transitions have already been set up for you. When you are finished, press <**Esc**>.

5. Close the presentation, selecting **No** at the save prompt if any changes were made.

6. Explore the many other templates available. If you are connected to the Internet, a wide variety of additional templates are also available under the **Microsoft Office Online** heading.

7. When you are finished, close *PowerPoint* and any open templates.

5.29 Presentation Tips

You've created a great presentation, memorized your speech, practiced giving your talk, and now the big day has arrived. Before you step up, consider the following suggestions for a successful presentation:

✱   Turn up early to your presentation and give yourself plenty of time to set up

✱   Check that all of the hardware you will need to use works correctly

✱   Disable the computer's screen saver (and standby features) to avoid interruptions

✱   Run through your presentation to check that it works as you expect

✱   Leave the presentation on slide 1, ready for your audience as they arrive

✱   Leave plenty of time for questions at the end of your presentation

✱   Try to be confident and enthusiastic; avoid simply reading your slides to the audience

✱   Speak slowly and loudly! Inexperienced speakers tend to talk too fast and mumble

✱   Pause from time to catch your breath and allow the audience to consider your words

5.30 Next Steps

Well done! You have now completed all of the exercises in this section. If you feel you are ready to test your knowledge and understanding of the topics covered, move on to the following **Develop Your Skills** activities. If there are any features of *Microsoft PowerPoint* that you are unsure about, you should revisit the appropriate exercises and try them again before moving on.

If you are interested in exploring some of *Microsoft PowerPoint's* more powerful features, why don't you use the Internet to find out a little more about the following advanced topics.

Feature	Descriptions
PowerPoint Show	A presentation can be saved as a **PowerPoint Show** so that it always runs in **Slide Show** view when opened. This is useful for sending your presentation to others (and discouraging any changes).
Package for CD	A presentation can be saved to a CD or DVD for use on another computer. All files that your presentation needs are copied, including a presentation viewing program for computers without *PowerPoint*.
SmartArt	**SmartArt** lets you create diagrams from within *PowerPoint* using a variety of different layouts and visual styles. This feature is really useful for creating flow and relationship diagrams.
Advanced Animation	Build on the lessons learned in 5.22 and create your own custom animations using the **Animation Pane**. These give you far greater control over your chosen effects, how and when they occur, and the exact order that they appear. You can also add sound effects to each effect.
Rehearsing	*PowerPoint* can automatically record the time it takes you to move from slide to slide during a **rehearsal**. These durations are then used to create more exact slide timings.
Action Buttons	Buttons can be added to slides which, when clicked, advance the presentation to any other slide (or opens a website or file).
Custom Slide Show	Custom shows allow only specific slides to be seen when a presentation is run. This saves the need to create multiple versions of the same presentation for different audiences.
Web Pages	A presentation can be saved as a web page so that others can access and view it online.
Custom Templates	*PowerPoint's* presentation templates work in generally the same way as *Word's* document templates. Any normal presentation can be saved as a template allowing you to create a standard layout that can be used as a basis for future slide shows.
Permissions	You can password protect your presentations or mark them as final.

At the end of every section you will get the chance to complete two full tasks without my assistance. This will help to reinforce learning and develop your skills. Don't forget to use the planning and review checklists at the back of the book to organise and evaluate your work.

> **Note:** Sample solutions for both tasks are provided in this section's data files folder.

Level 1: Staff Presentation

In this task you will be asked to create a simple presentation for *Yan*. You will need to use the ICT skills you have learned in this section to plan, develop and present an appropriate solution. You can ask for help from friends, colleagues or a teacher if you get stuck.

Level 1 Task

The *Big Planet Theme Park* management loved the *Demon of the Deep* presentation that you created earlier and approved my redesign plans on the spot – well done! However, before any work can begin, we need to inform the ride's current staff that we intend to close the attraction for refurbishment.

To do this, I've been asked to give a five minute presentation on our plans. I've already worked out what I need to say and have created an outline for the presentation in *Word*. Will you take this outline and create the presentation for me?

Information for the presentation is available in the following files:

* **Initial Ideas**   A document containing *Yan's* notes for the new presentation

* **Sketch**   A sketch of the proposed ride changes

Start by creating a new, blank presentation. Then add the contents of the **Initial Ideas** file on to new slides (as suggested in the **Initial Ideas** file). You will need to choose appropriate slide layouts for each individual slide and use two levels of bullets where indicated. Next, insert the **Sketch** image file in a suitable position on slide **4**. As the presentation will be seen by all of the ride team it needs to look professional – apply a suitable theme (I recommend **Flow**) and then save the presentation as **staff presentation**.

Level 2: Marketing Presentation

In this task you will be asked to update a draft presentation for *Yan*. You will need to use the advanced ICT skills that you have learned in this section to create a suitable solution (you may need to break the problem down into smaller parts first). Only level 2 students should attempt this task and it should be completed without help from others.

Level 2 Task

I've just received a telephone call from *Julia* at the *Laser Show*. I've been asked to prepare a presentation on the new *Demon of the Deep* ride for the park's marketing department, including a brief overview of our redesign plans and available budget.

I've made a start on the presentation, but I'd like you to finish it for me. The files that you will need are shown below:

* **Marketing**   The unfinished draft of the marketing presentation

* **Photo**   A photograph of the *Demon of the Deep* ride

* **Logo**   An image file containing the theme park's logo

First, using **Slide Sorter** view, move slide **4** (**Any Questions?**) to the end of the presentation. Next, add a new slide between slides **1** and **2** with a **Title Only** layout.

In **Normal** view, add the slide title **An Old Favourite** and insert the **Photo** image. Reposition and resize the image so that it fits neatly on the page (I recommend a **Shape Height** of **10cm**). Apply a **Simple Frame, White** design to the picture.

Next, rearrange the bullets on slide **6** so that they appear in order. Then, insert a new slide after slide **4** with a **Title Only** layout. Add the slide title **Marketing Budget** and insert a table (in a suitable position) containing the following information:

Item Description	Number	Cost
Mailings	240,000	5,000
Posters & Leaflets	10,000	4,000
Banners	20	1000

Using the **Slide Master**, add the theme park's **Logo** to the bottom right corner of every slide in the presentation. Also add a transition effect of **Fade** between each slide.

Finally, run the spell checker on the presentation and correct any mistakes found. Preview the presentation, check it works as expected (correcting any problems that you find), and then save it as **marketing presentation**.

6 | Microsoft Publisher

Hi, my name's Julia...

I'm the manager of the marketing department at *Big Planet Theme Park*. I'm currently working with staff at the *Laser Show* to help advertise their brilliant new attraction, *The Light Fantastic*.

This amazing show uses the latest computer technology to control hundred of lights and lasers in time to music. Lasting 20 minutes, the performance combines pictures and special effects to recreate famous cities and landmarks from around the world – it really is an unmissable event. In fact, park management expects *The Light Fantastic* to be so popular that they have decided to run the show six times each day.

Working in marketing, it is my job to create an advertising campaign to publicise the new attraction and its show times. To do this, I plan to use the desktop publishing application *Microsoft Publisher* to create a range of eye-catching and informative posters, flyers, brochures, leaflets and newsletters. There's a lot of work to do and a lot of different types of advertising publication to create – maybe you can help?

What you will learn:

In this chapter you will use the program *Microsoft Publisher* to help *Julia* complete a number of everyday tasks at *Big Planet Theme Park*. You will see how to use simple desktop publishing techniques to design, create and edit professional publications for a variety of purposes.

Knowledge, skills and understanding:

* Use *Microsoft Publisher* to create and edit professional publications

* Manipulate graphics and text using a range of editing, formatting and layout techniques

* Understand house styles and recognise best design practices

Data files

Data files needed to complete the activities in this section are provided in the **Section 6** data files folder. Publications that you create or edit can be saved to the same folder.

6.1 Using Microsoft Publisher

Desktop publishing programs allow you to create high-quality documents using a range of advanced text and image layout tools. These documents are traditionally printed, but they can also be saved in a simple picture format for use on websites or in e-mail marketing campaigns. Typically, desktop publishing software is useful for creating:

* Leaflets, flyers, greeting cards, business cards and headed letters

* Brochures, magazines, certificates, menus and newsletters

* Advertisements, posters, signs and banners

Unlike word processors, desktop publishing applications place a far greater emphasis on page layout and design, giving you much more control over the positioning and appearance of text and images on the page.

> Note: For professional publications, a dedicated printing company is often used to produce large quantities of a publication quickly and cheaply.

Microsoft Publisher is a desktop publishing application which is an appropriate choice for any task that requires an illustration or well-designed document containing a lot of pictures or graphics. The entry, layout and formatting of text is easily handled by such a program, as is the ability to import and arrange different types of object such as images, tables and charts.

> Note: *Microsoft Word* and *Publisher* both look and work in very similar ways. However, each application is better suited to creating specific types of document. As a simple rule of thumb, if your planned document is mainly text based, use *Word*; if it is largely visual with lots of images, use *Publisher*.

6.2   Creating a Publication

When you create a new publication, you must first choose a **page size** using one of *Publisher's* built-in templates. The most commonly used page size is **A4**.

Activity:

1. Start *Microsoft Publisher*. When the application opens, the **Getting Started with Microsoft Office Publisher 2007** window is automatically displayed. Examine the various types of publication available in the **Publication Types** list on the left.

2. As part of her advertising campaign, *Julia* would like to create a new poster for the *Laser Show*. She wants it to be A4 in size so that she can print it on her office printer. Select **Blank Page Sizes** from the list.

3. From the list of blank publication types that appear in the centre of the window, select **A4 (Portrait)** by clicking it once. Notice the **Page Size Information** box that appears on the right.

A4 (Portrait)
21 x 29.7cm

4. For now, simply click the **Create** button at the bottom of the window. A new blank publication is created, ready to add your own text and graphics.

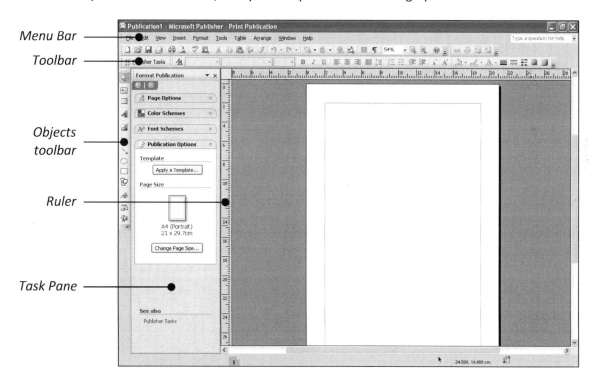

Menu Bar

Toolbar

Objects toolbar

Ruler

Task Pane

5. Examine the *Publisher* window. In particular, notice that this application uses **Menu bars** and **Toolbars** rather than the more common *Microsoft Office* **Ribbon**.

> Note: Menu bars group related options, tools and commands together under common headings (e.g. **File, Edit, View, Insert**). The most useful tools are also available as icons on the various toolbars that appear at the top and left of the window.

6. Locate the **Task Pane** on the left of the window (if this is not open, select **View | Task Pane** from the **Menu Bar**). As you will see later, this pane can be used to set up a publication and apply a variety of clip art, fonts, colours and background designs.

7. Locate the **Rulers** at the top and left of the editing window. These can be used to position objects on the page and control text indentation (similar to *Microsoft Word*).

8. Leave the blank publication open for the next exercise.

6.3 Text Boxes

Unlike *Microsoft Word*, text in *Publisher* is not simply typed directly onto the page. Instead, it needs to be placed in one or more **text boxes**. Each box can be resized and repositioned any way you like, and there is no limit to the number of boxes that can appear on a page.

Activity:

1. With the blank publication created in the previous exercise still on screen, click the **Text Box** button, [A], on the **Objects** toolbar.

2. The mouse pointer changes to a crosshair, ✛. In the centre of the current page, click and drag to create a text box of any size. Notice that, as you create the text box, its exact position and size are displayed on the **Status Bar**.

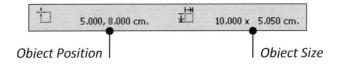

Object Position | Object Size

> **Note:** An object's position, measured by default in centimetres, is the precise location of the *top left* corner of the object in **x** (across) and **y** (down) coordinates.

3. When you release the mouse button a text box appears on the page with the cursor flashing inside it, ready for text to be entered.

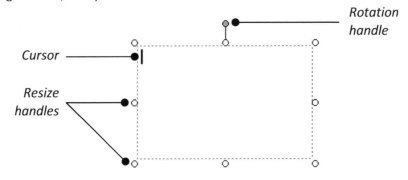

Rotation handle

Cursor

Resize handles

4. Press the <F9> key on your keyboard. The view zooms to **100%** on the current text box.

> **Note:** Pressing <F9> again returns to the previous zoom level.

5. Notice that the text box has standard resize and rotation handles. These will always appear when a text box (or any other object) is selected.

6. With the new text box still selected, display the **View** menu on the **Menu Bar** and select **Toolbars | Measurement**.

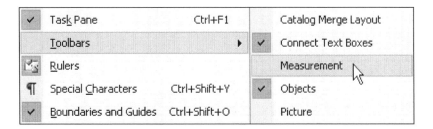

7. The options shown here can be used to precisely position, rotate and resize *any* object on a page. Change the value in the **Width** box to **17 cm** and the value in the **Height** box to **5cm**. Notice the effect that this has on the text box.

8. Next, change the **x** value to **2 cm** and the **y** value to **2 cm**.

9. Click the **Close** button, ✖, on the **Measurement** dialog box to hide it. The text box has now been precisely resized and positioned on the page. Notice the object's location and size on the **Status Bar**.

10. Leave the publication open for the next exercise.

6.4 Zoom Levels

You have already used <**F9**> to zoom in and centre on a selected object. As with other *Microsoft Office* applications, more precise zoom levels can also be selected on the **View** tab.

Activity:

1. With the empty text box created in the previous exercise still selected, display the **View** menu and expand the **Zoom** group. Examine the options available, then click **Whole Page**.

2.   The zoom level is decreased so that the entire current page is displayed in the main editing window.

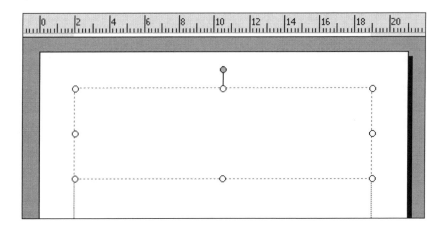

3.   Next, display the zoom options again and click **Page Width**. The full width of the page fills the main editing window.

4.   Finally, display the zoom options again and click **Selected Objects**. The zoom level is increased so that the selected text box fills the screen.

6.5   Entering Text and Best Fit

When you enter text into a text box, you can edit and format it using a range of standard **Font** and **Alignment** features. Also, a really useful tool called **Best Fit** (also known as **Autofit**) allows you to automatically increase a text box's font size to fill the space available.

Activity:

1.   With the empty text box created in the previous exercise still selected, type the following text as accurately as possible:

> **The Light Fantastic**
> **An Amazing New Show**

2.   Display the **Format** menu and expand the **AutoFit Text** group. From the options that appear, select **Best Fit**. The font size of the text is increased to fill the available space in the text box.

3. Using the bottom **Resize** handle, reduce the size of the text box to *approximately* **2 cm** (remember that you can use the **Object Size** information on the **Status Bar** to help).

4. The size of the text in the text box is automatically reduced to fit. Click **Undo**, , on the standard toolbar (at the top of the screen) to undo your last action.

5. To disable **Best Fit**, display the **Format** menu, expand the **AutoFit Text** group and select **Do Not Autofit**. The text box will no longer adjust its contents to fit.

6. Select the <u>first</u> line of text in the box and set the **Font Size** to **56** point. Then, select the <u>second</u> line of text and set the **Font Size** to **36** point.

7. Next, select <u>all</u> of the text in the box and, using the **Font** box, select the font **Impact**.

> **Note:**   It is important to select the right font for the job. **Impact** is a good, strong, sans serif font that will be easy to read from a distance – perfect for a poster.

8. With all of the text still selected, click the **Center** align button, , on the formatting toolbar (underneath the standard toolbar). The text is centred in the box.

> **Note:**   Familiar text alignment and formatting options such as **Bold**, **Italic**, **Underline**, **Font Color**, **Bullets** and **Numbering** are all available on the **Toolbar**.

9. Save the publication as **poster** in the data files folder for this section.

10. Leave the publication open for the next exercise.

6.6 Border and Shading Effects

A simple border of any colour or thickness can be added to a text box to mark its boundaries. A variety of shading effects can also be applied to improve the design of a publication.

> **Note:**   Borders can also be added to any other object (e.g. graphics, tables, charts, etc).

Activity:

1. With the **poster** publication open from the previous exercise, adjust the zoom level to **Whole Page**. Then, create a new text box with the following dimensions:

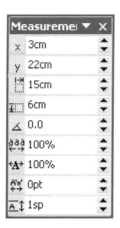

2. Zoom in on the new text box and enter the following text as accurately as you can:

    Now Showing
    at the Laser Show arena
    09:00, 10:30, 12:00, 13:30, 15:00, 16:30

3. Select all of the text, **Centre** align it, and then change the **Font** to **Impact**.

4. To centre the text vertically so that it appears in the very middle of the box, display the **Format** menu and select **Text Box**. When the **Format Text Box** dialog box appears, display the **Text Box** tab. Drop down the **Vertical alignment** box, select **Middle**, and click **OK**.

5. Apply a **Font Size** of **36** to the <u>first</u> line, **28** to the <u>second</u> line, and **20** to the <u>third</u> line. Adjust the zoom level to **Whole Page** to see the effect.

6. To apply a border to the selected text box, display the **Format** menu and select **Text Box**. Examine the various options available on the **Colors and Lines** tab.

7. In the **Line** group, expand the **Color** drop-down and select **More Colours**. From the **Standard** colours available, select a dark blue colour. Click **OK**.

> Note: You can also change line styles and weight here. You can even apply the selected border to specific sides of an object using the **Preview** and **Presets** buttons.

8. Increase the line **Weight** to **2 pt** to increase the border's thickness.

9. In the **Fill** group, expand the **Color** drop-down and select **More Colours**. From the **Standard** colours available, select a light blue colour. Click **OK**.

10. Click **OK** to apply these settings. The selected text box gains a dark blue border and a light blue background.

> **Note:**   **Fill Color** and **Line Color** buttons are also available on the **Toolbar**.

11. Click the drop-down arrow on the **Fill Color** button.

12. Select **Fill Effects** to open the **Fill Effects** dialog box. Display the **Texture** tab and select any of the textures shown. Click **OK** to apply the effect.

13. Open the **Fill Effects** dialog box again. Then, display the **Pattern** tab and select any of the patterns shown. Click **OK** to apply the effect.

14. Open the **Fill Effects** dialog box once again and display the **Gradient** tab. From the **Colors** group, select **Two colors**. Then, select white for **Color 1** and any blue colour for **Color 2**.

> **Note:**   You can also a use a picture as the background for a text box.

15. Click **OK** and a simple gradient effect is applied to the selected text box. Click away from the text box to see the effect.

Now Showing
at the Laser Show arena
09:00, 10:30, 12:00, 13:30, 15:00, 16:30

16. Save the publication and leave it open for the next exercise.

6.7 Background Effects

Gradients, textures, patterns and pictures can also be used as a page background. In this exercise you will apply a simple, custom gradient.

Activity:

1. Display the **Format** menu and select **Background**.

2. Examine the various background styles that can be applied. Select any that interest you to see the effect applied to the page.

3. Select **More backgrounds** to display the **Fill Effects** dialog box. Display the **Gradient** tab and select **Two colors** from the **Colors** group.

4. Next, select an orange colour for **Color 1** (from the **Standard Colours** palette) and white for **Color 2**.

5. From **Shading styles** group, examine the options available and then select **From corner**. From the **Variants** group, select the bottom right thumbnail.

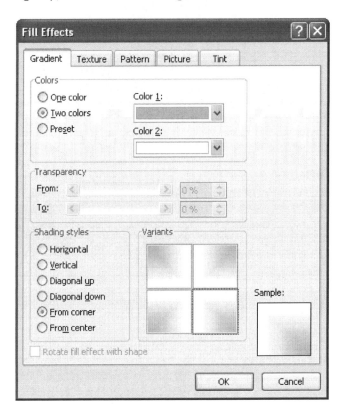

6. Click **OK** to apply the background effect. It fills the entire page.

7. Save the publication and leave it open for the next exercise.

6.8 Inserting a Picture

Any image file stored on your computer (or accessible from it) can be included in a publication. This includes pictures downloaded from the Internet (assuming you have permission to use them, of course), photos downloaded from your digital camera or mobile phone, or files produced by graphic image programs such as *Adobe Photoshop* or *Paint Shop Pro*.

Activity:

1. To insert a picture on the current page of the open **poster** publication, display the **Insert** menu and select **Picture | From File**. The **Insert Picture** dialog box appears.

2. Locate the data files folder for this section, select the **Rocket** image, and click **Insert** to import the file. A picture of a rocket appears in the centre of the page, and the **Picture** toolbar is shown floating on the screen.

> Note: The **Picture** toolbar will appear when a picture is selected. As with all objects in *Publisher*, pictures can be moved, resized and rotated.

3. By default, text in a publication is wrapped around an inserted image. From the **Picture** toolbar, click **Text Wrapping**, [image], and select **None**. The text wrapping is disabled.

4. From the **Picture** toolbar, click **Format Picture**, [image], to open the **Format Picture** dialog box. Display the **Size** tab and change the picture's **Height** to **17 cm**. The width of the picture will be automatically adjusted to keep the picture in *proportion*.

> Note: It is important to maintain the **proportions** of pictures and other objects such as charts when resizing them. If you do not they will become distorted.

5. Display the **Layout** tab and change the **Horizontal** value in the **Position on page** group to **2.4 cm** and the **Vertical** to **5.7 cm**.

6. Click **OK** and the picture is resized and repositioned. Notice, however, that part of the rocket appears on top of the lower text box.

7. With the picture selected, display the **Arrange** menu and select **Order | Send to Back**. The rocket image now appears behind the text box.

> Note: All objects on a page are placed on their own **layer** in a stack, rather like a deck of cards. The items higher up the stack appear on top of all other objects below. To move an object up or down the stack, use **Bring Forward** or **Send Backward**.

8. Well done! *Julia's* poster is now complete. Display the **File** menu and select **Print Preview** to see how this publication will look when printed.

> Note: A model solution named **Sample Poster** is available in this section's data files folder for comparison.

9. Click **Close** on the toolbar to close the **Print Preview**. Then save the publication and close it, leaving *Publisher* open for the next exercise.

6.9 Layout Guides

Layout Guides are lines on a page which act as visual aids to help you line up objects. More importantly, you can also **snap** objects to them using drag and drop.

> Note: The most useful **Layout Guides** are **Ruler Guides**, **Margin Guides** and **Grid Guides**. **Ruler** and **Margin Guides** are used in this exercise; **Grid Guides** are used in **6.10**.

Activity:

1. Open the file **Layout** from the data files folder. This simple publication features one text box and three shapes on a single page.

2. Display the **Arrange** menu and expand the **Ruler Guides** group. Select **Add Horizontal Ruler Guide** and a green dotted line appears across the middle on the page.

3.   This line is known as a **Ruler Guide**, and can be dragged up and down the page. Place your mouse pointer over the guide until it changes to a **Resize** cursor, ⬍.

4.   Using the left ruler as a reference, drag the **Ruler Guide** up to the **10 cm** mark.

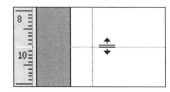

> Note: If the page rulers are not visible, display the **View** menu and select **Rulers**.

5.   Next, add a *vertical* **Ruler Guide** and place this at the **4 cm** mark using the top ruler as a reference.

6.   By clicking and dragging the object's border, move **Shape 1** left towards the vertical **Ruler Guide**. As the shape touches the guide, it "snaps" and sticks to it.

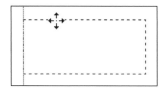

> Note: If snapping does not occur, display the **Arrange** menu and place a tick in both of the following **Snap** options: **To Ruler Marks** and **To Guides**.

7.   Release the mouse button to drop the shape.

8.   Next, move **Shape 2** left towards the vertical **Ruler Guide**. As the shape touches the guide, it again "snaps" and sticks to it.

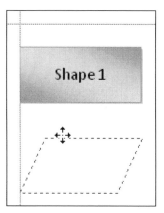

9.   Release the mouse button to drop the shape. Then move **Shape 3** left until it snaps to the vertical **Ruler Guide**. All three objects are now perfectly aligned with each other.

10. Next, drag the text box so that both the left and bottom sides line up with both the vertical <u>and</u> horizontal **Ruler Guides**.

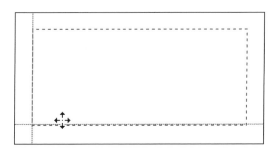

> **Note:**   Have you noticed the dotted blue border around the edge of the page? This is a **Margin Guide** and marks the border boundaries of the page.

11. Drop the text box. Now, use the top right **Resize** handle to increase the size of the text box. As it approaches both the top <u>and</u> right **Margin Guides**, it again snaps and sticks. Release the mouse button.

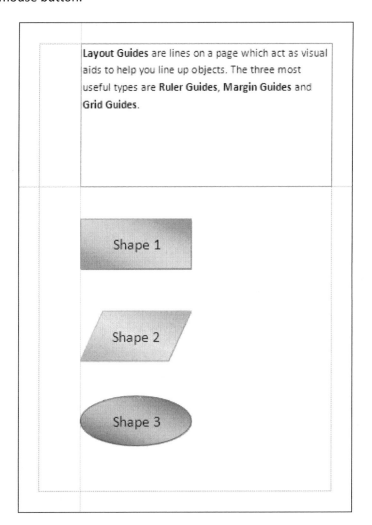

> **Note:**   All objects in *Publisher* can be aligned using the techniques described here.

12. Display the **File** menu and select **Print Preview** from the options shown. A preview of the page as it will be printed is shown; notice that the **Ruler** and **Margin Guides** do not appear. Click the **Close** button to return without printing.

13. Save the publication as **guides** and leave it open for the next exercise.

6.10 Multiple Pages

Single page publications are useful for creating posters and flyers, but publications such as newsletters and brochures will require many more pages.

Activity:

1. The **guides** publication should still be open. To insert a new page, display the **Insert** menu and select **Page**. The **Insert Page** dialog box appears, allowing you to add any number of extra pages to the publication.

2. Leave the default options (as shown above) and click **OK**. A new, blank page is added to the publication and is automatically selected.

3. Locate the **Page Selection** icons at the bottom of the screen. These show you how many pages are in a publication and allow you to move between them.

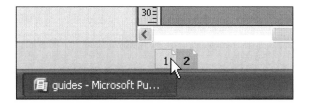

4. Select the **Page 1** icon to view the first page in the publication. Then select **Page 2** to move back to the new, blank page.

> Note: In the previous exercise you learned how to use **Ruler** and **Margin Guides** to help align objects. However, **Grid Guides** are also useful for creating layout guides which split a page into a number of columns or rows.

5. Display the **Arrange** menu and select **Layout Guides**. The **Layout Guides** dialog box appears.

---

6. On the **Grid Guides** tab, increase **Columns** to **2** and **Rows** to **3**, leaving the default **Spacing** between columns and rows as **0.2cm**. Notice the **Preview**, and then click **OK**.

7. The page is divided into two columns and three rows, with a small **0.2cm** gap between each "cell". Insert a text box with a black border in each of the six cells, and practice using the layout guides to make sure they fill all of the space available.

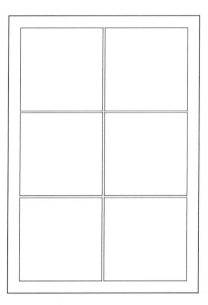

8. Display the **Insert** menu and select **Page** to open the **Insert Page** dialog box again.

9. Change the **Number of new pages** to **2**, make sure **After current page** is selected, and then select **Duplicate all objects on page (2)**.

10. Click **OK**. Two new pages are added containing copies of the objects on page **2**. The publication now contains 4 pages.

11. Select page **4**. To delete this page, display the **Edit** menu and click **Delete Page**. Read the message that appears and then click **Yes**. Page **4** is deleted from the publication.

12. Repeat this action to delete page **3** too.

Note: A page can be moved by clicking and dragging its **Page Selection** icon.

13. Save the publication and close it, leaving *Publisher* open for the next exercise.

6.11 Using Shapes and WordArt

It is possible to use the many design tools available in *Publisher* to create illustrations of your own. Shapes, pictures and **WordArt** can be combined to produce a range of impressive designs.

Activity:

1. Start a new, blank **A4 (Portrait)** publication.

2. *Julia* has had an idea for a logo for the new *Laser Show* attraction. She has sketched the logo on paper, and would now like you to create this in *Publisher*.

The Light Fantastic

3. Using the blank publication currently on-screen, select **AutoShapes**, , from the **Objects** toolbar. Expand **Basic Shapes**, select **Oval**, ⬭, and then draw a circle in the middle of the page.

> **Note:** Hold down <**Ctrl**> when drawing an object to maintain shape proportions (for example, to draw a perfect circle or a perfect square).

4. Use the **Measurement** box to set the shape's **Height** <u>and</u> **Width** to **6.5cm**. Apply a dark blue **Line Color** and select an appropriate **Gradient** fill effect (a white-to-blue, **Diagonal down** gradient works well).

> **Note:** *Publisher's* shapes and **WordArt** features are very similar to those you have used in previous *Microsoft Office* applications. If you feel confident using these features, you can try creating the logo without following the instructions in this exercise.

5. Next, insert a **Lightning Bolt** shape, ⚡, and position this on top of the circle shape. Set the shape's **Height** to **5cm** and **Width** to **3.5cm**. Apply an orange **Line Color** and a yellow **Fill Color**.

6. Next, insert the picture **Rocket** from the data files folder and set its **Height** to **6.5cm** and its **Width** to **6.173cm**.

7. Position the **Rocket** picture on top of the circle and lightning bolt shapes. Then, move, resize and rotate any object in the logo until you are happy that it best matches *Julia's* sketch.

8. Finally, click the **WordArt** button, [WordArt icon], on the **Objects** toolbar. Select the first available style in the **WordArt Gallery** and click **OK**.

9. In the **Edit WordArt Text** dialog box that appears, change the contents of the **Text** box to **The Light Fantastic** and change the **Font** to **Impact**, **Size 32**. Click **OK**. Position the new **WordArt** text below the logo, as suggested in *Julia's* sketch.

10. To edit the design of the **WordArt** object, click the **Format WordArt** button, , on the **WordArt** toolbar that has appeared. The **Format WordArt** dialog box appears.

11. From **Fill**, drop down the **Color** box and select **Fill Effects**. Then, create a light blue to dark blue gradient and click **OK**. From **Line**, drop down the **Color** box and select **No Line**.

12. Click **OK**. Well done, the logo is now complete and looks very impressive.

Note: You can **group** objects together so that they can be manipulated as one.

13. Press **<Ctrl A>** on your keyboard to select all objects that make up the logo.

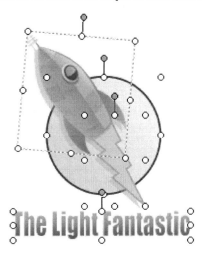

14. From the **Arrange** menu, click **Group**. All of the objects are now grouped into one.

15. Use the **Align or Distribute** options on the **Arrange** menu, to position the new logo object in the **Middle** and **Center** of the page (you may first need to select **Relative to Margin Guides** if these options are not immediately available).

Note: To remove a grouping and separate objects again, use **Arrange | Ungroup**.

16. Save your publication as **logo** and close it, leaving *Publisher* open for the next exercise.

Note: A model solution named **Sample Logo** is available in this section's data files folder.

6.12 Connecting Text Boxes

A really useful feature of *Publisher* is the ability to **Link** text boxes together. When this is done, the contents of one text box will automatically *overflow* into another.

Activity:

1. Open the publication **Leaflet**. In this two page publication (designed to be printed on both sides of a single A4 page), *Julia* has used your logo and set up a number of text boxes.

2. Use the **Page Selection** icons to show page **2**, and then select the first text box underneath the header. At the moment, any text entered here will be confined to the dimensions of the box (if too much text is entered it will disappear off the bottom).

3. Click **Create Text Box Link**, ⌨, on the toolbar. Notice that the mouse pointer changes to a "pouring jug" when it is placed over another text box.

4. To connect the first and second text boxes on this page, click anywhere inside the second text box. Any text placed in the first box will now overflow into the second.

5. Notice the **Go to Previous Text Box** button, ⬅, found just above the second text box. Click this once and the first text box is selected.

6. Click the **Go to Next Text Box** button, ➡, found just below the first text box. The second text box is selected again.

> Note: You will see the effects of entering text into all three boxes in the next exercise.

7. Save the publication as **leaflet final** and leave it open for the next exercise.

6.13 Importing Text

Instead of typing text into text boxes, existing text in different formats can be **imported** into *Publisher*. This is useful if large quantities of required text already exists in a different file.

Activity:

1. With the **leaflet final** publication open, place the cursor in the first text box on the second page. Then, display the **Insert** menu and select **Text File**.

2. The **Insert Text** dialog box appears. Locate and select the *Word* document **Leaflet Text** from the data files for this section and click **OK**. The document is imported into *Publisher* (a **Converting** message box may appear for a moment) and then the text is placed in the first text box.

3. **Zoom** in to **Page Width** and notice that the contents of the first text box **overflows** into the second text box (you will need to use the scroll bars to move up and down the page).

> Note: Notice also that the text formatting from the source document has been preserved.

4. Place the cursor in either the first or second text box and press <**Ctrl A**> to select all of the text in both boxes. Increase the **Font Size** to **18**. As text "falls off" the bottom of the first text box, it automatically appears in the second.

5. Now the text in the second box has overflowed. As it is not connected to another box, the **Text in Overflow** indicator, [A ⋯], appears below.

6. With the second text box selected, use the **Create Text Box Link** button to create a link to the third text box. The overflow text now appears here.

> Note: Text boxes can also be linked across different pages. To break a link between text boxes, simply use the **Break Forward Link** button on the toolbar.

7. Select all of the text and **Center** align it. The text now appears in the middle of each box.

8. Save the publication and close it, but leave *Publisher* open for the next exercise.

6.14 Font Schemes

A **font scheme** is a set of two fonts that can be applied to any publication. Within each font scheme both a *primary* font and a *secondary* font are specified. Usually the primary font is used for titles and headings and the secondary font is used for body text.

Font schemes are useful for ensuring that all of the fonts in a publication are consistent across pages, which is an important design consideration.

Activity:

1. Open the publication **Brochure**. This simple publication is designed to be printed on both sides of a single piece of A4 and then folded to create a leaflet. **Grid Guides** have been set up to help you visualise this simple layout.

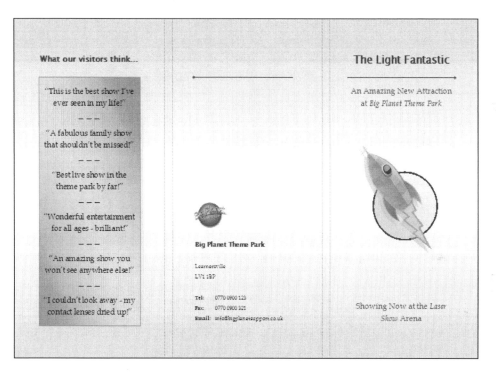

2. Examine both pages of the publication and notice that all of the headers use the font **Lucida Sans Unicode** and all the body text uses **Book Antiqua**.

> Note: Notice also that page **2** features a table. Tables can be easily created using the **Insert Table** button on the **Objects** toolbar.

3. To apply a new **Font Scheme** to the *entire* publication, display the **Format** menu and click **Font Schemes**. The available **Font Schemes** appear on the **Task Pane**.

4. Locate the style **Urban** (you may need to scroll down a little).

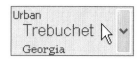

5. This scheme has **Trebuchet** as the *primary* font and **Georgia** as the *secondary* font. Click it to apply the scheme to every page in the publication; all fonts are updated.

> Note: By default, all new text added to this publication will now use the chosen scheme.

6. Notice that all of the headers in the publication now use the font **Trebuchet** and all the body text uses **Georgia**.

7. Leave the publication open for the next exercise.

6.15 Colour Schemes

All publications use a **colour scheme** to set the standard colours of text and objects. By default, *Publisher* uses a colour scheme called **Bluebird**, but this can be changed at any time.

> Note: Colour schemes coordinate all of the text and object colours in your publications, which helps to give them a more consistent and professional look.

Activity:

1. With the **Brochure** publication open, select the first page and then display the **Format** menu. Select **Color Schemes** and the available schemes appear on the **Task Pane**. Examine the various colour combinations available.

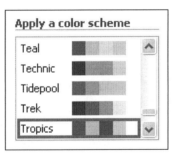

2. **Tropics** is the currently selected scheme. Find and select **Cherry**, and notice the effect this has on both pages of the publication.

3. Select a few of the other schemes to see their styles applied to the current page. Try to find and select a colour scheme that you feel works best with this publication.

4. When you are finished, save the publication as **brochure complete** and close it.

6.16 Columns

Columns can be used to split the contents of a text box into two or more vertical sections, exactly like the columns in a newspaper. This allows space to be used more effectively as you can often fit more words on a page.

> **Note:**   Text placed in columns is also much easier and faster to read.

Activity:

1. Open the publication **Newsletter**. This simple publication features a number of linked text boxes and is designed to be printed on both sides of a single piece of A4 paper (ignore any spelling errors that are present for now).

2. Click once in the large text box on page **1**. To arrange the contents of this box into two columns, click the **Columns Dialog** button, ⊞, on the standard toolbar.

3. From the options that appear, select **2 Columns**. The text is now divided into two columns (which is far easier to read as the eye has to move less to read a full line).

> **Note:**   Linked text boxes do not need to share the same alignment or formatting settings.

4. Display page **2** and notice that the first two text boxes, although linked to the text box on page **1**, are still arranged using a single column layout. Notice also that the text in the second text box has overflowed due to a lack of space.

5. Use the **Columns** button to set the second text box on this page to use **Two Columns** also. Notice that the text overflow has now been resolved.

6. Save the publication as **newsletter final** and leave it open for the next exercise.

6.17 Hyphenation

To improve the layout and readability of text, *Publisher* will sometimes **hyphenate** single words at the end of lines. This splits the words in two so that space is used more effectively.

Activity:

1. With the **newsletter final** publication open, select the text box on page **1** and then press <**F9**> to zoom in. Notice that a number of words have been split in two; the hyphen symbol, **-**, is used to indicate that a word continues on the following line.

> ## What's New
>
> It's been an exciting month at *Big Planet Theme Park!* A new rollercoaster called *Rumbling Rails* has opened, the *Haunted Castle* has seen a number of major improvements, and a brand new show has opened at the *Laser Show* arena.
>
> ## Haunted Castle
>
> The engineering and maintenance team at *Big Planet Theme Park* have done an excellent job improving the quality and overall safety of the rides at the *Haunted Castle*. Well done.

> Note: In this example, the words **improvements** and **excellent** have been hyphenated.

2. To stop automatic hyphenation, display the **Tools** menu and then select **Language | Hyphenation**. The **Hyphenation** dialog box appears.

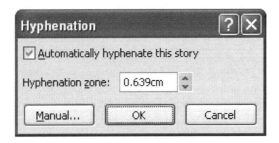

3. The **Hyphenation** dialog box appears. Remove the tick from **Automatically hyphenate this story** and click **OK**. Automatic hyphenation has now been disabled and words will no longer be split.

> Note: Hyphenation settings apply to all linked text boxes.

4. Save the publication and leave it open for the next exercise.

6.18 Cropping

When a picture is inserted into a publication, only a small part of it may be needed. If this is the case, the picture can be **cropped** to remove any unwanted areas from view.

Activity:

1. With the **newsletter final** publication open, display page **2** and insert the picture **Scanned**. *Julia* scanned this image into her computer from a printed leaflet, but it includes a lot of unwanted detail around the edges.

2. Zoom to **Whole Page**. Then, with the picture selected and the **Picture** toolbar displayed, click the **Crop** button, [icon]. Crop handles appear around the image.

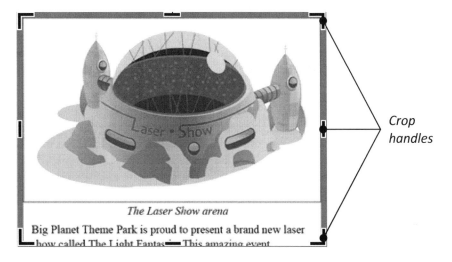

Crop handles

3. Click and drag the *top*, *left*, *right* and *bottom* crop handles inwards to frame the picture of the *Laser Show* arena only.

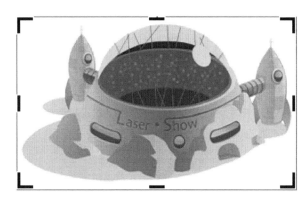

4. When you have finished, click the **Crop** button again. The picture is cropped and the unwanted areas removed from view.

> Note: The cropped areas of a picture are not deleted, only hidden. To remove the crop, click the **Reset Picture** button, [icon].

5. Next, use the **Measurement** box to set the cropped picture's **Height** to **7cm** and the **Width** to **11.5cm**. Position the image in the centre of the page underneath the first text box.

> Note: You can also crop images using this technique in other *Microsoft Office* applications.

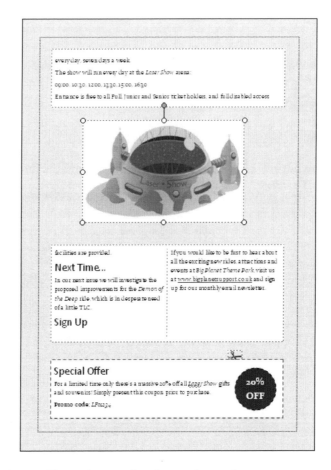

6. Save the publication and leave it open for the next exercise.

6.19 Clip Art and Wrapping

As you have already seen, text in a publication is wrapped around an image by default. However, there are many other text wrapping options available.

Activity:

1. With the **newsletter final** publication open, select page **1**. Then, display the **Insert** menu and select **Picture | Clip Art** to show the clip art search tools on the **Task Pane**.

2. *Julia* would like the newsletter to contain an image of a rocket ship on the first page. In the **Search for** box enter the keyword **rocket** and click **Go**.

Note: If you are prompted to search online, click **Yes**.

3. The results are displayed in the pane. Examine the various **Clip Art** illustrations found (notice that you can scroll down the list of results).

4. Select an appropriate **Clip Art** illustration by clicking it once (*Julia* recommends the clip art illustration shown on the following page). The picture appears in the centre of the current page.

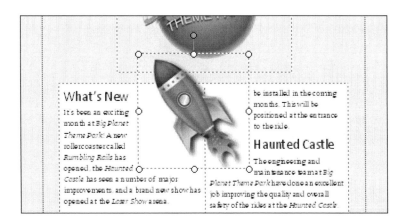

5. Notice that the text wraps around the inserted **Clip Art**. Click and drag the **Clip Art** object around the page to see the affect it has on the text underneath.

6. Display the **Arrange** menu and, from the **Text Wrapping** group, notice that **Square** is already selected. Select **None**.

7. The picture now appears floating above the text. Click and drag the **Clip Art** object around the page to see the affect it has.

8. Display the **Text Wrapping** options again and select **Top and Bottom**. Again, click and drag the **Clip Art** object around the page to see the affect it has on the text underneath.

9. Next, use the **Measurement** box to set both the **Height** and **Width** of the picture to **3cm**. Place the **Clip Art** object in the centre of the second column.

What's New

It's been an exciting month at *Big Planet Theme Park!* A new rollercoaster called *Rumbling Rails* has opened, the *Haunted Castle* has seen a number of major improvements, and a brand new show has opened at the *Laser Show* arena.

Rumbling Rails

Big Planet Theme Park unveiled its latest ride this month: *Rumbling Rails* – a thrilling high speed train ride through rocky canyons and icy mountain passes. Now open to the public, this ground-breaking new roller coaster is a massive 100 metres high and reaches speeds of 80 miles per hour.

To help manag queues during the summer months, a *Fast Ticket* service will be installed in the coming months. This will be positioned at the entrance to the ride.

Haunted Castle

The engineering and maintenance team at *Big Planet Theme Park* have done an excellent job improving the quality and overall safety of the rides at the *Haunted Castle*. Well done.

The Light Fantastic

Big Planet Theme Park is proud to present a brand new laser show called *The Light Fantastic*. This amazing event combines pictures and special effects to recreate famous cities and landmarks from around the world!

108 computer controlled lights and lasers

10. Save the publication and leave it open for the next exercise.

6.20 Spelling Check

Similar to other *Microsoft Office* applications, *Publisher's* spelling check feature can check the spelling of all words in a publication.

Activity:

1. With the **newsletter final** publication open on page **1**, place the cursor at the start of the text in the large text box. Then, display the **Tools** menu and select **Spelling | Spelling**.

2. *Publisher* will now automatically check for errors in the *current* "story" only.

> Note: In *Publisher*, a **story** is the name given to the contents of a text box. If two or more text boxes are linked then they share the same story.

3. If any errors are found, the **Check Spelling** dialog box will appear.

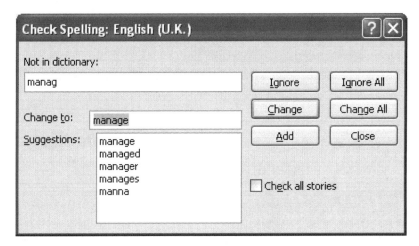

> Note: The **Check Spelling** dialog box is similar to the familiar spell checking feature available in *Microsoft Word*. If an error is found, you can choose to **Ignore** it or **Change** the selected word to one of the **Suggestions** given.

4. Correct any errors found. When the spelling check reaches the end of the current "story", a message appears. Click **Yes** to continue checking the rest of the publication.

> Note: If **Check all stories** is checked in the **Check Spelling** dialog box, then the prompt to continue checking the rest of the publication will <u>not</u> appear.

5. When no more errors are found, a message appears informing you that **The spelling check is complete**. Click **OK** to close it.

6. Save the publication and leave it open for the next exercise.

6.21 Printing

Once you have created a publication you will probably want to print it. *Publisher's* **Print** options offer a number of features to make this task easy.

Activity:

1.   Display the **File** menu and select **Print** from the options on the left to display the **Print** dialog box (alternatively, press <**Ctrl P**> on your keyboard). A preview of the first page as it will be printed is shown on the right.

2.   The print options that appear on this screen depend on the printers that you have available. Select the printer that you generally use, and then examine the print options on show, most of which you should be familiar with by now.

> Note: If your publication's size is small enough, you can print more than one copy on a single side of paper using the **Multiple copies per sheet** option. If applicable, this setting will appear under **Printing options**.

3.   Check that the **1** copy of the publication will be printed in **Portrait** orientation on **A4** paper, and that all pages in the range will be printed.

4.   Drop down the **2-sided printing options** box and examine the settings that appear. Select **Two-sided** to print the current publication on both sides of a single piece of paper.

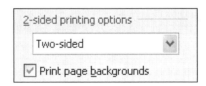

> Note: If your printer does not support double-sided printing, you will need to print the first page and then manually flip the paper over and print the second page. A dialog box may appear instructing you to do this.

> Note: If you need help printing on both sides of a piece of paper, the useful **Two-Sided Printing Setup Wizard** can help. To use this, select **Show how to insert paper** under **Preview** and then click the link that appears.

5.   Click the **Print** button, [Print], to print a copy of the newsletter on your chosen printer. You will automatically return to the main publication view.

> Note: Alternatively, click **Cancel** to return without printing.

6.   Close the **newsletter final** publication, saving any changes.

6.22 Save As

As well as printing publications, you can also save them in different **file formats** for use outside of *Publisher*. For example, you can save a simple one page publication as a picture (that can be used on a website) or as a document (that can be downloaded and viewed online).

Activity:

1. Open the **poster** publication that you created earlier. *Julia* wants to place a preview of this publication on the *Big Planet Theme Park* intranet site for all staff to see.

2. Display the **File** menu and select **Save As**. The **Save As** dialog box appears.

3. Navigate to the data files folder for this section. Then, locate the **Save as type** drop-down box below **File name**. Notice that the default file type, **Publisher Files**, is selected.

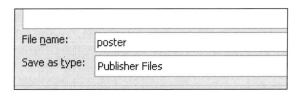

4. Click the **Save as type** drop-down button once to display a list of different file types. Examine the file types available. The most useful at this level are described below.

PDF	Creates a small document for downloading and viewing on the web. This is the best format to save in if you want to distribute your publication electronically, or if you wish to send it to others who may not have *Publisher* available to open and view your files.
Plain Text	Creates a small file containing only the text in a publication. All images, layout and text formatting are lost.
Web Page, Filtered	Creates a web page out of your publication that can be uploaded to the Internet and viewed by others.
JPEG	Converts your publication into an image that can be used elsewhere in other applications. As this type of file is compressed to save space and make it easier to use online, you may notice the quality of the image decreases a little.
PNG	Converts your publication into an image that can be used elsewhere in other applications. Unlike JPEG, the quality of the file does not decrease, but the file size usually remains too large to use online.

5. Select **JPEG File Interchange Format** from the list of file types available. Notice that a **Resolution** area has now appeared below the **Save as type** drop-down.

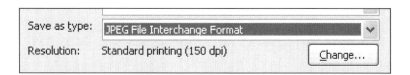

> **Note:** An image's **resolution** refers to how detailed the image is when printed, and is measured in **Dots Per Inch (DPI)**. The higher the DPI, the better the quality of the printed image but the larger the file size will become.

6. As this preview image of the **poster** publication will not be printed, you can choose a low resolution; click the **Change** button and select **Web (96 dpi)** and click **OK**.

7. Change the **File name** to **poster preview**.

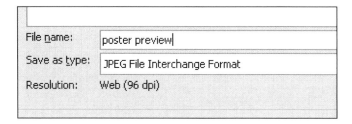

8. Click the **Save** button to save the publication. Note that this does not affect your original saved *Publisher* file, which remains on screen.

9. Close the **poster** publication without saving any changes, and then close *Publisher*. Open your **My Documents** folder and navigate to the data files for this section.

10. Notice that a new file, **poster preview**, is present. Double click this to open the image in your computer's default picture viewing application.

> **Note:** Notice that the text is now part of the image; it can no longer be edited.

11. Close your picture viewing application, and then close your **My Documents** window.

6.23 Templates

Templates are useful *Publisher* designs that can be used as a basis for new publications. *Publisher* includes a wide variety of built-in templates, but many, many more are available at **Office Online**. Although many templates look very impressive, you should ensure that any design theme you choose is suitable for the target audience.

Activity:

1. Start *Publisher*. The **Getting Started with Microsoft Office Publisher 2007** window is automatically displayed.

2. Examine the various templates available in the **Publication Types** list.

> **Note:** If you are connected to the Internet, a wide variety of additional templates are also available online. To view these, click the **View templates from Microsoft Office Online** link that appears at the top of the selected publication type's window.

3. Click once on **Brochures** to view the selection of templates that are available. Select **Arrows** from the list.

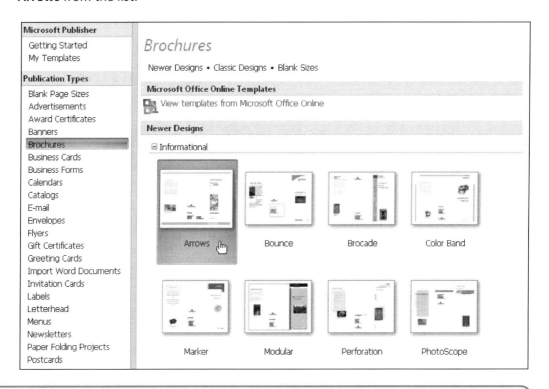

> **Note:** Notice the options on the right of the screen to customise the selected template's **Color scheme** and **Font scheme** before creating a publication.

4. Click the **Create** button on the right of the screen and a new publication is created based on the selected **Arrows** template.

5. Examine the contents of both pages in this publication, and feel free to alter any of the default text (the original template will not be affected).

6. Close the publication, selecting **No** at the save prompt if any changes were made.

7. Explore the many other templates available. In particular, view templates for **Advertisements, Award Certificates, Business Cards**, **Calendars**, **Greeting Cards** and **Resumes** to get a flavour of some of the other publication design types not covered in this section.

8. When you are finished, close *Publisher* along with all open templates without saving any changes.

6.24 Design Tips

When creating a new publication, visual impact is everything. Consider the following points of good practice when designing your pages:

* Keep things simple and try not to use too many different colours, fonts and fancy background designs.

* A simple, consistent design should be used *throughout* a publication. Empty areas (known as **white space**) can also make your publication more attractive to the eye.

* As some people have difficulty separating certain colour combinations (especially red-green), be careful when using these colours to describe important information.

* Focus on what is important and don't try to cram too much information onto one page. Long sentences and paragraphs are often boring to read.

* Consider where your publication will be seen. If it will be a poster on a wall, use eye-catching headlines and keep font sizes big enough to see from a distance.

* Avoid dark text on dark backgrounds and light text on light backgrounds.

* Sans serif fonts (e.g. Arial) are often easier to read that serif fonts (e.g. Times).

* Use pictures and simple charts rather than complicated tables of figures.

* Use guides to line up objects and help maintain consistency between pages.

6.25 House Styles

A **house style** (also known as a "style sheet") is a set of rules that specifies exactly how promotional materials such as publications, presentations and documents should look. A company will frequently have a house style linked to their corporate image or range of products. This helps to make sure that a recognisable, consistent brand is communicated to customers.

House styles can include guidelines on the following:

* Font types, sizes, alignment, positions and colours

* Background designs and colours

* Margins, spacing and page sizes

* Position and size of company logos

* Spelling preferences (e.g. US or UK) and the format of times, dates and currencies

* Addresses and other contact details

House styles also help to reduce the amount of time you need to spend creating a design as all of the hard decisions have already been made for you. If you are asked to follow a house style in your own work, make sure you find and follow the relevant guidelines for your publication type.

6.26 Next Steps

Well done! You have now completed all of the exercises in this section. If you feel you are ready to test your knowledge and understanding of the topics covered, move on to the following **Develop Your Skills** activities. If there are any features of *Microsoft Publisher* that you are unsure about, you should revisit the appropriate exercises and try them again before moving on.

If you are interested in exploring some of *Microsoft Publisher's* more powerful features, why don't you use the Internet to find out a little more about the following advanced topics.

Feature	Description
Design Gallery	**Design Gallery Objects** are ready-made illustrations such as calendars, sidebars, borders and advertisements that you can use in your own publications.
Business Information	*Publisher* has a feature which allows personal information to be recorded, which can then included in any publication created from a template. This is called **Business Information** and it can be edited to suit your own needs.
Styles	Similar to *Microsoft Word*, *Publisher's* **Styles** are specific combinations of font types, sizes and alignments. When they are applied, text will adopt all of the style's formatting settings. This helps ensure consistent formatting throughout a publication.
Master Pages	When each page in a publication has common elements (e.g. the same background, headers, footers, logos, etc.) then creating a **Master Page** is useful. Whatever appears on the **Master Page** will also appear automatically on every page in that publication.
Headers and Footers	**Headers** and **Footers** are text areas which appear at the top and bottom of every page in a publication (and are set on the **Master Page**). They can contain fixed items of text such as publication title or author name, or **fields** such as the date and time or page number.
Pack and Go	This useful feature can be used to prepare your publication to be sent to and printed by a commercial printing company.
Design Checker	Once a publication has been created it can be automatically checked for common problems such as low quality images, poor use of colour, layout issues, and badly aligned or resized objects.
Placeholders	**Picture Placeholders** can be used to reserve an area in your publication for an image that you want to add later.
Mail Merge	*Publisher's* **Mail Merge** feature is used to combine a main publication (a flyer, for example) with a separate list containing names and addresses. These two files, when merged, create a personalised copy of the main publication for everyone on the list.

At the end of every section you will get the chance to complete two full tasks without my assistance. This will help to reinforce learning and develop your skills. Don't forget to use the planning and review checklists at the back of the book to organise and evaluate your work.

> Note: Sample solutions for both tasks are provided in this section's data files folder.

Level 1: Advertising Poster

In this task you will be asked to create a simple advertising poster for *Julia*. You will need to use the ICT skills you have learned in this section to plan, develop and present an appropriate solution. You can ask for help from friends, colleagues or a teacher if you get stuck.

Level 1 Task

The *Laser Show* arena has a special offer running at the moment: 20% off all souvenirs and gifts. I've sketched an idea for an *A4* poster to advertise the promotion, but I need you to create it for me in *Publisher*.

Start with a new, **Blank A4 (Portrait)** publication. Use three separate text boxes for the **"Special Offer"**, **"20% Off"** and **"All Gifts and Souvenirs"** text.

For the illustration in the middle of the page, use an **Explosion** shape. The following picture of a space rocket can be inserted from the data files folder:

✳   **Rocket**

Apply an orange outline colour to the explosion shape and fill it with a white/yellow gradient. Finally, save the publication as **advertising poster** in the data files folder for this section.

Level 2: Product Catalogue

In this task you will be asked to create a well-designed product catalogue for *Julia*. You will need to use the advanced ICT skills that you have learned in this section to create a suitable solution (you may need to break the problem down into smaller parts first). Only level 2 students should attempt this task and it should be completed without help from others.

Level 2 Task

To accompany our latest "20% Off" promotion at the *Laser Show* arena, we are looking to create an exciting new product catalogue. This simple two sided A4 publication will include information about the show and the products on offer in our gift shop.

I've made a start on the new publication, but I'm going to need your help to finish it. As our printing department wants it ready in 30 minutes, we've not got much time!

Information you will need is available in the following files:

* **First Draft**   A publication containing all of the text with the correct layout

* **Arena**   An image file to be used on page 1

* **Logo**   The *Big Planet Theme Park* logo for use on page 2

Start by opening the **First Draft** publication and inserting the **Arena** picture in the white space that is available. You should resize the image to approximately *8 cm* high by *14 cm* wide. The text on the first page also needs to appear in *two* columns.

On page 2, the text in the first text box under the title has overflowed. To correct this, create a *link* to the empty text box at the bottom of the page. Then, insert a relevant piece of **Clip Art** in the white space available (I suggest searching for **gifts**). You should resize and reposition the image for best effect.

Next, insert the **Logo** illustration on page *2*. Resize the image to *3 cm* high by *4.2 cm* wide, and use the margin guides to align the object towards the *bottom left* corner. Set the logo's text wrapping to **None** so that is doesn't effect the content of the text boxes.

As the newsletter will be seen by customers, it needs to look professional and contain no spelling or grammar errors. Run the *spell checking* feature and correct any errors that you find. I also recommend proof reading the text yourself to make sure it reads correctly.

We're also getting *ten thousand* product catalogues printed tonight, so you need to get everything right first time! Print a proof of this publication on your own printer to check that everything appears exactly as you would expect. Finally, save the publication as **product catalogue** in the data files folder for this section.

Microsoft Access

7 | Microsoft Access

I'm manager of the *Active Leisure* team here at *Big Planet Theme Park*. My staff and I are based in the *Pirate's Cove* section of the park, which is a fun leisure pool and fitness area for visitors of all ages and abilities.

Starting next week we will begin offering a range of exciting new activities for visitors to take part in. Although some will be based in the pool, most will take place in one of our popular health and fitness halls. All of the activities will also be run by highly trained and experienced trainers and will occur at the same time every day, Monday to Friday. However, due to limited availability, we expect that visitors will need to book their places well in advance.

Of course, this means there is going to be a lot of booking information to keep track of. Visitor and trainer details will need to be recorded along with all of the activities and their times. To help make sure that both trainers and visitors meet up in the right place at the right time, I'm going to use the application *Microsoft Access* to create a database to manage bookings. Maybe you can help me?

What you will learn:

In this section you will use the program *Microsoft Access* to help *Zahra* create a new, fully functional database. You will also see how to use a range of useful database techniques to enter, store, edit and analyse large amounts of complex information.

Knowledge, skills and understanding:

* Use *Microsoft Access* to design and construct a simple database for a purpose

* Enter, maintain and work with large amounts of data

* Build and run queries to retrieve information and create reports

Data files

Data files needed to complete the activities in this section are provided in the **Section 7** data files folder. Databases that you create can be saved to the same folder.

7.1 Using Microsoft Access

A **database** is a simple storage system designed to hold large amounts of information. The possible uses of a database are endless. In business you will often find them used for any task that requires a lot of information to be recorded or accessed quickly and easily. For example, databases are ideal for storing:

* Staff, customer and student records

* Stock, product, order and shipping details

* Lists, diaries and schedules

* Website content and user login data

Microsoft Access is a program that allows you to design and build databases. It is known as a **Database Management System** because it also allows you to access and update the information held in a database and to display that data in a variety of useful ways.

> **Note:** If you are new to the world of databases, you may find them a little overwhelming at first. Don't worry – most beginners experience the same difficulties when they first start out. However, with a little time and practice you'll soon be able to create and use databases like a professional.

In this section you will create a new database to store visitor booking information at *Pirate's Cove*. You will also get the opportunity to open and explore a few ready-made databases.

7.2 Tables, Fields and Records

If you were to crack open a database and take a look inside, you would find all of the information stored within one or more **tables** (which appear very similar to worksheets in *Excel*).

Employee Name	Date of Birth	Department	Salary
Jack Grimes	27/03/87	Fitness	£15000
Shona Piquet	03/12/90	Aqua	£13500
Tariq Hussan	15/06/84	Sport	£18000
Ivan Hendle	15/08/82	Sport	£13500

In those tables, information would be split up into a number of columns known as **fields**. Each field represents a single, separate piece of information (such as the four fields in the example above: **Employee Name**, **Date of Birth**, **Department** and **Salary**).

> **Note:** As all data held in a database is stored within tables, it makes sense that all databases must contain *at least one* table.

Information is added to a table in rows known as **records**, where each record represents a single complete set of fields. In the previous example, the four fields containing information for **Jack Grimes** is a single record.

Jack Grimes	27/03/87	Fitness	£15000

Activity:

1. Start *Microsoft Access* and open the database **Staff Members** from the data files folder. This is a working database containing information about staff members and their jobs.

2. Locate the **Navigation** pane on the left of the screen, labelled **All Access Objects**, which lists all of the objects present in the current database. One table called **Trainers** is listed.

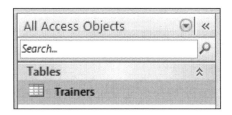

Note: In *Access*, any item contained in a database (such as a table) is called an **object**. You will learn more about other types of object later in this section.

3. Double click on the **Trainers** table object. It is opened in the main part of the window and all of the records contained are shown in a list. This is known as **Datasheet View**.

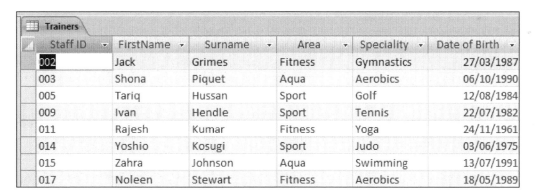

Staff ID	FirstName	Surname	Area	Speciality	Date of Birth
002	Jack	Grimes	Fitness	Gymnastics	27/03/1987
003	Shona	Piquet	Aqua	Aerobics	06/10/1990
005	Tariq	Hussan	Sport	Golf	12/08/1984
009	Ivan	Hendle	Sport	Tennis	22/07/1982
011	Rajesh	Kumar	Fitness	Yoga	24/11/1961
014	Yoshio	Kosugi	Sport	Judo	03/06/1975
015	Zahra	Johnson	Aqua	Swimming	13/07/1991
017	Noleen	Stewart	Fitness	Aerobics	18/05/1989

4. The table contains records for each of the trainers in the *Active Leisure* team at *Pirate's Cove*. Records can easily be added, altered and deleted from here.

5. On the **Home** tab, click the drop-down arrow on the **View** button and then select **Design View**. This view allows you to edit the design of the table by defining the various fields that should appear in it.

Note: Clicking the **View** button instead of the drop down arrow will switch directly from **Datasheet View** to **Design View** (and vice versa).

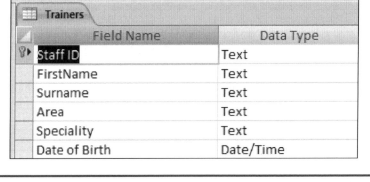

> **Note:** You will learn more about a field's **Data Type** and **Properties** in a later exercise.

6. Click the drop-down arrow on the **View** button and select **Datasheet View** to view the table's data again.

7. Close the database (this is an option on the **Office Button**). As no changes have been made to the design of any objects, there will be no prompt to save changes.

> **Note:** Other *Microsoft Office* programs such as *Excel* can be used to store information in tables, so why use a database? The answer is simple: a well-designed database allows you to record, update, manage and search through vast amounts of information very quickly and efficiently.

7.3 Creating a Database

In most *Office* applications, files are created during the **Save** process (for example, saving a new document in *Word* will create a document file). In *Access*, however, a blank database is created and saved <u>before</u> any changes are made to it.

Activity:

1. With the *Access* **Getting Started** screen displayed, select **Blank database** under **New Blank Database**.

2. The panel on the right allows you to name the new database and specify where it will be located (your default file name and path may appear differently).

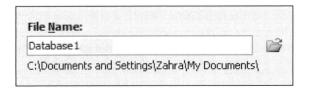

> **Note:** The default is to create your new database in your **My Documents** folder.

3. Click the **Browse** button, 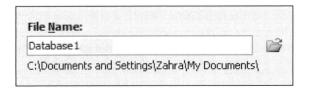, to display the **File New Database** dialog box.

4. Navigate to the data files folder for this section, and then replace the default database **File name** with the text **activity list**.

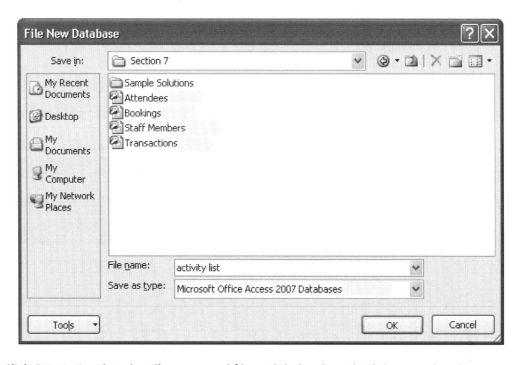

5. Click **OK**. Notice that the **File name** and file path below have both been updated.

6. Click the **Create** button. The new database is created and saved (even though there is no content yet). A new default table is opened in **Datasheet View**.

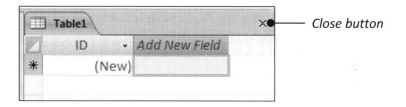

Close button

7. In order to demonstrate the general method for creating tables, close the default table by clicking the **Close** button found to the right of the **Table1** tab.

8. Leave the **activity list** database open for the next exercise.

7.4 Creating a New Table

Before creating a new database table you first need to consider all of the fields that it will contain. This is a very important stage in the design of a database as the chosen fields will define the *exact* types of information that can be stored.

For example, if you want to record information about customer telephone numbers, at the very least you will need a field for the customer's name and another for their telephone number.

> **Note:** Fields can also be added and edited at any time in **Design View**.

Activity:

1. With the **activity list** database open, display the **Create** tab and click the **Table Design** button. A new table appears in **Design View**, which allows the structure of the table to be created.

Table Design

> **Note:** The **Design View** is divided into two main areas. The upper half of the screen allows each field in the table to be defined, whereas the lower half shows more details about the currently selected field.

2. In the first **Field Name** row, enter **Code** as the name of the field.

3. Press **<Enter>** to move to the **Data Type** column. The default type **Text** appears.

> **Note:** You will learn more about **Data Types** in the next exercise.

4. Move to the **Description** column and enter **Activity code**.

Field Name	Data Type	Description
Code	Text	Activity code

Table1

> **Note:** This **Description** text is displayed in the **Status Bar** whenever this field is accessed in **Datasheet View** (recall that **Datasheet View** is the view used to view and enter data into a database).

5. Click in the **Field Name** for the second row to start the next field. Enter the following fields, choosing a default **Data Type** of **Text** for each.

Field Name	Data Type	Description
Activity	Text	Activity name
Staff ID	Text	Trainer for this activity
Location	Text	Activity location
Time	Text	Starting time (daily)
Cost	Text	Cost per person
Discount	Text	Big Planet Club discount
Maximum	Text	Maximum participants

> **Note:** You can use the **<Tab>** key to move to the next column/field.

6. Leave the table open for the next exercise.

7.5 Data Types

Every time you add a new field to a table you must also select an appropriate **Data Type**. There are many different **Data Types** available to choose from, and each can be used to restrict the type of information allowed in a field. The most useful types are listed below:

Data Type	Description
Text	Any combination of letters, numbers or punctuation can be entered into fields of this type.
Number	Only numbers can be entered into fields of this type. Letters and punctuation are rejected.
Date/Time	Only accepts values in time or date format (e.g. 08:00).
Currency	Only accepts values in currency format (e.g. £12.50).
AutoNumber	Fields of this type include a single number that is automatically increased by 1 each time a new record is added to the table.
Yes/No	Displays a checkbox which can be either on or off.

Activity:

1. The **activity list** database currently contains 8 fields. For each field, the default **Data Type** of **Text** has been selected.

2. Click once in the **Data Type** column for the **Time** field, and then click the drop-down arrow that appears to right of the selection.

3. Examine the various **Data Types** available, and then select **Date/Time**.

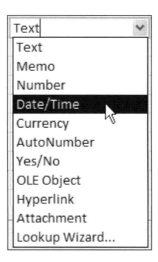

4. Now only valid dates and times can be entered into this field (e.g. **08:00** or **04/04/2012**). Any invalid dates and times will be rejected.

5. For the **Cost** field, choose a **Data Type** of **Currency**. Now only valid money amounts can be entered into this field (e.g. **£15.50**).

6. Finally, for the **Discount** and **Maximum** fields, choose a **Data Type** of **Number**. Now only numbers can be entered into these fields.

> **Note:** Choosing a **Data Type** of **Number** is useful if you need to perform calculations on the contents of a field.

Field Name	Data Type	Description
Code	Text	Activity code
Activity	Text	Activity name
Staff ID	Text	Trainer for this activity
Location	Text	Activity location
Time	Date/Time	Starting time (daily)
Cost	Currency	Cost per person
Discount	Number	Big Planet Club discount
Maximum	Number	Maximum participants

7. Leave the table open for the next exercise.

7.6 Field Properties

Depending on the **Data Type** selected, a field can also have a number of additional **properties** applied to it. These properties specify exactly what values are permitted for a field and allow you to customise how the data appears in the database.

Activity:

1. With the **activity list** database open, select the field **Code** (to do this click once in any of the columns for that row).

2. Notice the **Field Properties** panel which fills the bottom half of the screen. A number of customisable properties for the selected field are shown in a list.

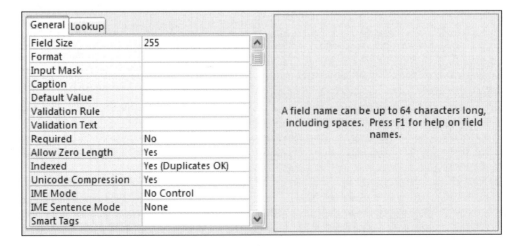

3. Examine the field properties shown. Notice the **Field Size** property is currently set to **255** (the maximum). This means that 255 individual characters can be entered into this field.

4. *Zahra* informs you that all course codes are only 4 characters long. Change the value in the **Field Size** property to **4** so that *no more* than 4 characters can be entered.

> **Note:**   Notice the useful description of the selected property that appears in the box on the right of the **Field Properties** panel.

5. Set a **Field Size** of **3** for the **Staff ID** field, and **50** for the **Activity** and **Location** fields.

6. Next, select the field **Time**.

7. Click once in the **Format** property box and read the short description that appears on the right of the **Field Properties** panel.

8. Click the small drop-down arrow found towards the right edge of the field. Examine the available formats and then select **Short Time**. The contents of the field will now be displayed in the format **17:34**.

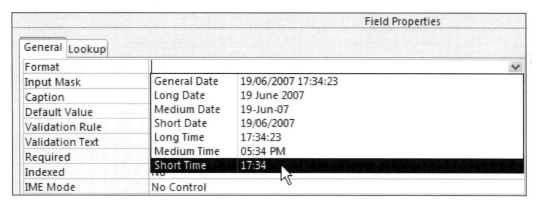

9. Next, select the **Cost** field. Click once in the **Decimal Places** property box and click the drop-down arrow that appears on the right edge of the field.

10. From the options displayed select **2**. The contents of this field will now <u>always</u> be formatted to 2 decimal places (e.g. **£32.00**).

11. Select the **Discount** field, and then set the **Format** property to **Percent**. Values placed in this field will now always be displayed as a percentage (as shown in the example below).

12. The default **Field Size** for a number, **Long Integer**, is appropriate for most uses. However, for percentages to display correctly, it is recommended that you choose **Double** instead. Use the drop-down menu for this property and select it now.

13. Select the **Maximum** field, and then set the **Decimal Places** property to **0**. Now only whole numbers will be displayed in this field.

14. In the **Default Value** property box type in **0**. Now, for every new record created, the **Maximum** field will automatically contain the default starting value **0**.

> **Note:**   If the **Required** field property is set to **Yes**, a new record cannot be saved unless a valid value has been placed in this field.

15.   Leave the table open for the next exercise.

7.7 Primary Keys

It is an advantage to have one field which *uniquely* identifies each individual record in a table. That way, any record in the table can be referred to individually and with absolute certainty. This field is referred to as the **primary key** for the table.

For example, in a table of motor vehicles, registration number would be a good choice for primary key because the values it will contain will always be unique for each record.

> **Note:**   Some tables do not have a suitable or obvious field to use as a primary key. For example, in a table of employee records, names and personal details may not be unique. In this case, a new field can be created which contains a custom, unique value for every record. A **Data Type** of **AutoNumber** is useful here.

Activity:

1.   The new table should be open in **Design View** from the previous exercise. Which field would you say is best suited for use as a primary key?

> **Note:**   Remember: the primary key field must contain unique values for each record in a table. If you attempt to enter a new record into a database with a duplicate primary key value, the new record will be rejected.

2.   The **Code** field would make an ideal choice for a primary key. It is unique for all activities.

3.   Click anywhere in the **Code** field in order to select it.

4.   With the **Table Tools - Design** tab selected on the **Ribbon**, click the **Primary Key** button in the **Tools** group. The **Code** field is now defined as the primary key for this table, which is indicated by a small icon next to the field.

Primary Key

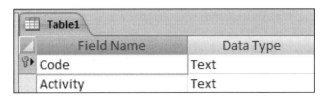

> **Note:**   Notice that the **Code** field property **Indexed** has changed to **Yes (No Duplicates)**. This is used make sure that the primary key values are all unique.

5.   Leave the table open for the next exercise.

> **Note:**   Primary keys are useful in a single table databases to help maintain data integrity, but they are essential for linking tables in a multi-table database. You will learn more about this in a later exercise.

7.8 Saving Tables

When a table, or any other database object, has been created or edited in **Design View**, it must be saved so that the changes are applied.

Activity:

1.   To save the newly created table, click on the **Save** button on the **Quick Access Toolbar**.

Save button ———

2.   As the table has not been saved yet, the **Save As** dialog box is displayed. Enter the **Table Name** as **Activities**.

3.   Click **OK** to confirm the table name and close the dialog box.

> **Note:**   If you had not yet chosen a primary key for this table, you would now be prompted to do so before saving.

4.   The table is saved. Notice the new **Activities** table now appears in the **Navigation** pane, and the tab for the table now displays the table's saved name.

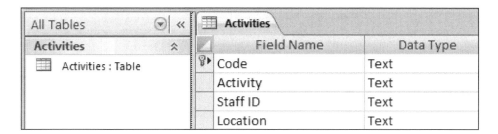

5.   The design of the table is now complete. Using the **View** button, return to **Datasheet View**. The table's fields appear across the top of the screen.

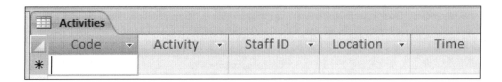

6.   Leave the database open for the next exercise.

7.9 Entering Records

Once the design of a table has been finalised, records can be entered. A simple way to do this is in **Datasheet View**. It is important to enter data accurately – records added to a table are *automatically* saved in the database.

Activity:

1.   The **Activities** table should currently be open in **Datasheet View**. There are no records saved in this table yet.

2.   Click in the first field (**Code**) and type **A001**.

> Note: As the **Code** field has been defined with a maximum size of 4, only the first 4
>   characters of any value you enter into this field will be accepted.

3.   Press <**Enter**> to move to the next field (**Activity**). Type **Aqua Fit** and press <**Enter**>.

4.   Using <**Enter**> (or <**Tab**>) to move between fields, enter the **Staff ID** as **003** and the **Location** as **Large Pool**.

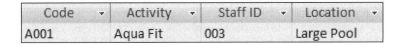

5.   In the **Time** field, enter **800** and press <**Enter**>. An error message appears because this is not a valid entry for the data type. Select **Enter new value** from the options.

6.   Type **8.00** then press <**Enter**>. *Access* displays this as **08:00**.

7.   In the **Cost** field, type **15.5** and press <**Enter**>. *Access* displays this as **£15.50** according to the formatting options chosen for this field.

8.   In the **Discount** field, type **20** and press <**Enter**>. Again, *Access* displays this as **20.00%** because of the formatting options chosen for this field.

9.   In the **Maximum** field, type **Ten** and press <**Enter**>. An error message appears as only numbers are allowed in a **Number** field. Select **Enter new value** and type **10**.

10. Press <**Enter**>. This is the last field in the table and so the record is complete. The first field in the next record is automatically selected.

> **Note:** New records are always added at the bottom of a table and are automatically saved by *Access*. There is no need to save manually.

11. Let's try another one. Leave the **Code** field empty for now and enter the following values:

Starting Yoga; 011; Hall 2; 8:00; 10; 15; 12

12. When you press <**Enter**> after the last field an error message will appear.

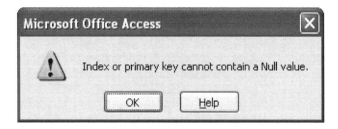

13. Remember, **Code** was defined as the primary key for this table and is therefore required on every record. It cannot be left empty (or **Null**).

14. Click **OK** and enter a value of **A001** in the **Code** field, and then click once in the row below to accept that change. Another error message is displayed as a **Code** of **A001** already exists in the table (recall that primary keys must be unique).

15. Click **OK**, delete the text in the **Code** field, and then type **Y001**. Click in the field below this one. At last everything is fine and the record is added successfully.

16. Leave the table open for the next exercise.

7.10 Editing Table Design

The design of a table can be easily altered after it has been created. However, if records have already been added to the table, there are a number of issues which must first be considered:

✱ If an existing field is deleted, any data in that field will be lost for all records

✱ If an existing field's **Data Type** or **Field Properties** are changed (e.g. if **Field Size** is reduced), any existing data may be permanently lost

✱ If a new field is added to the table, it will be empty for all existing records

Activity:

1. The **Activities** table should be open in **Datasheet View**. Use the **View** button to switch to **Design View**.

2. The **activities list** database also needs to keep track of the minimum number of people recommended for each activity. In the first empty row at the bottom of the table, click once in the **Field Name** column and type **Minimum**. Set the **Data Type** to **Number** and **Description** to **Minimum participants**.

| Maximum | Number | Maximum participants |
| Minimum | Number | Minimum participants |

3. In the next row, enter a **Field Name** of **Fully Booked** and select a **Data Type** of **Yes/No**.

4. To see the effect, click the **View** button to switch to **Datasheet View**. A message is displayed before the **Datasheet View** is shown.

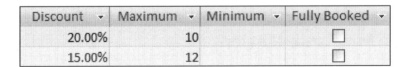

5. The table design has changed and the changes must be saved before the effects can be seen. Click **Yes**. The table is saved and the **Datasheet View** is displayed.

6. The **Datasheet View** now has 2 extra columns on the right (you may need to use the horizontal scrollbar to see these).

> **Note:** Notice that the two new fields for all existing records are empty. This may seem obvious and of little concern, but if the table had thousands of records it may have to be considered.

Discount	Maximum	Minimum	Fully Booked
20.00%	10		☐
15.00%	12		☐

7. It is just as easy to remove fields from a table. Switch back to **Design View** and click in the **Fully Booked** row to select it (if it is not already selected).

8. With the **Design** tab displayed, click the **Delete Rows** button, 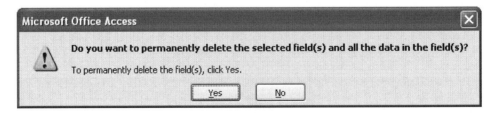. A warning message is displayed.

9. All data in this column of the table will be permanently lost. Again, this is not really a problem here but in a large table it may need to be considered.

10. Click **Yes**. The field is deleted.

> **Note:** Tables must be saved after making design changes.

11. Switch to **Datasheet View**. You will have to click **Yes** to save the table design changes again. The **Fully Booked** column is no longer shown.

12. Leave the table open for the next exercise.

7.11 Column Widths

In **Datasheet View**, values or field names are sometimes longer than the default column width of a table. This causes the data display to be **truncated** (cut off). The truncated data is not lost; it is just hidden. Fortunately it is an easy matter to display all of the content by simply changing the width of the columns.

Activity:

1. The **Activities** table should be open in **Datasheet View**. Let's add another record. Click in the first field of the first blank record in the table and enter the following values:

   Z001, Introduction to Judo, 014, Small Sports Hall, 19:00, 12, 10, 8, 2

2. Depending on your screen resolution, the **Activity** and **Location** fields may not be fully displayed (if they are fully displayed, you can simulate this problem by reducing the size of the *Access* window). There are two ways to deal with this.

3. First, place the cursor on the bar between the column headers **Activity** and **Staff ID** as shown below. The cursor changes to a double-headed arrow.

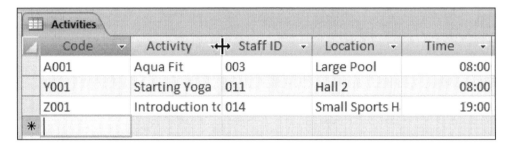

4. Double click and the column width will increase automatically to accommodate the largest value in this field.

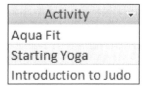

5. Column width can also be changed manually. Place the cursor on the bar between the column headers **Location** and **Time** so that it changes to a double-headed arrow.

---

6. Click and drag to the right to increase the column width by a small amount. Release the mouse button to see the effect. You may need to repeat the process until all of the text in the field can be seen.

Location	Time
Large Pool	08:00
Hall 2	08:00
Small Sports Hall	19:00

7. Leave the table open for the next exercise.

7.12 Editing Records

In addition to adding new records, one of the strengths of *Access* is that it is also easy to amend or remove records that already exist. Remember, data changes made in **Datasheet View** are automatically saved as they happen.

Activity:

1. The **Activities** table should be open in **Datasheet View**. Click in record **2** for activity **Y001** (**Starting Yoga**). Then, find the **Record** navigation buttons which are located at the bottom of the table.

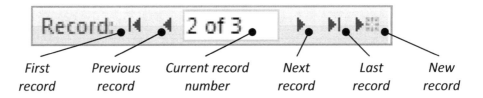

| First record | Previous record | Current record number | Next record | Last record | New record |

2. Click the **Next record** button to move to record **3**, then click the **First record** button to move to record **1**. Finally, click the **Next record** button again to move back to record **2**.

3. Move the mouse pointer over the start of the **Staff ID** field for this record until it changes to a large cross icon.

Code	Activity	Staff ID	Location
A001	Aqua Fit	003	Large Pool
Y001	Starting Yoga	011	Hall 2

4. Click with the mouse to select the whole of the field. Press the **<Delete>** key. The entire contents of the field are deleted.

5. Click the **Undo** button, on the **Quick Access Toolbar**. The action is reversed and the **Staff ID** field returns to its original value.

6. A data entry error has been made: the starting time of **Starting Yoga** should be **10:00**. Click in the field and edit the value to **10:00**. Press **<Enter>** to confirm the change.

> **Note:**   Standard editing functions such as **Cut**, **Copy**, **Paste** may also be used.

7.   It has been decided that all activities should be priced at **£8.00**. First, change the value in the **Cost** field for record **1** to **£8.00**.

8.   Next, highlight the new value using click and drag.

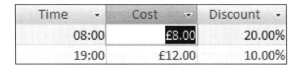

9.   Click the **Copy** button, , in the **Clipboard** group of the **Home** tab.

10.   Highlight the activity cost in the record below and click the **Paste** button. The copied price replaces the original value. Repeat this for record **3**.

> **Note:**   Standard **Find** and **Replace** techniques also work for databases.

11.   Leave the table open for the next exercise.

7.13 Deleting Records

Records can easily be deleted in **Datasheet View**. Deleting a record removes it and all of its data from the table. There is a warning prompt and then the record is removed permanently.

Activity:

1.   The **Activities** table should be open in **Datasheet View**. Move your mouse pointer over the **Record Selector** bar until an arrow cursor appears, ➡. Click once on record **2** (**Code Y001**) to select the whole of that record.

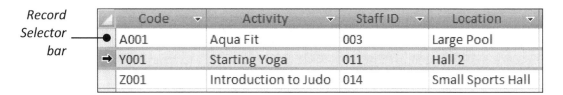

2.   Click the **Delete** button, , in the **Records** group of the **Home** tab.

---

3. Read the confirmation message that appears and then click **Yes** to permanently remove the record. Use the same technique to delete the other two remaining records.

4. Well done. The database is now ready to be used by staff at *Pirate's Cove* to record new activities. *Zahra* thanks you for your help.

5. Close the database, saving any changes that have been made to the table's design.

7.14 Sorting Records

In a large table it can sometimes be useful to **sort** all of the records into a specific order. For example, you could sort all employee records alphabetically by name or numerically by age. This technique allows you to group records in a way that helps you find the information you need quickly and easily.

Records can be sorted in **ascending** or **descending** order using any field in a table. Ascending sorts for a text field will be alphabetical, A-Z. For a numeric field it will be lowest to highest, and for a date field will be oldest to newest. Descending order applies the opposite sort.

> Note: By default, the records in a table are arranged in ascending order by the contents of the primary key field.

Activity:

1. Open the **Attendees** database.

> Note: If a **Security Warning** appears under the **Ribbon**, simply click **Options**, select **Enable this content** and then click **OK**. Because of the risk of viruses, always be careful enabling content if you do not fully trust the source of the database.

2. Using the **Navigation** pane, open the **Visitors** table. This table contains details of park visitors who have recently attended activities at *Pirate's Cove*. The **Visitor** field is defined as the primary key for the table.

3. Move your mouse pointer over the field header **Last Name** until it changes to a downward arrow, ↓.

Last Name ↓ ▾	Ticket Type ▾
McKnight	Full
Robson	Junior

4. Click once to select this field, and then click the **Ascending** button, ⁤, in the **Sort & Filter** group on the **Home** tab. The table is instantly sorted into ascending (alphabetical) order of name.

> **Note:**   Entire records are sorted, not just the contents of the selected field.

Visitor ▾	Title ▾	First Name ▾	Last Name ⇟	Ticket Type ▾
HC173	Mr	Saeed	Akram	Full
HC168	Mr	Jahved	Ali	Junior
HC145	Miss	Brenda	Appleby	Full
HC106	Mr	Tariq	Assiz	Senior
HC157	Mr	Bill	Barnacle	Full

> **Note:**   A small arrow icon in the **Last Name** heading indicates a sort is active on this field.

5.   With the **Last Name** field still selected, click the **Descending** button, $\boxed{\substack{Z \\ A\downarrow}}$. The table is now sorted in reverse order of name (notice the arrow icon has reversed).

6.   Click the **Remove Sort** button, $\boxed{\substack{A \\ Z}}$, from the **Home** tab. The sort is removed and the records are displayed in their original order.

7.   Next, select the **Age** field and select **Ascending** from the **Ribbon**. The table is sorted by increasing age. Select **Descending** to reverse the sort.

8.   Click the **Remove Sort** button, $\boxed{\substack{A \\ Z}}$, and leave the table open for the next exercise.

7.15 Filtering Records

Filtering is a quick way to find records in a table that match certain selection criteria. Only the records that match the criteria are displayed (the records that do not match are hidden).

Activity:

1.   The **Visitors** table of the **Attendees** database should be open in **Datasheet View**. Place the cursor in the first record's **Ticket Type** field (**Full**).

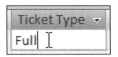

2.   From the **Sort & Filter** group on the **Home** tab, click the **Selection** button. Examine the various options that are listed based on the selected field.

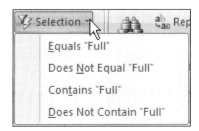

---

3. Select **Equals "Full"**. Only records with **Ticket Type** fields of **Full** are displayed. The **Record** navigation buttons at the bottom of the table show **Record 1 of 34** and the text **Filtered**.

> **Note:** When a filter is applied, the **Record** navigation buttons will show the number of filtered records only, not the number of records in the database.

4. From the **Home** tab, click **Toggle Filter**, [Toggle Filter]. This switches off the filter but does not delete it.

5. Click the **Toggle Filter** button again. The last filter used is applied once again.

Visitor	Title	First Name	Last Name	Ticket Type	Age
HC050	Mr	Charles	McKnight	Full	41
HC108	Mr	John	Hooper	Full	39
HC111	Mr	Tazeen	Raman	Full	24
HC115	Mrs	Gita	Patel	Full	28
HC116	Mrs	Jean	Kilroy	Full	31

> **Note:** A small icon in the **Ticket Type** heading indicates a filter is active on this field.

6. To remove the filter completely, click **Advanced** on the **Home** tab and select **Clear All Filters**. All 65 records appear again.

7. Next, place the cursor in the first record's **Age** field (**41**). Click the **Selection** button and select **Less Than or Equal To 41**.

8. Only visitors whose age is 41 or under will now appear (47 records). Click **Advanced** and select **Clear All Filters**.

9. Using the same technique, apply a filter so that only visitors whose age is **Greater Than or Equal to 41** are displayed (21 records). Click **Advanced** and select **Clear All Filters**.

10. Using the same technique again, apply a filter so that only visitors whose age is **Equal to 41** are displayed (3 records). Click **Advanced** and select **Clear All Filters**.

11. You can also apply more specific filters. Click the drop-down arrow on the **Visit Date** field header, ·, and move your mouse pointer over **Date Filters**.

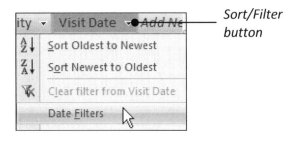

Sort/Filter button

12. From the submenu that appears, select **Before**. A **Custom Filter** dialog box appears.

13. In the **Visit Date is on or before** box, enter **13/05/2011** and click **OK**. Only records with a **Visit Date** earlier than May 13, 2011 will be displayed (21 records).

> **Note:** You can also apply more than one filter at a time.

14. With the previous filter still active, click the drop-down arrow on the **Ticket Type** field header and move your mouse pointer over **Text Filters**.

15. Select **Contains**. In the **Custom Filter** dialog box enter the text **Full** and click **OK**.

16. Only records with a **Visit Date** earlier than **13/05/2011** and with a **Ticket Type** of **Full** are now displayed (9 records).

17. Click **Advanced** from the **Home** tab and select **Clear All Filters**. Examine the various filter types available for other fields in the table. Feel free to try out a number of different filters, but make sure you select **Clear All Filters** before continuing.

18. Leave the table open for the next exercise.

7.16 Queries

For more control over sorting and filtering in a table, you can use a **query**. A basic query **selects** specific fields and records from a database table and displays them in another table. The original table is not affected by the query.

> **Note:** Queries simply provide a different view of a table's data. However, editing the results of a query will also change the original table's content.

One of the biggest advantages of a query is that it is saved as a separate object and can be used again at any time. Of course, every time you open the query, it will always show the most current information stored in the database.

Activity:

1. The **Visitors** table should still be open in **Datasheet View**. You have been asked to quickly produce a list of all **Junior** visitors to *Pirate's Cove*, showing their **First Name**, **Last Name** and **Ticket Type**. The results should be shown in order of **Age** with the youngest visitors first. This can be done easily using a simple query.

2. Display the **Create** tab and select **Query Design** from the **Other** group.

Query
Design

3. A query design tab (**Query1**) is displayed and the **Show Table** dialog box appears on top.

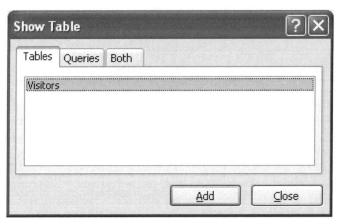

4. The **Show Table** dialog box is used to select which tables should be used as the basis for this query. With the **Visitors** table highlighted, click **Add** to add the table to the query.

5. Click **Close** in the **Show Table** dialog box to close it.

6. Examine the new **Query1** tab. The top half contains a list of all fields available in the selected table. The lower half allows you to select which fields to include in the query.

7. From the lower query grid, click the drop-down arrow button on the first column's **Field** property box. From the list of fields displayed, select **First Name**.

Field:	First Name ⌄		
Table:	Visitors		
Sort:			
Show:	☑	☐	☐
Criteria:			
or:			

8. Use the same method to select **Last Name** in the second column.

> **Note:** An alternative method for adding a field to your query is to double click the field name in the field list at the top of the page. The field is added in the next column. You can also drag and drop fields from the field list to an available query column.

9. Add the fields **Ticket Type** and **Age** to the query.

Field:	First Name	Last Name	Ticket Type	Age
Table:	Visitors	Visitors	Visitors	Visitors
Sort:				
Show:	☑	☑	☑	☑
Criteria:				
or:				

> **Note:** The query will display fields in the order that they appear in the query design. This can be different to the order that they occur in the original table.

10. Display the **Query Tools - Design** tab and click **Run** to run the query. All 65 records contained in the **Visitors** table are shown, but only the four selected fields appear here.

11. Click **Save**, 💾, on the **Quick Access Toolbar** to save the query. Enter **Visitor Query** as the **Query Name**.

12. Click **OK** to save the new query, and leave it open for the next exercise. Notice that the query now also appears on the **Navigation** pane.

7.17 Sorting in Queries

Records selected using queries can also be automatically sorted (in either ascending or descending order) based upon the contents of one or more of the included fields.

Activity:

1. Using **Visitor Query**, switch to **Design View**. Click in the **Sort** box of the **Last Name** field, then click the drop-down arrow on the right and select **Ascending** from the list.

Field:	First Name		Last Name		Ticket Type		Age	
Table:	Visitors		Visitors		Visitors		Visitors	
Sort:			Ascending	▼				
Show:		☑		☑		☑		☑
Criteria:								
or:								

2. Run the query. All 65 records are shown again, but now they are sorted alphabetically by **Last Name**.

3. Switch back to **Design View**. Change the **Sort** field of **Last Name** to **(not sorted)** and then select **Descending** in the **Sort** box for the **Age** field.

4. Run the query again. The selected fields are now displayed in descending order of **Age** (eldest first). Save the query and then close it.

5. A saved query can be run at any time. Double click the **Visitor Query** object in the **Navigation** pane. The query runs automatically and once again selects and sorts all records in the **Visitors** table.

> **Note:** It is important to remember that a query can be run at any time. If new records are added or removed, the query will always show the most up-to-date information.

6. Leave the query open for the next exercise.

7.18 Selection Criteria

Queries are of most use when used to filter records based on specific selection criteria. When added to a field, only the records that match these criteria are shown.

Activity:

1. **Visitor Query** should be open in **Datasheet View**. Click the **View** button on the **Home** tab to switch to **Design View**.

2. Click in the **Criteria** box for the **Ticket Type** field and type **Junior**. Press <**Enter**>. This will now restrict the query to records which contain the text **Junior** in the **Ticket Type** field.

Field:	First Name	Last Name	Ticket Type	Age
Table:	Visitors	Visitors	Visitors	Visitors
Sort:				Descending
Show:	☑	☑	☑	☑
Criteria:			"Junior"	

> **Note:** In queries, **junior** is the same as **Junior** or **JUNIOR**. The speech marks, if not entered manually, will be added automatically by *Access*.

3. Click **Run** on the **Query Tools - Design** tab again to run the query. 21 records are selected.

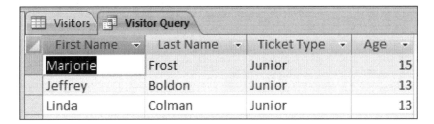

4. Click the **View** button on the **Home** tab to return to **Design View**.

5. When the **Show** checkbox is ticked for a field, ☑, it indicates that the field will be displayed in the query. Click the checkbox for the **Ticket Type** field to remove the tick.

Field:	First Name	Last Name	Ticket Type	Age
Table:	Visitors	Visitors	Visitors	Visitors
Sort:				Descending
Show:	☑	☑	☐	☑
Criteria:			"Junior"	

6. Run the query. The **Type** field is no longer displayed, but it is still used in the query to select records.

7. Switch back to **Design View** and replace the tick in the **Show** checkbox for **Ticket Type**.

8. This now completes the query - well done. Save and close the query and then close the **Attendees** database (saving any changes, if prompted).

7.19 Numerical Criteria

Query selection criteria can also be applied to numerical fields (including currency and date fields). To do this you can use the following mathematical operators to select records that lie in a specific range:

<	less than
>	greater than
>=	greater than or equal to
<=	less than or equal to

Activity:

1. Open the database **Transactions** and double click on the **Invoices** table to open it. This table contains records of supplier invoices (bills) that *Zahra* has recently received. Running *Pirate's Cove* is an expensive business!

2. Display the **Create** tab and select **Query Design**. Create a new query based on the **Invoices** table and close the **Show Table** dialog box.

3. Place the fields **Company Name**, **Town**, **Amount**, **Date** and **Type** into the query grid in that order.

4. Position the cursor in the **Criteria** box for **Amount** and type **<500**.

Town	Amount	Date
Invoices	Invoices	Invoices
☑	☑	☑
	<500	

> **Note:** Currency symbols such as £ or $ do not need to be included when entering query criteria. Only the number itself is required.

5. Run the query. All invoices for less than **£500** will be selected (16 records).

6. Switch back to **Design View**.

7. Change the criteria in the **Amount** field to **<=500** and run the query. All orders worth up to and *including* **£500** will now be selected. As there are 17 records found – one more than last time – one invoice must be for exactly **£500**. Can you find this?

> **Note:** The **equals** operator, =, is not required by itself. This will simply be assumed when you enter a value directly into a field's **Criteria** box.

8. Switch to **Design View** and delete the selection criteria in the **Amount** field. Type the following criteria in the **Date** field: **<01/01/2011** and press <**Enter**>.

Town	Amount	Date
Invoices	Invoices	Invoices
☑	☑	☑
		<#01/01/2011#

> **Note:** The **#** symbols are added automatically by *Access* to indicate that the selection criteria will be based on a date value.

9. Run the query. All orders dated before 1st Jan 2011 will be selected (31 records).

10. Save the new query as **Dates** and close it.

11. Leave the **Invoices** table open in **Datasheet** View for the next exercise.

7.20 Wildcards

Wildcards are special symbols that can be used to select records containing values which are *similar* but not *exactly* the same. The most useful wildcard symbol is the asterisk, *****, which can be used in place of one or more characters in a query. For example, the query criteria **Yo*** will select any values that start **Yo**, including words such as **York**, **Yorkshire**, **yolk**, **yoga**, **yo-yo**, and so on.

Activity:

1. With the **Transactions** database open, create a new query in **Design View** based on the **Invoices** table.

2. Place the fields **Type**, **Company Name**, **Town**, **Amount** and **Date** into the query grid.

3. Place the cursor in the **Criteria** box for **Company Name**, type **b*** and press **<Enter>**. *Access* changes the criteria to **Like "b*"**.

Type	Company Name	Town
Invoices	Invoices	Invoices
☑	☑	☑
	Like "b*"	

4. Run the query. All orders for companies whose name starts with **B** are selected (11 records).

> **Note:** The wildcard symbol **?** can be used in place of a single letter. For example, the criteria **Yo?k** would match the values **York** and **yolk**.

5. Switch back to **Design View** and remove the query criteria from **Company Name**.

6. Leave the query open for the next exercise.

7.21 Not and Between

Two particularly useful operators for use in query selection criteria are **Not** and **Between**. The **Not** operator can be used to select records that *do not* match a certain criteria. The **Between** operator can be used to select values *within* a specific range.

Activity:

1. In the **Criteria** box for the **Type** field, enter **not supplies** (i.e. not equal to supplies) and press <**Enter**>.

Field:	Type	Company Name	Town	Amount
Table:	Invoices	Invoices	Invoices	Invoices
Sort:				
Show:	☑	☑	☑	☑
Criteria:	Not "supplies"			
or:				

2. Run the query. All invoices that are <u>not</u> for supplies will be selected (61 records).

3. Switch back to **Design View**. Delete the selection criteria from **Type** and, in the criteria for the **Amount** field, enter **between 500 and 900**.

Field:	Type	Company Name	Town	Amount
Table:	Invoices	Invoices	Invoices	Invoices
Sort:				
Show:	☑	☑	☑	☑
Criteria:				Between 500 And 900
or:				

4. Run the query. 9 records will be selected.

5. The **Between** operator is also useful for selecting date ranges. Switch back to **Design View** and remove the selection criteria from **Amount**. In the **Criteria** box for the **Date** field, enter **between 01/04/2011 and 30/04/2011**.

6. Select a **Descending** sort on **Date**.

7. Run the query. All orders with dates in **April 2011** will be selected (4 records) and displayed in date order with the latest first.

8. Save the query as **April Invoices** and close it. Leave the **Transactions** database open for the next exercise.

7.22 Multiple Criteria

Multiple query criteria can be combined with an **AND** relationship. For example, you can select records where the **Type** field is **Supplies** <u>AND</u> the **Amount** is **>£2000**. Each extra **AND** criteria will usually narrow the selection and produce fewer results.

Criteria can also be combined with an **OR** relationship. For example, you can select records where the **Type** field is **Supplies** <u>OR</u> the **Amount** field is **>£2000**. In this case, each extra **OR** criteria will usually widen the selection and produce more results.

Activity:

1. In the **Transactions** database, create a new query in **Design View** based on the **Invoices** table. Add the fields **Type**, **Company Name**, **Town**, **Amount** and **Date** to the query.

2. Position the cursor in the **Criteria** box for the **Type** field and enter **supplies**. In the **Criteria** box for **Amount** type **>2000**.

Field:	Type	Company Name	Town	Amount
Table:	Invoices	Invoices	Invoices	Invoices
Sort:				
Show:	☑	☑	☑	☑
Criteria:	"supplies"			>2000
or:				

3. Run the query. 1 record is found where the **Type** is **Supplies** <u>AND</u> the invoice **Amount** is more than **£2000**.

4. Switch back to **Design View**. Delete the query selection criteria from the **Amount** field and enter **>2000** in the **or** row directly below.

Field:	Type	Company Name	Town	Amount
Table:	Invoices	Invoices	Invoices	Invoices
Sort:				
Show:	☑	☑	☑	☑
Criteria:	"supplies"			
or:				>2000

5. Run the query. 52 records are now found where the **Type** is **Supplies** <u>OR</u> the invoice **Amount** is more than **£2000**.

6. Switch to **Design View** and remove the query criteria from both the **Type** and **Amount** fields. Type **Alton** in the **Criteria** box for **Town** and type **Hadsley** in the **or** box below.

Field:	Type	Company Name	Town	Amount
Table:	Invoices	Invoices	Invoices	Invoices
Sort:				
Show:	☑	☑	☑	☑
Criteria:			"Alton"	
or:			"Hadsley"	

7. Run the query. All invoices from either **Alton** <u>OR</u> **Hadsley** are listed (12 records).

> **Note:** Entering the text **Alton or Hadsley** in the **Criteria** box would produce the same result.

8. Save the query as **Towns** and leave it open for the next exercise.

7.23 Printing Query Results

Once you have created and run a query to select specific records from a table, it is then very easy to print a copy of those results.

Activity:

1. The **Towns** query should be open in **Datasheet View**.

2. Click the **Office Button** and expand **Print**. Examine the options that are displayed on the right and then click **Print Preview**.

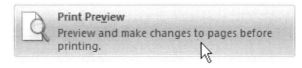

3. A preview image of how the query results will appear when printed is displayed. Clicking the mouse button with the pointer on the page preview will toggle a magnified view.

	Towns			05/08/2011
Type	**Company Name**	**Town**	**Amount**	**Date**
Buildings	Bob's Builders	Alton	£650.00	23/09/2010
Training	Precision Pools	Alton	£457.00	27/09/2010
Supplies	Chapel Garden Supplies	Alton	£419.00	14/10/2010
Buildings	Hadsley Builders	Hadsley	£15,600.00	23/10/2010
Buildings	Bob's Builders	Alton	£158.00	04/12/2010
Supplies	Chapel Garden Supplies	Alton	£325.00	06/12/2010
Buildings	Hadsley Builders	Hadsley	£15,600.00	03/01/2011
Buildings	Bob's Builders	Alton	£158.00	20/03/2011
Supplies	Chapel Garden Supplies	Alton	£225.00	24/03/2011
Training	Precision Pools	Alton	£457.00	25/03/2011

> **Note:** Notice the name of the query and the date are added to the page header and a page number is added to the page footer.

4. Click the **Print** button from the left of the **Print Preview** tab. A print dialog box is displayed with options to change printer settings. Click **Cancel** to close the dialog box *without* printing.

5. Click the **Close Print Preview** button from the right of the **Print Preview** tab to return to the **Datasheet View**.

6. Close the query.

> **Note:** The print technique described here can also be used to print any database table.

7.24 Reports

Printing queries (or tables) does not allow any real control over the appearance of the final printed document. To produce more professional looking output it is better to create a **Report**.

Reports are separate objects in *Access* (just like tables and queries) and once created can be run at any time. You can choose to create a report using selection criteria and sorting features, or you can create a report based on a query which already does this for you – the choice is yours.

Activity:

1.	In the **Transactions** database, click <u>once</u> to select the **Dates** query in the **Navigation** pane. This is a query that you created in an earlier exercise.

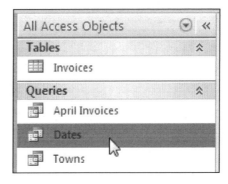

2.	Display the **Create** tab and select **Report** from the **Reports** group. A new report is generated based on the currently selected object (the **Dates** query).

3.	Notice new **Report Layout Tools** tabs have appeared on the **Ribbon**.

4.	You can customise the default titles that appear. Click on the report title, **Dates**, to select the text box. Click again to edit the content. Replace the text with **Old Invoices**.

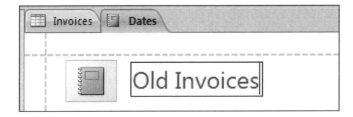

5.	Change the column heading **Company Name** to **Supplier Name**.

6. The broken lines near the edges of the display indicate the printed page boundaries. It currently looks like the report will overflow the right edge of the paper (and go onto a second page). Display the **Page Setup** tab on the **Ribbon**.

7. Select **Landscape** from the **Page Layout** group. The orientation of the page is changed.

8. Display the **Format** tab and click the **View** drop-down button. The currently selected view is **Layout View**, which includes query data and also allows some basic report formatting.

9. Select **Design View**. This view shows the design of the report without any data. All parts of the report's design may be changed from here including which fields are displayed.

10. Each part of the report can be customised. Click in an empty area of the screen to deselect all of the text boxes, then find the **Detail** area (which will contain all of the selected records when printed) and click in the **Amount** box.

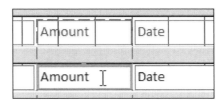

11. Click the drop-down arrow on the **Font Color** button, ![Font Color button], in the **Font** group of the **Design** tab. Select a red colour of your choice.

12. Find the **Page Header** area and click the **Amount** label (this represents the column heading on the report). Use the **Font Color** button to select any blue colour.

> **Note:**   Standard **Font** type, size and alignment features are also available in this view. Individual boxes and labels can also be repositioned on the report.

13. Click the **View** button and select **Print Preview**. The **Amount** column heading is shown in blue and the **Amount** data fields in red.

14. Click **Close Print Preview**. Save the report as **Old Invoices** and close it, leaving the database open for the next exercise.

7.25 Report Wizard

There is a **Report Wizard** feature in *Access* which allows more control over the data that goes into a report and how it is presented. To use this feature, you simply complete a series of dialog boxes which guide you step-by-step through the report creation process.

> **Note:**   A **Wizard** is a part of a computer program designed to simplify a complex task for new users. It will guide beginners through a number of simple steps, gather information, and then perform the task automatically for them.

Activity:

1. With the **Transactions** database open, display the **Create** tab and select 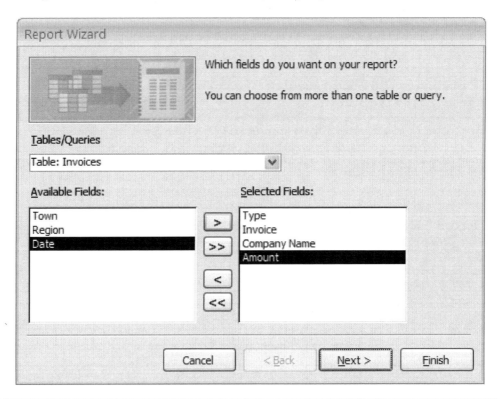 Report Wizard. The first screen of the **Report Wizard** is displayed.

2. Read the text on this screen and then click the drop-down arrow on **Tables/Queries** box. Click **Table: Invoices** to select it. The available fields in the table are listed.

3. From the **Available Fields** area, select **Type**. Click > to move it to **Selected Fields** area on the right. Select and move the fields **Invoice**, **Company Name**, and **Amount** also.

Note: The >> button will move all fields from left to right. The < and << buttons will move fields from right to left. Double clicking on any field will also move it from one side of the dialog box to the other.

4. Click **Next**. This screen can be used to group records in the report.

5. At the moment, all selected fields are grouped together. With **Type** selected, click > . Records will now be grouped by invoice **Type**.

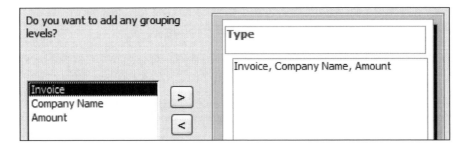

6. Click **Next**. This screen allows you to select the order in which the records will be displayed in the report. Up to four levels of sorting can be applied.

7. Select **Company Name** in the first drop-down box.

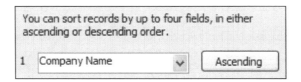

8. Click **Next**. This screen allows you to customise the report's layout. Preview the types of layout by selecting each one in turn, and then finally choose a **Layout** of **Stepped** and an **Orientation** of **Landscape**.

9. Make sure the **Adjust the field width…** check box is checked (this prevents fields from being truncated in the final report).

10. Click **Next**. On this screen you can select a design for your report. Select any styles to preview them, and then finally select **Office** and click **Next**.

11. On this final screen, change the report title to **Invoice List**. The **Report Wizard** is now complete. Click **Finish** to automatically create the report and **Print Preview** the results.

12. Examine the layout of the report (you can zoom in if necessary). All invoices of the same type are grouped together and sorted by **Company Name**.

> **Note:**   *Access* is not always perfect in its report layout. For example, some fields may be displayed as ######## which means there is not enough space allocated to a field to display all of its contents. If this happens, you can adjust the size of the boxes in **Design View**.
>
>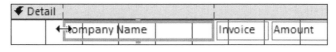

13. Close **Print Preview**. The report is displayed in **Design View**. Once again, any aspect of the report layout can be changed from here.

> **Note:**   Reports can also be built entirely from scratch in **Design View**.

14. Close the report, saving any changes, and then close the **Transactions** database.

7.26 Linked Tables

Data in a database can be stored in more than one table, and if there is a logical relationship between them, they can be linked together (these are called **Relational Databases**). By using this technique of linking simple tables together, the real power of databases is revealed.

Activity:

1. Open the **Bookings** database. *Zahra* has linked the **Activities**, **Trainers** and **Visitors** tables that you used in previous exercises to create a more practical database. It has been in use for a few days now and contains a lot more activity information.

2. Display the **Database Tools** tab and click the **Relationships** button. A picture of the database **structure** is displayed showing how the tables are linked. This diagram is sometimes called a **database schema**.

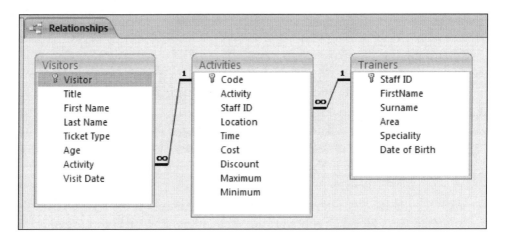

3. This relationship diagram shows that every **Activity** code in the **Visitors** table links to a full record for that activity in the **Activities** table. Each **Staff ID** in the **Activities** table also links to a full record for that staff member in the **Trainers** table.

> **Note:** This simple approach means you only have to create a single record for each activity in the **Activities** table. Every time this activity in used in the **Visitors** table, all of the information it contains is immediately available.

4. Let's take a look at some of the advantages of linking these three tables. Close the **Relationships** window and open the **Activities** table. As this table is now linked to the **Visitors** table, you can now see all visitors who have signed up for each activity.

5. A **Subdatasheet** button, ⊞, appears next to each activity record. Click the **Subdatasheet** button next to the first record. The related **Visitors** record(s) for this activity are shown. Only one person has registered for this activity.

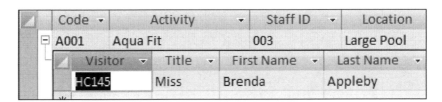

6. Click the **Subdatasheet** button next to the second record. Two people have registered for this activity.

7. Close the **Activities** table.

> **Note:**   Even though data is held in individual linked tables, queries and reports can present the data in one view.

8.   Display the **Create** tab and select **Query Design** from the **Other** group.

9.   In the **Show Table** dialog box, select **Activities** and click **Add**, then select **Visitors** and click **Add**. Close the dialog box. Both tables are added to the query and they are shown as linked.

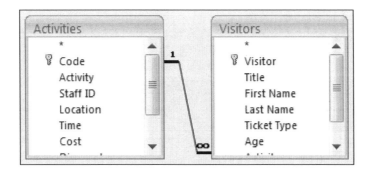

10. Include **First Name** and **Last Name** from the **Visitors** table in the query grid, then **Location** and **Activity** from the **Activities** table. Select an **Ascending** sort for **Location**.

Field:	First Name	Last Name	Location	Activity
Table:	Visitors	Visitors	Activities	Activities
Sort:			Ascending	
Show:	☑	☑	☑	☑
Criteria:				
or:				

11. Run the query. The visitor records are displayed in order of their activity location, even though location information is not present in the visitor records themselves.

12. Save the query as **Locations** and close it.

13. Another useful feature of linking tables involves **data integrity**. Open the **Visitors** table and click **New** from the **Records** group of the **Home** tab. Enter the following data:

HC174; Mr; John; Smith; Full; 45; F009; 21/04/2011

14. Click **Save** from the **Records** group of the **Home** tab to add the record (or simply click in another row to commit the changes). Read the message that is displayed.

15. This means that, because the tables are linked, you cannot use an activity code in the **Visitors** table that has not first been defined in the **Activities** table. This can be a big help in avoiding data entry errors.

16. Click **OK** to remove the message, then change **Activity** to **F003** and save the new record. It is added successfully to the database as **F003** is a valid activity code.

17. Close the table and the database, and then close *Access*.

7.27 Next Steps

Well done! You have now completed all of the exercises in this section. If you feel you are ready to test your knowledge and understanding of the topics covered, move on to the following **Develop Your Skills** activities. If there are any features of *Microsoft Access* that you are unsure about, you should revisit the appropriate exercises and try them again before moving on.

If you are interested in exploring some of *Microsoft Access's* more powerful features, why don't you use the Internet to find out a little more about the following advanced topics.

Feature	Description
Forms	Forms are another object in an *Access* database. They can be thought of as an interface to your database and are often used to control data entry or to present information to users in a very specific way. They are generally used to show and edit one record at a time, and are extremely useful when designing a database for other people to use.
Validation	Simple validation rules can check values entered into a field for accuracy. For example, validation rules can check that a telephone number is a certain length or that a postcode uses the correct pattern of letters and numbers. Custom error messages can then be displayed if the requirements are not met.
Lookup	One of the most useful data integrity techniques is the **Lookup** feature. Instead of typing an entry into a field it can instead be selected (looked up) from a predefined list of possible values. This avoids typing errors and data "guessing". The list of values can be defined in a field's properties or can be stored in another table in the database.
Advanced Queries	In addition to the queries described in this section, you can also create queries which summarise data or perform actions such as creating tables, updating records in a table, adding records to a table or deleting records from a table.
Calculated Fields	Queries and reports can include calculated fields. These are fields which are calculated whenever needed, but do not exist as separate fields on any table. For example, if a table contains a **Price** field and a **Discount** field, it is not necessary to have a **Discounted Price** field. This value can (and should) be calculated wherever it is needed.
Macros	Macros are a powerful feature of most practical databases. They are commands which can be triggered by buttons on forms (e.g. press a button to close a form and open a different one) or by events (e.g. when a table is updated, run a report).
SQL	**Structured Query Language**: the database programming language which *Access* uses behind the scenes to produce most of its query and report results. You do not need to know anything about **SQL** in order to use *Access*, but you should at least be aware of it.

At the end of every section you will get the chance to complete two full tasks without my assistance. This will help to reinforce learning and develop your skills. Don't forget to use the planning and review checklists at the back of the book to organise and evaluate your work.

> **Note:**   Sample solutions for both tasks are provided in this section's data files folder.

Level 1: Event Booking Database

In this task you will be asked to create a simple database for *Zahra*. You will need to use the ICT skills you have learned in this section to plan, develop and present an appropriate solution. You can ask for help from friends, colleagues or a teacher if you get stuck.

Level 1 Task

Next month we're planning to host a number of special evening events for visitors attending the *Pirate's Cove* pool. As space will be strictly limited at each event, we will need to create a database to record visitor bookings – can you help?

Start by creating a database called **evening events** in the data file folder for this section, and then add a table called **Bookings**. The table design will need a 4-digit *event code*, an *event name*, a *location*, a start *date*, a start *time*, and an event *duration* (in minutes). Set up the appropriate fields, data types and properties. You will also need to choose a suitable field to be primary key.

The first event we have planned is for a show called **Pirates have Talent**. The event has a code *E001* and is a *1.5* hour show in the *Large Pool* at *8pm* on the *first* day of next month. Enter the record and make sure all the data is fully displayed in the table.

Oh, I forgot to mention that we will be charging *admission* to each event. Add another field to the table and include the charge *£8.50* for the first show.

Enter a new event, *E002*, called **Celebrity Walk the Plank**. The event costs *£9* and is a *2* hour show in the *Large Pool* at *6pm* on the *third* day of next month. Enter the record and make sure all the data is fully displayed. Print the table and then close the database.

Level 2: Age Analysis

In this task you will be asked to create a detailed database report for *Zahra*. You will need to use the advanced ICT skills that you have learned in this section to create a suitable solution (you may need to break the problem down into smaller parts first). Only level 2 students should attempt this task and it should be completed without help from others.

Level 2 Task

You have just received the following note from *Zahra*:

> I need to find out how many Junior and Senior ticket holders have attended an activity at Pirate's Cove. Can you find out this information for me please? Thanks, Zahra.

Using the **Bookings** database, create a query based on the **Visitors** table that selects all records where **Ticket Type** is either **Junior** or **Senior**. Run the query, note the number of records selected (31), and then save the query as **Tickets**.

> I forgot to mention, from the records found, can you also tell me how many attended an activity on or before August 1st 2011, and what that activity's code was? Thanks again, Zahra.

Edit the **Tickets** query so that only records where the **Visit Date** field is less than or equal to **01/08/2011** are selected. Add the **Activity** field to the query and run it (25 records).

> One last thing – for the records you have found, can you include the names of each visitor and then sort the list alphabetically by surname? Can you then create a report based on this data? Z.

Edit the **Tickets** query so that the **Title**, **First Name** and **Last Name** fields are included in the query, and sort the **Last Name** field in ascending order. Run and save the query, and then create a new report based on it. Change the title to **Concessions** and the page orientation to landscape. Save the report as **Concessions** and print it for *Zahra*.

8 | Internet & E-Mail

8

I work in the *IT Centre* at *Big Planet Theme Park's* head office – a building that only staff members are allowed to enter. It is my job to make sure all of the ICT systems in the park work properly by fixing problems and keeping everything up to date with the latest hardware and software upgrades.

A lot of my time is spent providing IT support directly to park staff via e-mail, which is a really quick and easy way to communicate with people. However, even though I'm a computer expert, I'm still often faced with problems I don't know how to fix. Fortunately, the answers can usually be found on the Internet... if you know where to look, of course.

It is worth remembering that using e-mail and the Internet in education or at work is slightly different to using it at home. As you will find out in this section, to protect you and your place of study or employment, there are usually strict rules on what you can and can't do online.

What you will learn:

In this chapter you will use an Internet browser and the *Microsoft* e-mail program *Outlook* to help *John* complete a number of everyday tasks at *Big Planet Theme Park*.

Knowledge, skills and understanding:

* Use an Internet browser to successfully search for and download information

* Learn to evaluate the relevance of the information that you find online

* Avoid common pitfalls and be aware of copyright and other legal issues

* Use e-mail and the Internet to communicate with others

* Work accurately, safely and securely

Data files

 Data files needed to complete the activities in this section are provided in the **Section 8** data files folder. Files that you create (or e-mail file attachments that you receive) can also be saved to the same folder.

8.1 Internet Basics

The **Internet**, or net for short, is a global network of linked computer systems that allows people from all over the world to communicate and share information. Many different types of computer equipment are able to connect to the Internet, from desktop and laptop computers to mobile phones and printers. By connecting to the Internet, both you and your devices are able to interact with and benefit from the many features and services that it offers.

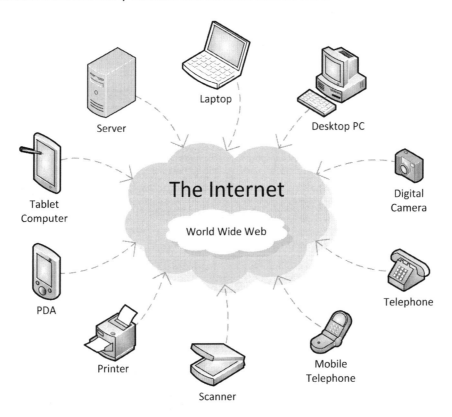

Most people use the Internet to access the **World Wide Web**; a vast collection of interconnected files called **web pages**. At its most basic, each web page is simply a document containing information in the form of text and images. However, most web pages today also contain a variety of other multimedia features including video, music, and interactive programs.

> **Note:**   The World Wide Web is not the same thing as the Internet – in fact, "the web" is just one of the many services that runs on the Internet.

To move between web pages on the Internet you use **hyperlinks**. With a single click of the mouse, a hyperlink allows you to quickly and easily move to another web page anywhere else on the World Wide Web. As each page links to other pages, which in turn link to many more, you can see where the concept of a "web" of information comes from.

> **Note:**   Web pages are stored on computers called **servers**. These are very similar to your own home or work computer, but they are always connected to the Internet and usually have vastly more storage space.

When combined, two or more related web pages form a **website**. This is a fairly loose term which refers to any collection of web pages that belong together (in the same way that the individual pages of a printed magazine belong together). Most web pages in a website also share the same basic design features and are usually located on the same server.

8.2 Surfing the Web

The World Wide Web contains an enormous amount of information covering almost every subject you can think of. If that wasn't enough, vital services such as online banking, shopping, health care, news, and even education can now all be accessed online. In fact, as the Internet has no international boundaries, you can interact with websites *anywhere* in the world, from local councils and businesses to multinational companies and organisations.

To access this vast worldwide "web" of information, you must use a special type of software known as a **web browser**.

Activity:

1. *John* has created a website which he uses to help train new staff members at *Big Planet Theme Park*. It contains a lot of interesting information including files to download and links to other useful websites.

2. Start the *Internet Explorer* application.

> **Note:** *John* recommends that you use the popular *Internet Explorer* web browser. If you choose to use a different application, some of the features mentioned in this section may appear and function slightly differently to that described.

3. Click once in the **Address Bar** at the top of the browser window and enter the following website address: **www.bigplanetsupport.co.uk**

Address
Bar

> **Note:** Always make sure you enter a web address *precisely*. One character out of place and you may be taken to another website.

4.   Press <**Enter**>. The *Big Planet Support* website's home page is downloaded and displayed.

Navigation links

5.   Locate the **Navigation** hyperlinks on the left of the home page. These "links" will appear on every web page on the *Big Planet Support* website.

6.   Move your mouse pointer over **Hyperlinks**. The pointer changes to a hand, 👆, indicating this is a link to another web page.

7.   Click <u>once</u> to display the **Hyperlinks** page (you should not double click links), and then read the information about the types of hyperlink that exist.

8.   Click the browser's **Back** button, ⬅, to return to the previous page.

9.   Notice that the browser's **Forward** button, ➡, is now available. Click this once to revisit the **Hyperlinks** page again.

> **Note:**   If you move back to a previously viewed web page, the **Forward** button can be used to move forward again (unless another link is clicked). If there are no more pages to move back or forward to, these buttons will become ghosted (inactive).

10.   Next, click **Image Gallery** link from the **Navigation** hyperlinks on the left of the page and then follow the **Cartoons** hyperlink.

> **Note:**   Notice that the **Cartoons** hyperlink appears as a subentry under the **Image Gallery** hyperlink. This is a common technique for allowing visitors to quickly "drill down" to increasing levels of detail with each click.

11.   Use the **Back** button to return to the *Big Planet Support* website's home page.

> **Note:**   As you browse the web you will probably visit web pages that you would like to return to later. If so, use your browser's **Favorites** (or **Bookmarks**) feature to record a link to the site.

12.   Leave the *Big Planet Support* website open for the next exercise.

8.3   Tabbed Browsing

Normally, when you click a hyperlink, the web page it connects to is downloaded and displayed (replacing the web page that was previously open). However, it is possible to have more than one page open at the same time, each contained within its own **Tab**.

> **Note:**   Tabs are a useful way to explore links without needing to navigate away from a web page. They can really help improve your productivity when browsing.

Activity:

1.   With the *Big Planet Support* website open, right-click once on the **Image Gallery** hyperlink. A pop-up shortcut menu appears.

> **Note:**   Notice that you can open the link in a new *window* which will appear as a separate item on the *Windows* **Taskbar**. There is not much difference between opening new tabs and opening new windows. However, you will often find it easier to open new tabs as this keeps all of the websites you are browsing in one place.

2.   For this exercise, select **Open in new tab**.

> **Note:**   If you chose to use a web browser other than *Internet Explorer*, specific menu options such as **Open in new tab** may appear slightly differently to that described.

3. The **Image Gallery** web page is opened in a new tab which appears at the top of the browser window.

4. If the new tab is not automatically selected, click it once now to activate it.

Close
Tab

5. Click the **Computers** hyperlink shown on the **Image Gallery** page. Then, select any of the image previews (known as "thumbnails") to open a larger version of that picture.

> **Note:**   Each tab maintains its own list of recently viewed web pages that can be accessed using the **Forward** and **Back** buttons.

6. Click the **Back** button once to return to the previous page (**Computers**).

7. Notice that the active tab has a **Close Tab** button. Click this once to close the new tab and return to the first tab (which still shows the site's home page).

8. Next, click the **Useful Links** hyperlink. A page containing a number of hyperlinks to other websites is downloaded and displayed in the current tab.

> **Note:**   The creator of a web page can design a link to always open in a new tab/window.

9. Click any hyperlink that interests you from the **News and Current Affairs** group. This time, the linked web page is opened automatically in a new **Tab** (which may appear in its own window). The links were set up by *John* to do this when clicked.

> **Note:**   Each web page that you visit is recorded in your browser's **History**. This list of recently viewed items is stored for 20 days (by default) and can be used to revisit web pages again at a later date. If you would like to delete this log of your online activity, you can do so at any time from within your browser settings.

10. Feel free to explore the content of the selected website.

> **Note:**   To reload a page and download the most up-to-date information, click the browser's **Refresh** button, ↻ (also sometimes known as the **Reload** button).

11. When you are finished, close the new tab (or window, if the new tab appeared in one).

12. You can explore some of the other hyperlinks on the **Useful Links** page, but remember to close each tab when you are finished.

> **Note:** Within your browser settings you can also set up a favourite website as your default **Home** page. This will always be displayed when you start the browser and can be returned to again at any time using the **Home** button, .

13. Leave the *Big Planet Support* website open for the next exercise.

8.4 Copying Text and Pictures

Text and pictures can easily be copied from the World Wide Web and used in other *Windows* applications. However, unless you have the permission of the owner or creator of these items, international **copyright** restrictions prohibit you from using them in your own work.

> **Note:** It is <u>very important</u> that you do not use or distribute any material obtained from the Internet unless you are totally sure that copyright restrictions do not apply.

Activity:

1. The *Big Planet Support* website should still be open. As *John* created this website, he has given you permission to copy content from it during this exercise.

2. Click the **Information** hyperlink, and then follow the link to **Internet**.

3. Select the main body of text on this page (i.e. from "**This page contains information about the Internet**…" to "…**explore the World Wide Web for yourself.**").

> **Note:** There are two ways of copying selected text from a web page: use either <**Ctrl C**> or right click and choose **Copy** from the shortcut menu that appears.

4. Press <**Ctrl C**> on your keyboard. The selected text is copied to the **Clipboard**.

5. Start *Microsoft Word* (and a new blank document).

6. With the cursor flashing at the beginning of the empty document, click the **Paste** button on the **Ribbon**. The copied text from the web page is pasted into the new *Word* document.

> **Note:** Notice that the formatting of the text is preserved. **Paste Special** can be used if **Unformatted Text** is required.

7. Without closing *Word*, use the **Taskbar** to return to your web browser application. Visit the **Image Gallery** page and then follow the link to **Places**. Click any picture that you like to view a larger version.

8. Right click the picture and select **Copy**. The selected picture has now been copied.

> **Note:** **Save picture as** (or similar, depending on your chosen browser) can also be used to save a picture directly to your computer's **My Pictures** folder.

9. Return to *Word* and paste the copied picture at the end of the document.

> **Note:** This technique can be used to copy and paste text and pictures into most other *Microsoft Office* applications.

10. Save the document as **information** in the data files folder for this section, and then close *Word*.

11. Click the hyperlink labelled **Home** to return to the *Big Planet Support* home page.

> **Note:** Nearly all web pages feature a link back to a website's main home page. Hint: if you can't find this, try clicking the site's logo at the top of the page.

8.5 Downloading Files

Information on the World Wide Web is not just available as simple text and images. Many types of multimedia files that contain video and audio content can also be downloaded. In addition, you can also download documents, spreadsheets, presentations, publications and databases that you can open and use in *Microsoft Office*.

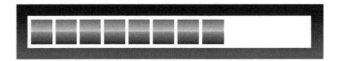

Furthermore, new software programs and updates can be downloaded and installed on your computer to add new features (but this is usually not allowed on shared or public computers).

Activity:

1. The *Big Planet Support* website should still be open. Visit the **Downloads** page using the **Navigation** hyperlinks.

2. This page contains a number of files that you can download. Click on the hyperlink **Apollo.wav** (under **Audio**) to start downloading a small sound clip.

Audio:

- Apollo.wav: A small audio clip (67Kb)
- Berlio.wav: A small audio clip (114Kb)

> **Note:** Your browser's security settings will ask you to confirm that you really want to download this file. As you will find out later, file downloads from the Internet can be a potential source of viruses that can damage your computer. However, the files available on the *Big Planet Support* website are quite safe to use.

3. When a security message appears, select **Open** (or similar, depending on your chosen browser) from the list of options available. The file is downloaded and plays automatically in your computer's default music player (you may need to **Allow** this file to play).

> **Note:** Files downloaded in this way are only saved *temporarily* on your computer.

4. When the music finishes playing, close the media player to return to your web browser.

5. Next, download and open the video file **Ocean.avi**. The file is downloaded and plays again automatically in your computer's default video player (you may need to **Allow** this first).

6. When the video finishes playing, close the media player. Then, download the document **Testimonial.doc**. When opened, this document appears in *Microsoft Word*.

7. Close *Word* to return to your web browser.

8. Files can also be downloaded and saved to your computer in a specific folder. Right click on the hyperlink **Turnover.xls** and select **Save target as** (or similar).

9. In the dialog box that appears, locate the data files folder for this section and click **Save**. The spreadsheet file **Turnover.xls** is saved to your computer.

10. Use the **Start Menu** to open the **My Documents** folder and navigate to the data files for this section. Double click the **Turnover** file to open it in *Microsoft Excel*.

11. Close *Excel* and your **My Documents** folder, leaving only your web browser open.

8.6 Search Engines

The Internet can be used to find information on almost any subject you can think of. However, finding the exact information you want from the billions and billions of websites on the World Wide Web is not always so easy. To help, you can use a **search engine**.

As you probably already know, a search engine is a website that you can use to search for **keywords** on other web pages. Although a search engine may look simple, behind the scenes it is connected to a very large and complex database. When you perform a search, the search engine *very quickly* selects every web page in the database that contains your keywords. These pages are then presented to you as a list of hyperlinks.

> **Note:** The web pages that a search engine finds are often referred to as **hits**.

There are many useful search engines available on the web, some of which are more specialised that others. Today, the best and most popular *general* search engines include:

Google	**www.google.co.uk**
Bing	**www.bing.com**
Yahoo	**www.yahoo.co.uk**
Ask	**www.ask.com**

In this exercise you will only use the *Google* search engine. This is probably the best search engine available and *John* highly recommends it for general everyday use. Of course, the search techniques that you learn in this exercise will apply equally well to any other search engine that you choose to use in the future.

Activity:

1. Your web browser should still be open. Enter **www.google.co.uk** in the **Address Bar** and press <**Enter**>. The **Google** search engine appears.

Search box

> **Note:** All search engines have a search box where you can enter keywords, and a button to start the search. However, as websites change frequently, the page you see may not exactly match the screens shown in this section.

2. *John* is working on a research project and needs to find the names of other competing *theme parks* in the *UK*. In the **Search** box, enter **park** and press <**Enter**>.

> **Note:** *Google* may automatically start searching as you enter keywords. It may also provide a number of search suggestions as you type. If the search text you are entering appears, you can simply select it to save time.

3. *Google* finds every site in its database which contains the required keyword **park**. Make a note of the number of results found (which will be shown at the top of the page).

park

About 2,990,000,000 results (0.10 seconds)

4. All of the web pages found are placed in order of relevance, with the first ten or so *most* relevant pages shown first. Scan the results and notice that a number of pages have been found which have nothing to do with theme parks.

> **Note:** As well as providing hyperlinks to web pages where your keywords were found, *Google* also shows a small extract of the text on those pages.

5. Let's try to make your search a little more specific. At the top of the page, change the current keyword text to **theme park** and press <**Enter**>.

6. The number of results found is now far smaller. Scan the results and notice that the web pages now seem much more relevant.

> **Note:** The best way to find accurate and relevant information on the web is to use the most suitable keywords in your searches.

7. To narrow the search even further, change the keyword search text to **UK theme park** and press <**Enter**>. The results found are again fewer and more relevant.

8. However, have you noticed that the search keywords can appear in any order in the results? To search for the specific phrase **UK theme park** only (with all of the words in that *exact* order) place quotation marks around the keywords in the search box at the top of the page and press <**Enter**>.

> "UK theme park"
>
> About 41,600 results (0.15 seconds)

> **Note:** The quotation mark symbol can usually be inserted by pressing <**Shift 2**>.

9. The number of results will be further reduced and only web pages that feature the exact phrase "UK theme park" somewhere in the text will be displayed.

10. Remember that *John* was searching for the names of other theme parks in the UK. Examine the results found, and then visit the web page that seems most relevant.

> **Note:** If you find it difficult to read the text on a web page you can adjust the **Zoom** level in your browser's settings.

11. If the selected web page does not contain the information *John* requires, click the **Back** button and try another. If the first set of *Google* search results is not relevant you can view more by clicking the **Next** link at the bottom of the page.

> **Note:** The first page you visit on a website may not contain all of the information you need, but other pages on that website might. You may need to explore.

12. When you are finished, use the **Back** button to return to *Google*.

13. For his research project, *John* wants you to find out about the history of the *Ferris wheel*. In particular, he wants to know when the first one was created and who built it.

14. Use *Google* now to find out this information before moving on.

15. How did you do? Although there are many ways to search for this information, *John* used the search **ferris wheel created by** to find out that George W. Ferris created the first Ferris wheel in 1893.

16. Next, *John* wants to see if you can use *Google* to find out about the first ever *steel roller coaster*. He wants to know when it was built and what is was called, but isn't at all interested in wooden roller coasters. Try to find this out now.

17. Did you find the relevant information? *John* used the search **first steel -wooden roller coaster** to find out that the first tubular steel roller coaster, the *Matterhorn*, was opened in 1959.

18. Finally, *John* recalls a famous quote he would like to include in his research project: *"Here age relives fond memories of the past, and here youth may savor the challenge and promise of the future"*. So that *John* can use this quote, can you use *Google* to find out who said it?

19. *John* used the search **"age relives fond memories of the past" quote** to find out that that it was *Walt Disney* who said this.

20. Well done. Close your web browser and any open tabs.

8.7 Search Tips

When you use a search engine such as *Google* to find information, remember these following useful tips:

✱ Keep your search simple and only use keywords that are important and relevant (search engines will generally ignore common words like **and, an, of, where, when, is,** etc).

✱ The more precise your keywords, the more likely you are to find useful results. For example, **theme park** will produce more specific results than just **park**.

✱ Be descriptive and enter keywords as you think they will appear on a web page. For example, **park admission prices** will produce better results than **park entry costs**.

✱ If initial results are too broad, you can refine your search by adding more keywords.

✱ Remember that you can use quotation marks to find specific phrases.

✱ Use the minus operator to exclude results that contain keywords you do not want.

* It doesn't matter if you use upper or lower case text.

* Don't bother to include general punctuation marks as these are usually ignored.

* Be prepared to follow more than one search result to find the information you need. It really does pay to be patient and explore a selection of results.

> **Note:** These search techniques will work with all general search engines, not just *Google*.

8.8 Evaluating Information

Don't believe everything you read on the Internet! Unlike professionally published material such as books and newspapers, there is no quality control online – the contents of a website do not need to be reviewed, approved or checked for accuracy. As such, you need to stop and consider how trustworthy information is <u>before</u> you use it. This is not always easy to do, but the following useful tips will help:

* Consider the source of the material that you are reading. Who has written it and why, and do they have any evidence to support their claims?

* Consider the publisher's authority in their area. Are they well known for producing reliable and credible information?

* What is the intention of the publisher? Is the information they are providing aimed at informing you of facts, presenting a viewpoint, persuading you of a belief, or trying to sell you something?

* Forums or "blog" posts will most likely be based on biased, one-sided opinion. You should take care when using information of this type.

* The articles stored on editable web pages or "wiki" sites (i.e. *Wikipedia*) are created by the general public – not experts – and should not be fully trusted.

* Well known and legitimate business websites are much more trustworthy, but they are also likely to be biased towards promoting their own products and company goals.

* Materials obtained from well known government or scientific sources (e.g. the *National Geographic* website) are usually a good source of reliable and accurate information.

* Consider the age of the information you find. It could be out of date and no longer relevant.

* Finally, try to confirm specific details by visiting more than one web page.

Remember, someone may ask you to justify your findings (or they may even make decisions based upon them) so you need to be confident that the facts and figures you use are totally reliable, accurate, and fit for purpose.

8.9 Communicating Online

There are many ways to interact with other people online. As the Internet has no international boundaries, you can talk freely to friends, family, colleagues, organisations and services throughout the world – instantly and with little or no cost. In fact, modern ICT has completely changed the way we communicate with each other and do business, giving us access to a worldwide network of advice, debate, feedback, opinion, conversation, support and knowledge. The following table briefly describes the most popular technologies available today.

Technology	Description
E-mail	Short for electronic mail, this basic ICT system for sending short messages and files to other people online is still the most dominant form of online communication – especially in business. You will find out a lot more about e-mail from exercise 8.12 onwards.
Instant Messages	With *Instant Messaging* tools you always know when your contacts are online and can easily start a text or video based conversation in "real-time". These tools are very useful for communication with colleagues instantly and can be used to request help and support.
Skype	*Voice over Internet Protocol* (VoIP) software such as *Skype* can turn your PC into a phone, allowing you to talk to friends, family, colleagues and customers anywhere in the world.
Forums	Businesses and people with similar interests can share their views and post messages on specifically dedicated websites called forums or discussion boards. These can also be used for requesting help and support from others who are often experts in their own fields.
Social Networking	Social networking sites such as *Facebook* and *Twitter* allow people to communicate with friends and family online (by sharing photos and comments). As this is a recreational service, social networking is regarded as an inappropriate use of time at work.

Note: Many Internet technologies can be really useful for working with other people online. However, it is very important that you respect the **Internet usage policy** of the organisation or business that is providing your access. This document will tell you what you can and can't do online and is designed to prevent damaging, illegal, inappropriate or unacceptable use of the Internet.

For beginners, getting involved in e-mail discussions and posting messages online can often be a very daunting and scary prospect. Fortunately, a few simple rules exist to help you use these technologies safely and considerately (which you will learn more about in the next exercise).

Note: Always remember that your views and opinions are as valid as anyone else's, and your contributions or requests for help and advice are very welcome.

8.10 Netiquette

When you are working online it is very easy to forget your basic manners and say things that you would never say in a face-to-face conversation. Therefore, before you interact with others online or via e-mail, try to familiarise yourself with the rules of **netiquette** - "network etiquette":

* Behave online as you would in real life, and respect other people and their opinions.

* Be clear and keep your contributions brief, accurate and relevant.

* Be tolerant of others, and never send angry messages (known as **flames**).

* Use appropriate language (especially when representing a business).

* Don't use UPPERCASE words – this is the same as shouting.

* Make sure your contributions are spelled correctly and make sense.

* Avoid forwarding irrelevant junk e-mail, jokes and chain messages.

* Always respect copyright and data protection laws.

* Don't post anything that could get you into trouble or embarrass you in the future!

> **Note:**   Whether at work or in education, you have a responsibility to act professionally and make a good impression when communicating with others.

Unfortunately, no matter how well-mannered you are online, you will eventually read comments or interact with others who are not so considerate. Inappropriate behaviour and offensive material is a constant problem on the Internet and you will do well to simply ignore it. However, if any behaviour or content is particularly offensive or worrying (for example, if you feel you are being bullied or that another person is at risk) you <u>must</u> report this to a person in authority.

8.11 Staying Safe

The Internet is an amazing resource and people find new uses for it every day. However, all of this potential and freedom does have a price – your privacy and safety.

Fortunately, you can avoid many of the risks involved in using ICT with a little common sense:

* Firstly, always be careful when downloading files of any sort from the Internet. Unless you *completely* trust the source of the file, it may contain damaging viruses and other malware that can harm your computer or allow criminals to steal information from it.

* Always run up-to-date antivirus software. If you do download a file, scan it <u>first</u> using the antivirus software before you open or run it (if you are using a computer outside of the home, locate the antivirus software that is installed and learn how to scan files with it).

✱ To prevent other people from accessing your computer and stealing the data it contains, always make sure your **Windows Firewall** is running. Furthermore, if you receive any security alerts from *Windows*, attend to them immediately.

✱ Keep your computer up-to-date with the latest security updates.

✱ Treat your own (and other people's) personal information with the respect it deserves. Don't give out private information online unless you <u>fully</u> trust the person or company who is receiving it and you completely understand what it will be used for.

✱ Always ignore invitations to win prizes and download free software and files – these will often contain viruses and other malware. Also keep an eye out for fake websites and only purchase items from legitimate and well known sources.

✱ If you ever submit private information online (for example, when purchasing items on shopping websites), make sure the padlock symbol, 🔒, appears in your browser's **Address Bar**. This helps guarantee that nobody else can see what you are doing and stops criminals getting hold of your personal details.

✱ Don't trust that people are who they say they are. This may seem obvious, but people can very easily exaggerate or lie about their identities to mislead you. <u>Never</u> give personal contact details to – or arrange to meet – people you don't know.

✱ When at work or in education, do not use the Internet for personal activities.

✱ Avoid downloading copyright music or videos. As well as being illegal (and you can get into a lot of trouble for doing it), these files can often contain viruses and malware.

Remember that it is your responsibility to protect your own safety and that of others who you work or study with. If you allow a virus to gain access to and damage your own computer, it can also spread and cause harm to other systems that you share a network with – so be careful! Also remember that the *Data Protection Act* requires you to treat other people's information and customer data with care.

8.12 E-mail Basics

By far the most popular use of the Internet today is sending and receiving electronic mail (**e-mail**). E-mail is an extremely important communication tool that allows people to send messages to other ICT users anywhere in the world instantly. Think about how much more quickly business documents can be sent using e-mail rather than by surface or airmail.

The following exercises will introduce you to *Microsoft Outlook*, a popular e-mail program that allows you to send, receive and organise e-mail messages. *Outlook* can also be used to attach files to messages and maintain an address book of contacts.

> **Note:** There are many online services that you can use to send and receive your personal e-mail. However, in most professional situations, an e-mail program such as *Outlook* is used.

8.13 E-mail Addresses

Before you can fully use *Outlook* or any other e-mail system, you will first need your own **e-mail address**. In the same way that a phone number uniquely identifies you on a telephone network, your e-mail address uniquely identifies you on the Internet. E-mail addresses all follow the same general format, as the following example shows:

john@bigplanetsupport.co.uk

The **@** symbol is pronounced "at" and is used to separate a person's username from the name of their organisation or Internet Service Provider (ISP).

> **Note:** If you do not know your own e-mail address, contact the person who runs your computer network. If you are a home user, contact your Internet Service Provider.

8.14 Using Microsoft Outlook

Outlook stores all of your e-mail messages in a number of different folders. This folder structure is known as your **mailbox**.

Activity:

1.   Start *Microsoft Outlook*.

> **Note:** If you are prompted to connect to the Internet or select a profile, do that now.

> **Note:** If the **Internet Connection Wizard** or **Add New Account** dialog box appears when you start *Outlook*, your computer is not ready to use e-mail. It is recommended that you find somebody who can help you set up an account.

2.   Examine the *Outlook* window. Notice that this view features **Menu Bars** and **Toolbars** rather than a **Ribbon** (the **Ribbon** will appear when creating a new e-mail or contact).

> **Note:** The various panes can be resized or hidden by dragging their boundary bars.

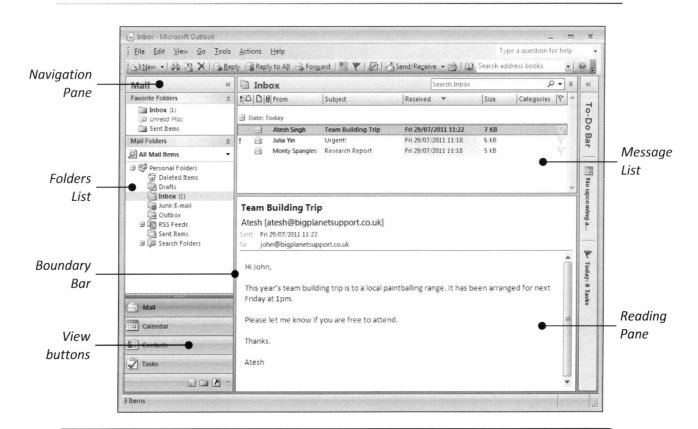

> **Note:**   Your screen may not look exactly like that shown above as there are many display options available.

3.   Locate the **Navigation Pane** on the left of the window. If your **Inbox** folder is not currently selected in the **Folders List**, select it now (make sure the **Mail** view button is selected, as shown above).

> **Note:**   If your screen does not match *John's*, display the **View** menu and make sure **Navigation Pane** is set to **Normal**, **To-Do Bar** is set to **Minimized**, and **Reading Pane** is set to **Bottom**.

4.   All messages that you receive are placed in your **Inbox** folder. These will appear in the **Message List**. Any message selected in the **Message List** will be previewed in the **Reading Pane**.

5.   You will explore other mailbox folders and features in later exercises. For now, leave *Outlook* open for the next exercise.

8.15 Creating a Message

New e-mail messages can be created easily in *Outlook*. All you need is the e-mail address of the recipient (the person you are sending the message to). Always be careful when you enter an address, however, as one letter out of place will result in the message being returned "undelivered" or – even worse – going to the wrong person.

Activity:

1. With *Outlook* open and your **Inbox** selected, click the **New** button, 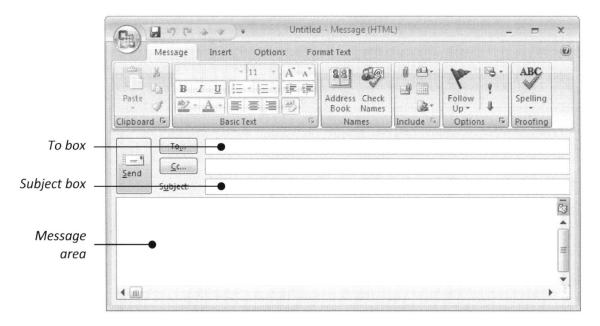, on the **Toolbar** to start a new e-mail message. An **Untitled Message** window appears.

> **Note:** To give you more space to work in, you can **Maximize** the message window.

2. Notice that the cursor is currently flashing in the **To** box (if it is not, click inside the **To** box now). The **To** box is where you enter the e-mail address of the person who will receive the message. For this exercise, type in <u>your own</u> e-mail address.

> **Note:** Entering your own e-mail address in the **To** box will cause any message you send to be immediately returned to you. This allows you to observe the results of sending messages. Sending a message to another person follows exactly the same steps.

3. Click once in the **Subject** box. The text you enter here is used to briefly describe the content of your e-mail message; it allows the person who receives your message to see at a glance what it is all about.

4. Enter the following subject text: **Functional Skills**.

> **Note:** It is good practice to always enter a short but <u>relevant</u> subject for every new message that you create.

5.   Click once in the **Message Area**. Notice that the title of the e-mail, shown on the **Title Bar**, now changes to **Functional Skills**.

6.   Type the following message (including the obvious spelling mistakes):

> **I am sendin this e-mail messige as part of my studies for Functional Skills. I hope it meets with your apruval.**

Note: Notice that the spelling mistakes are underlined in red as you type. These will be corrected in the next exercise.

---

7.   Press <**Enter**> twice and type your name. Leave the message open for the next exercise.

8.16 Sending a Message

Before you send any e-mail message, you should first use *Outlook's* spell checking feature to check for errors. Once an e-mail has been sent, it is practically impossible to get it back again!

Activity:

1.   The **Functional Skills** e-mail created in the previous exercise should still be open. On the **Ribbon**, click the **Spelling** button (not the drop-down arrow).

2.   The **Spelling and Grammar** dialog box appears. If an error is found, you can choose to **Ignore** it or **Change** the selected word to one of the **Suggestions** given.

3.   Correct any errors found. When a message appears informing you that **The spelling check is complete**, click **OK** to close it. The message is now ready to be sent.

> I am sending this e-mail message as part of my studies for Functional Skills. I hope it meets with your approval.
>
> John|

4.   Click the **Send** button (found to the left of the **To** box).

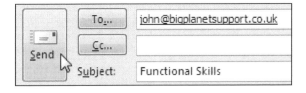

5.   The message window is closed automatically and the e-mail is sent to your **Outbox**.

Note: E-mail messages that you send are first moved to your **Outbox** folder. If you are connected to the Internet they will be sent immediately from there. If you are not, messages will remain in your **Outbox** until you do connect.

---

6. Select the **Outbox** folder in the **Folders List**. Any messages waiting to be sent are shown.

7. If your **Outbox** is empty then your message has already been sent. If it is not empty, then click the **Send/Receive** button on the **Toolbar**.

> **Note:** The **Send/Receive** button forces *Outlook* to send any waiting messages. A progress dialog box (or message on the **Status Bar**) may appear for a moment as the message is sent. If you are prompted to connect to the Internet, please do so.

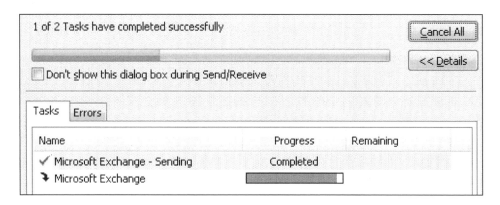

8. Your message has now been sent. Select the **Sent Items** folder in the **Folders List**. A copy of the **Functional Skills** message is saved here.

9. Return to your **Inbox** folder and leave it open for the next exercise.

8.17 Receiving a Message

When you receive an e-mail it is stored in your **Inbox** folder. New and unread messages are shown in the **Message List** in bold type with an unopened envelope icon, ✉. Once you read the message its icon changes to an open envelope, 📨.

> **Note:** When you are not using *Outlook*, messages are stored for you until they are collected. You do not need to keep the program running all of the time.

Activity:

1. After a short time you will receive the message that you sent to your own address in the previous exercise. If it has not appeared in your **Inbox** yet, use the **Send/Receive** button to check for new messages.

> **Note:**   It sometimes takes a little while for messages to be sent and returned to you.

2.   Notice the closed envelope icon and bold text for this message on the **Message List**. This indicates that the received message has not yet been read.

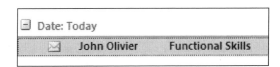

> **Note:**   E-mail messages are stored on a mail server where they will remain until you download them. *Outlook* will regularly check for new messages automatically, but clicking the **Send/Receive** button forces it to check immediately.

3.   The name on the message indicates who the e-mail was sent from, next to the time it was received (and date if received on a previous day). Click the message once on the **Message List**, if it is not already selected, to preview its contents in the **Reading Pane**.

4.   Double click the e-mail on the **Message List** to open it in a new window. Notice the features available on the **Ribbon**.

5.   Close the e-mail by clicking the **Close** button, ⊠, found towards the top right corner of the message window.

6.   Notice the **Functional Skills** e-mail on the **Message List**. The closed envelope icon will have changed to an open envelope and the bold formatting will be removed. This indicates that the message has now been read.

> **Note:**   Sometimes you will open an e-mail but not have time to read it. Being able to mark items as **Unread** so that you can return to read them later is a very useful feature.

7.   To mark the **Functional Skills** e-mail as **Unread** again, display the **Edit** menu and select **Mark as Unread**. The open envelope icon changes back to a closed envelope and the text to bold.

8.   Leave your **Inbox** open for the next exercise.

8.18 Replying to Messages

When you receive an e-mail message, it is very easy to create and send a reply. A message window will appear where your reply text can be entered.

Activity:

1. With the **Functional Skills** e-mail still selected, click the **Reply** button, 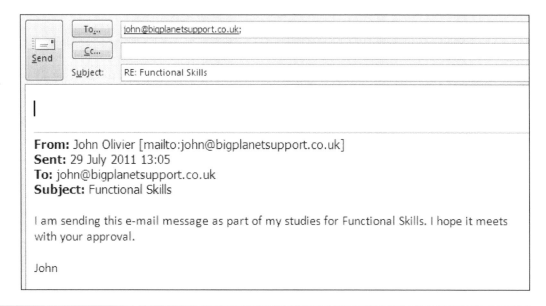, on the **Toolbar**. A message window, addressed to the sender of the original message (you), will appear.

To... john@bigplanetsupport.co.uk;

Cc...

Subject: RE: Functional Skills

From: John Olivier [mailto:john@bigplanetsupport.co.uk]
Sent: 29 July 2011 13:05
To: john@bigplanetsupport.co.uk
Subject: Functional Skills

I am sending this e-mail message as part of my studies for Functional Skills. I hope it meets with your approval.

John

> **Note:** For reference, the text of the original message is displayed below your reply.

2. Notice that the **Subject** begins with **RE:** indicating a reply to a previous message.

3. Enter the following text in the **Message Area** (above the original message):

    Thank you for your message. Good luck.

> **Note:** Notice that your reply appears in a different colour to the original message text.

4. Send the e-mail. After a moment you will receive the e-mail reply (which was again addressed to yourself). Remember to use the **Send/Receive** button if necessary to check for new messages.

5. Select the reply in the **Message List** to examine it.

    ### RE: Functional Skills

    John Olivier [john@bigplanetsupport.co.uk]

    Sent: Fri 29/07/2011 13:31
    To: john@bigplanetsupport.co.uk

    Thank you for your message. Good luck.

6. Leave your **Inbox** open for the next exercise.

8.19 Forwarding Messages

A message that you receive can also be forwarded to another person. In business, always consider the *Data Protection Act* and be careful to only forward messages to authorised people.

Activity:

1. The reply that you sent in the previous exercise should currently be selected in your **Inbox**. To forward this message, click the **Forward** button on the **Toolbar**. Notice that the **Subject** now begins with **FW:** indicating a forwarded message.

2. Enter your <u>own</u> e-mail address in the **To** box again so that you can observe the results of this exercise. In the **Message Area**, enter the following text:

    Here is a copy of a message I thought might interest you.

3. Send the e-mail.

4. After a moment you will receive the forwarded e-mail (which was again addressed to yourself). Remember to use the **Send/Receive** button if necessary to check for new messages.

5. Select the forwarded message in the **Message List** to open and examine it, and then leave your **Inbox** open for the next exercise.

8.20 Creating Contacts

Over time you will find that many of the e-mail messages that you create will be sent to the same group of people (your "contacts"). Often these will be friends, family, or work colleagues. To avoid having to remember their e-mail addresses and contact details, you can store them in *Outlook's* **Contacts** (also known as the **Address Book**).

Activity:

1. From the *Outlook* **Navigation Pane**, click the **Contacts** view button.

2. The **Contacts** view appears. If you have never used this view before it is likely that the list will be empty.

3. To create a new **Contact**, click the **New** button on the **Toolbar** (the default action of the **New** button changes depending on the current view).

4. An **Untitled Contact** window appears. Enter your own personal details into the text boxes (you do not need to complete every box). Make sure you enter your real e-mail address correctly, however, as this will be used in later exercises.

> **Note:** If any further dialog boxes appear (e.g. prompts to check full name or conversion of telephone numbers), click **Cancel** to continue.

5.   After all of the information has been entered, click the **Save & Close** button in the **Actions** group. A personalised contact has now been created for you.

6.   The new contact will appear as a "virtual" **Business Card**. If it does not, make sure **Business Cards** is selected in the **Current View** group on the **Navigation Pane**.

7.   *John* often sends information to *Fiona* at reception. Click the **New Contact** button again and enter her contact details:

Full Name:	**Fiona Jones**
Company:	**Big Planet Support**
Job Title:	**Reception Manager**
E-mail:	**fiona@bigplanetsupport.co.uk**
Business Phone:	**0770 0900 823**

> **Note:** Always make sure you enter details accurately, especially e-mail addresses and phone numbers. Personal details such as date of birth, nickname, spouse's name or anniversary can also be included by selecting **Details** in the **Show** group.

8.   **Save & Close** the new contact. The contact's business card is created.

9.   Click the **Mail** view button on the **Navigation Pane** to return to your mailbox, and then leave your **Inbox** folder open for the next exercise.

8.21   Using Contacts

When you create a new e-mail message (or forward a message to another person), you can use your list of **Contacts** to quickly look up and select e-mail addresses.

Activity:

1.   *John* wants to send a very important message to *Fiona* about a new computer that has arrived for her department. Use the **New** button to start a new message.

2.   Locate the **To** button. This can be used to select one or more e-mail addresses of people in your **Contacts** list.

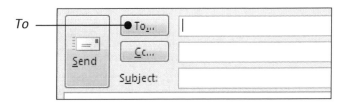

3.   Click the **To** button to display your list of contacts.

> **Note:**   It is possible to have more than one list of contacts. For example, if your computer is connected to a network, other lists containing the details and e-mail addresses of other users may appear in the **Address Book** drop-down box.

4.   Select the entry for **Fiona Jones** and then click the **To** button, To ->. Her e-mail address is copied to the **To** box.

5.   Click **OK**. Her e-mail address now also appears in the e-mail's **To** box.

> **Note:**   If you would like other people to receive a copy of a message, their e-mail addresses can be entered in the **Cc** box (which stands for **Carbon copy**). Typically, recipients of carbon copies are not regarded as participants in a conversation but as observers. For example, if you send an important e-mail to a customer, you could also send a carbon copy to your manager for information purposes.

6.   Click the **Cc** button (below the **To** button) to open your list of contacts again.

7.   Select your own contact record and click the **Cc** button, Cc ->. Your e-mail address is copied to the **Cc** box. Click **OK**.

8.   Enter the e-mail message subject: **Your new computer**. Then, enter the following message in the **Message Area**:

> **Hi Fiona,**
>
> **The new computer that you requested for reception is now ready to collect from head office. Could you please pick it up before 5pm today?**
>
> **Thanks.**

9.   Leave the message open for the next exercise.

> **Note:**   It is best to use as little formatting as possible in e-mail messages. Fancy fonts and colours look very unprofessional, can be distracting for the reader, and don't always appear correctly. However, simple formatting such as bold, italic and underline – used sparingly – can be used to help emphasize important points.

8.22 Message Priority

It is possible to change an e-mail message's priority to either **High Importance** or **Low Importance**. This does not mean the message is sent any more quickly or slowly, only that a flag is placed on the message that alerts the recipient to its importance.

Activity:

1. The e-mail to *Fiona* created in the previous exercise should still be open. On the **Ribbon**, click the **High Importance** button in the **Options** group on the **Message** tab.

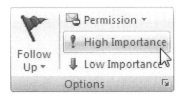

> **Note:**   Notice that the button stays highlighted to indicate the message has high priority. Clicking it again will reset the message to normal priority.

2. Click **Send** to send the message. This will send the message to *Fiona* and a **Carbon copy** back to you.

> **Note:**   *Fiona's* e-mail address is a <u>real</u> address that can be used to practice sending messages to. The first message you send may receive an automatic reply, but all others will go unanswered and will be deleted immediately.

3. After a moment you will receive your carbon copy of the message back in your **Inbox** (use the **Send/Receive** button if necessary to check for new messages).

4. Notice that the message appears with an exclamation mark, [!], indicating that it has been sent with high importance.

Date: Today		
! ✉ John Olivier	Your new computer	

5. Preview the message in the **Reading Pane**. An **Information Banner** appears at the top of the message.

> **Note:**   The process of making a message low priority is very similar. Simply click the **Low Importance** button in the **Options** group when creating a new message. The message will have a low priority icon when it is received, [⬇].

6. Leave your **Inbox** open for the next exercise.

8.23 Attaching Files

It is possible to attach files stored on your computer to an e-mail message in *Outlook*. The attached files are then sent along with the message and can be saved or opened by the person who receives it. This makes it easy to send documents, spreadsheets, presentations, publications or pictures anywhere in the world.

In this exercise you will attach a simple *Word* document to a message. When the message reaches its destination, a paperclip icon, , will let the recipient know there is an attachment.

Activity:

1.   Start a new message and address it to yourself so that you can observe the results of this exercise. Enter the subject as **Upgrade Schedule** and, in the **Message Area**, enter the following text:

   Please find attached this year's computer upgrade schedule.

2.   Click the **Attach File** button in the **Include** group on the **Ribbon**.

3.   The **Insert File** dialog box appears. Select the location where the data files for this section are stored, and then click **Schedule** once to select it.

4.   Click the **Insert** button and the *Word* document is attached to the e-mail. The attachment appears in a new **Attached** box under the **Subject**.

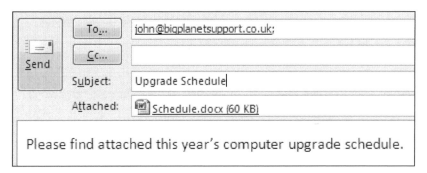

> **Note:**   Depending on your default settings, attachments may appear as icons in the **Message Area**. You can also add more than one attachment to a message.

> **Note:**   If you are sending multiple files, it is often a good idea to **zip** them up together. This reduces the overall file size and makes the message much quicker to send.

5.   Send the message and leave *Outlook* open for the next exercise.

> **Note:**   When attaching files to e-mail, you must ensure that the recipient has the same version of the software installed on their computer in order to open and view them. If the software is not installed, the file will not open.

8.24 Receiving Attachments

When you receive an e-mail containing an attachment, it will appear in the **Message List** marked with a paperclip icon, 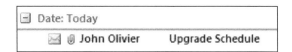. The attachment may then be opened and/or saved to your computer.

Activity:

1. After a moment you will receive the **Upgrade Schedule** message back in your **Inbox** (use the **Send/Receive** button if necessary to check for new messages). Notice that the message features a paperclip icon in the **Message List**.

2. Select the message to view its contents in the **Reading Pane**. The attached file appears on a bar at the top of the message.

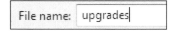

3. Click the **Schedule** item once to preview the contents of the file. If a warning appears, click the **Preview file** button.

> **Note:**   E-mail attachments are one of the biggest sources of computer viruses. Never open an e-mail attachment unless you know and fully trust the person who sent it to you. Even then, you should save the attachment to your computer first and scan it with your antivirus software before opening it.

4. To save the attached file to your computer (outside of your *Outlook* mailbox), display the **File** menu and select **Save Attachments**. Then select the attached **Schedule.docx** file.

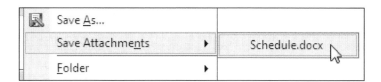

5. The **Save Attachment** dialog box appears. Rename the file as **upgrades** by replacing the text in the **File name** box.

File name: upgrades

6. Locate the data files folder for this section, and then click **Save** to save the attached file.

> **Note:**   You can now find the file in **Windows Explorer** and check it for viruses.

7. Leave *Outlook* open for the next exercise.

8.25 Sorting Messages

To help you find messages quickly, you can sort the contents of a folder into order by sender name, date, subject, and so on. You can also quickly search through messages for keywords.

Activity:

1. With your **Inbox** selected, notice that information in the **Message List** is grouped into columns. At the top of the screen, these columns are labelled **From**, **Subject**, **Received**, **Size**, and so on.

> **Note:** Notice also that there are column headers with **Importance** and **Attachment** icons.

2. E-mail messages in your **Inbox** are currently shown in the order that they were received, with the newest at the top. This order of sorting is indicated by the small arrow, ▾, on the **Received** column header.

3. Click the **Received** column header once. The arrow turns upside down, indicating that the sort has been reversed. E-mails are now shown in reverse order with the oldest first.

4. Click the **Subject** column header. All e-mail messages are now sorted in alphabetical order by subject. Click the **Subject** column header again to reverse the sort.

5. Explore the other sorts available by selecting each of the column headers on view. When you are finished, click **Received** once to restore the original sort (newest first).

> **Note:** You can also quickly search for messages that contain specific keywords.

6. Click once in the **Search** box and enter the keywords **Functional Skills**. Press <Enter> and the current folder's **Message List** is *filtered* to display <u>only</u> those messages that match your search criteria (the keywords can appear in any part of the e-mail message).

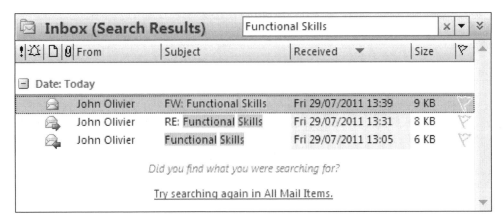

7.   Replace the search text with the keyword **upgrade**, press <**Enter**>, and notice the effect. Feel free to experiment with other search keywords and options.

8.   To close the search and remove the filter, click the **Clear Search** button, ⊠, to the right of the **Search** box. All messages in the folder reappear.

> **Note:**   It is often useful to **flag** important e-mail messages so that you can "follow them up" later. For this reason, *Outlook* allows you to add a small coloured flag to the item in the **Message List**, ⚑. When you have taken action on or responded to the message, you can then mark it as complete, ✔.

9.   Leave *Outlook* open for the next exercise.

8.26 Organising Messages

To help organise your mailbox folders, it can sometimes be a good idea to create a system of subfolders in which to store specific types of e-mail (e.g. **personal**, **important**, **enquiries**, **orders**, **newsletters**, etc). Messages can then be moved between folders as required.

Activity:

1.   As *John* receives a lot of e-mail messages about *Functional Skills* training, he would like to store them in their own folder (to make them easier to find later).

2.   Display the **File** menu and select **Folder | New Folder**.

3.   The **Create New Folder** dialog box appears. Notice that the **Inbox** folder is currently selected in the folder list (if it is not selected, select it now).

4.   Enter the name for the new folder as **Training**.

5.   Click **OK**. The new folder appears directly beneath the **Inbox** folder in the **Folders List**.

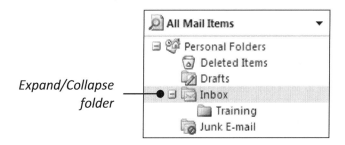

Note: If the **Training** folder is hidden, show it by clicking the **Expand/Collapse** toggle button, ◢, found to the left of the **Inbox** folder.

6.   Within your main **Inbox** folder, select the message **Functional Skills** that you sent to yourself earlier. You are going to move this message to the new **Training** folder.

7.   On the **Toolbar**, click the **Move to Folder** button, [icon]. From the submenu that appears, select the **Training** folder.

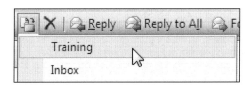

8.   The selected message is moved. Open the **Training** folder from the **Folders List**. The message appears in the **Message List**.

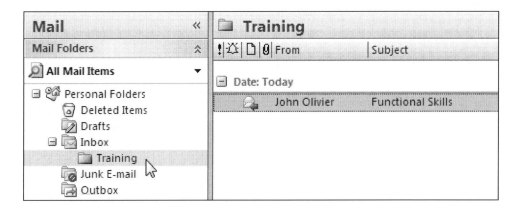

Note: You can also drag and drop messages from the **Message List** to any other folder.

9.   Use the same technique to move the two e-mail messages **RE: Functional Skills** and **FW: Functional Skills** to the new **Training** folder.

Note: Subfolders can be created within *any* of the folders on the **Folders List**, and messages can be moved freely from folder to folder.

10.   Return to the main **Inbox** folder and leave it open for the next exercise.

8.27 Deleting Messages

To help you to save space, when a message is no longer needed, you can delete it from your mailbox – simply select the unwanted message in the **Message List** and click the **Delete** button. A deleted message will be sent to the **Deleted Items** folder until it is permanently removed (or restored again if you change your mind and want it back).

Activity:

1. With your **Inbox** folder open, select the **Upgrade Schedule** e-mail message on the **Message List**.

2. To delete this message, click the **Delete** button, ☒ , on the **Toolbar**. The message is moved immediately to the **Delete Items** folder.

3. Next, select the **Your new computer** message and press the **<Delete>** key on your keyboard to remove it (this is an alternative method for deleting e-mails).

4. In the **Folders List**, right click the **Training** subfolder and select **Delete "Training"**. Click **Yes** at the prompt to confirm the deletion and remove the folder.

5. Open the **Deleted Items** folder. Notice that all of the deleted items are shown here. You could now restore any item by simply moving it to another folder.

> **Note:** All deleted *Outlook* items, including tasks and contacts, will also appear here.

6. To permanently remove all deleted messages from the **Deleted Items** folder, display the **Tools** menu and select **Empty "Deleted Items" Folder**. A prompt will appear asking you to confirm the deletion. Click **Yes** (or **No** if you'd rather keep the contents of this folder).

> **Note:** Only delete messages when you are <u>sure</u> you will never need them again.

7. Close *Outlook*.

8.28 E-mail Tips

The laws, company policies and basic netiquette rules discussed in this section provide you with a simple checklist of professional issues to consider when sending and receiving e-mail:

* Keep e-mail to the point and don't forget to add a meaningful subject.

* Do not send e-mails that are likely to offend the person receiving them (including discriminatory or inflammatory information or material).

* Use appropriate language and always spell check your messages (try to avoid overuse of fancy fonts and colours).

✱ Do not send large e-mail attachments (unless you first get permission).

✱ Do not send illegal information or material (i.e. material that is protected by copyright or the *Data Protection Act*).

✱ Respect others people's confidentiality and avoid inappropriate disclosure of information.

✱ Don't be distracted by irrelevant messages (especially jokes and junk mail), and <u>do not</u> use work e-mail for personal activities.

✱ Prioritise messages and respond to urgent requests first.

✱ Consider carefully who you copy in to e-mails.

> **Note:** Learn to deal with "e-mail overload". Research shows that people receive around 40 messages per day on average – it doesn't take long for your mailbox to fill up.

8.29 Phishing and Spam

Phishing (also known as **identity theft**) is the process of attempting to gain private information such as user names, passwords and credit card details by pretending to be a trustworthy business or organisation. If you ever receive an official-looking e-mail asking for this type of information, <u>delete it</u>. This includes requests to reset login information or verify an account.

> **Note:** Businesses will <u>never</u> ask for personal details to be confirmed by e-mail.

Although less of a security risk, junk mail can also be a nuisance and can take up a lot of your time. Also known as **spam**, these messages are often used by companies to advertise products. If they become a problem, anti-spam software can be used to filter out these unwanted messages before they even reach your Inbox.

8.30 Next Steps

Well done! You have now completed all of the exercises in this section. If you feel you are ready to test your knowledge and understanding of the topics covered, move on to the following **Develop Your Skills** activities. If there are any *Internet* and *E-mail* features covered in this section that you are unsure about, revisit the appropriate exercises and try them again before moving on.

If you are interested in exploring some of the more powerful features of your web browser or *Microsoft Outlook*, use the Internet to find out a little more about the following advanced topics.

Feature	Description
Favorites	Expand on the notes in 8.2 and learn to create, organise and delete **Favorites** (also known as bookmarks).
Web Tools	Web browser software features a number of settings and tools to customise your browsing experience.
History	Expand on the notes in 8.3 and learn to manage and delete your browsing **History** (including temporary internet files and cookies).
Home Page	Set up one or more favourite websites as your browser's default **Home** page(s).
Search Providers	Explore the various search providers that can be used to extend the functionality of your browser's built-in search facility.
Advanced Search	There any many other types of operators that can be used to help refine a search. You can see which ones are supported by following a search engine's "advanced search" link.
Calendars	*Outlook* features a handy **Calendar** tool. This can be used to plan your daily activities and schedule appointments and meetings with others.
Tasks	*Outlook's* useful **Tasks** feature can be used to create "to-do" lists and reminders.
Drafts	Unfinished messages can be saved so that they can be completed and sent at a later date. E-mails saved in this way are known as a **Draft** messages and are saved in your **Drafts** folder.
Rules	**Rules** can be created in *Outlook* to automatically perform actions when certain messages are received. For example, messages containing specific keywords can be automatically moved to a different folder or they can generate an automatic reply.
Signatures	An e-mail signature is a personalised block of text that is added to the end of an e-mail message. It usually contains your name and contact details, saving you the need to enter this information every time you create a message.

8

At the end of every section you will get the chance to complete two full tasks without my assistance. This will help to reinforce learning and develop your skills. Don't forget to use the planning and review checklists at the back of the book to organise and evaluate your work.

> **Note:**   Sample solutions for both tasks are provided in this section's data files folder.

Level 1: Pirate's Cove Quiz

In this task you will be asked to perform some simple online research for *John*. You will need to use the ICT skills you have learned in this section to plan, develop and present an appropriate solution. You can ask for help from friends, colleagues or a teacher if you get stuck.

Level 1 Task

Zahra at *Pirate's Cove* has created a brand new quiz for an event she is running next week. Unfortunately she has lost all of the answers, and has asked me to help her find them again online. I've not got much time, but maybe you can help? Information you will need is available in the following files:

✱   **Quiz Answers**   A *Microsoft Word* document containing *Zahra's* quiz (without the answers, of course).

Start by opening the file **Quiz Answers**. Notice that a space is available for you to enter each of the five missing answers. Use your favourite web browser and a search engine of your choice to find those answers and complete *Zahra's* document.

Notice the image of a pirate ship in the **Quiz Answers** document. You have reason to think *Zahra* has downloaded this from an Internet site. Why is this a problem?

Notes:

Level 2: Staying Safe

In this task you will be asked to compose and send an e-mail to *John's* friend. You will need to use the advanced ICT skills that you have learned in this section to create a suitable solution (you may need to break the problem down into smaller parts first). Only level 2 students should attempt this task and it should be completed without help from others.

Level 2 Task

I've just received the following e-mail from my friend *Pete* who works at *Reception*:

Peter is obviously wasting time and abusing his work e-mail account, and I'm worried that he will get into trouble if someone finds out. Create a new e-mail addressed to *Peter* and explain to him the following concerns:

✱   The park's rules and regulations do not allow personal use of e-mail.

✱   You should avoid forwarding e-mail of this type to others when at work.

✱   You shouldn't open e-mail attachments without checking them first.

In your message, describe why these issues are important and mention the best ways to deal with e-mail attachments. Make sure the final message looks professional and contains no spelling errors. When you are finished, send the message (*Peter's* e-mail address is a <u>real</u> address that can be used to practice sending messages to).

Planning Checklist

Before creating a solution to a problem it is always a good idea to spend a moment reviewing the task's requirements and planning how you will go about solving it. Consider what the solution you are creating will look like, who it is for, and what kinds of information it will contain?

	Issues to Consider	
	Using ICT	
1.	What are the exact ICT requirements of the task?	✓
2.	What are the stages of development and how will I approach the problem?	✓
3.	Does the task need to be broken down into smaller subtasks? What are they?	✓
4.	Do I need to prioritise one subtask before another?	✓
5.	Which software application(s) do I intend to use?	✓
6.	Who will use the solution? Will it work for them or is there a better way?	✓
7.	Do I have enough time to finish the task? If not, what should I do?	✓
	Finding and Selecting Information	
8.	Is all of the information that I need to solve the problem available?	✓
9.	If more information is needed, where and how will I find it?	✓
10.	Is the information that I have accurate and fit for purpose?	✓
11.	What pieces of information will I use? Only the relevant parts are needed.	✓
12.	What is the best way to store and manage the information on my computer?	✓
	Developing, presenting and communicating information	
13.	Are there any new skills that I need to learn to complete the task?	✓
14.	What skills and techniques will I use to create my solution?	✓
15.	What is the best way to organise and combine the information I have found?	✓
16.	Will the planned solution be suitable for the intended audience?	✓
17.	Do I have the necessary hardware and software to complete this task?	✓
18.	Are there any house styles and design guidelines that I need to follow?	✓
19.	What safety and security issues do I need to take into account?	✓
20.	Are there any laws or regulations that may affect the task or my solution?	✓
21.	Are there any ICT problems that I can expect to encounter?	✓
22.	If I encounter any problems, how will I resolve them? Who can I ask for help?	✓
23.	How will I deliver the solution (e.g. by e-mail or printed document)?	✓

Review Checklist

When you have created your solution, you should review the effectiveness of the choices you've made. Does the solution meet the requirements of the task, does it solve the problem correctly, and are there any improvements that can be made?

	Items to Evaluate	
	Using ICT	
1.	Was my initial understanding of the task's ICT requirements correct?	✓
2.	Did my solution actually solve the problem? If not, how can I improve it?	✓
3.	Did my approach allow me to tackle the problem in the best possible way?	✓
4.	Did I underestimate the time/resources needed to create the solution?	✓
5.	Would another software application have done the job better?	✓
	Finding and Selecting Information	
6.	Was I able to find all of the information that I needed for the task?	✓
7.	Was all of the information that I used relevant and appropriate?	✓
8.	Was the information that I used accurate and fit for purpose?	✓
9.	Was the information that I created or edited clear, accurate and correct?	✓
10.	Was the format that I used to present the information suitable?	✓
11.	Was my approach to data storage sufficient and could it be improved?	✓
	Developing, presenting and communicating information	
12.	Were there any additional skills that would have helped complete the task?	✓
13.	Were there any alternative ICT techniques that I could have used?	✓
14.	Do I need to learn or revise any functional skills for the future?	✓
15.	Was the person I created the solution for happy with the end result?	✓
16.	Was the solution that I created suitably professional?	✓
17.	Did I correctly resolve any safety or security issues that I encountered?	✓
18.	Did I correctly resolve any ICT problems that I encountered?	✓
19.	Am I certain that I followed all relevant laws and regulations during the task?	✓
20.	If applicable, have I tested the solution to make sure it works in all cases?	✓
21.	Was the chosen delivery method suitable or would an alternative be better?	✓
22.	For items 1 to 21, have I considered what I would do differently next time?	✓

Other Products

CiA Training is a leading publishing company which has consistently delivered the highest quality products since 1985. Our experienced in-house publishing team has developed a wide range of flexible and easy to use self-teach resources for individual learners and corporate clients all over the world. Supporting many popular qualifications including ECDL, CLAIT, ITQ and Functional Skills, our products are an invaluable asset to tutors and training managers seeking support for their programme delivery.

At the time of publication we currently offer materials for:

* Functional Skills ICT

* ITQ Level 1, Level 2 and Level 3

* New CLAIT, CLAIT Plus and CLAIT Advanced

* ECDL Syllabus 5.0

* ECDL Advanced Syllabus 2.0

* CiA Revision Series

* Start IT

* Skill for Life in ICT

* e-Citizen

* Open Learning Guides

* CourseNotes

* Trainers Packs with iCourse Professional

* Bank Safe e-learning

* And many more...

Previous syllabus versions are also available upon request.

We hope you have enjoyed using this guide and would love to hear your opinions about our materials. To let us know how we're doing and to get up-to-the-minute information on our current range of products, please visit us online at:

www.ciatraining.co.uk

Index

© CiA Training Ltd 2011